PROTESTANT BEGINNINGS
IN
JAPAN

JAPANESE CHRISTIAN LEADERS CONFERENCE, Tokyo, May 1883
Front row: Dr. Rikizo Fukashima, Rev. Masatsuna Okuno, Rev. Taka-
yoshi Matsuyama, Mr. Sen Tsuda, Mr. Jutei Ri, Mr. Jiro Yuasa, Rev. Saehachi
Kurimura, Rev. Danjo Ebina. *Second row:* Mr. Takei Morita, Rev. Hiroyasu
Hiraiwa, Mr. Tetsuya Makioka, Mr. Tokyu Tsuji, Mr. Kanzo Uchimura,
Rev. Joseph Hardy Neesima, Rev. Kumaji Kimura, Mr. Hisakichi Terasawa,
Rev. Yasutaro Ishihara. *Third row:* Rev. Motoichiro Ogimi, Mr. Yujro Kato,
Rev. Kajinosuke Ibuka, Mr. Junjiro Aoyama, Rev. Tsuneteru Miyagawa, Rev.
Tokio Yokoi, Rev. Arata Inagaki, Mr. Ichibei Koide. *Fourth row:* Mr.
Tokichi Ito, Mr. Tsuyoshi Nagasaka, Mr. Ayao Hattori, Rev. Hiromichi
Kozaki, Rev. Masahisa Uemura, Rev. Tsurin Kanamori, Rev. Masayoshi
Oshikawa, Rev. Hidetoyo Wada, Rev. Hōryu Uehara. *Last row:* Mr. Hiro-
mi Asakawa, Rev. Tōru Miura, Rev. Koki Yoshioka, Rev. Yushichi Kumano,
Rev. K. Minami, and name unknown. Photograph through the courtesy of
Frank Cary.

PROTESTANT BEGINNINGS

IN

JAPAN

The First Three Decades

1859-1889

by

WINBURN T. THOMAS, Ph. D.

CHARLES E. TUTTLE COMPANY

Tokyo, Japan　　　　　　　　　Rutland, Vermont

*Published by the
Charles E. Tuttle Company
of Rutland, Vermont & Tokyo, Japan
with editorial offices at
15 Edogawa-cho, Bunkyo-ku, Tokyo*

*Library of Congress Catalog Card
No. 59–6489*

First edition, 1959

*Printed in Japan by the
Obun Printing Company, Tokyo*

PROTESTANT BEGINNINGS IN JAPAN *was originally presented as a dissertation to the faculty of the Graduate School of Yale University in candidacy for the degree of Doctor of Philosophy.*

CONTENTS

FOREWORD

Some time ago while discussing the Christian movement in Japan with a group of postwar residents I was very much surprised to discover that few of them were at all well-informed on the beginnings of Protestantism in this country. To them the ninteenth century was very vague and unreal. The thrill of the pioneer days was unknown.

At the time, this greatly surprised me, yet after some reflection I realized that there is very little historical material on this period readily available to the modern reader. There has always been a paucity of scholarly study in this field. Today, most of the standard works are out of print.

Naturally, then, I responded favorably when Dr. Winburn Thomas requested my assistance in publishing his doctoral thesis which deals with *Protestant Beginnings in Japan*, 1859 –1889. During the first two decades the seed was sown and then slowly germinated in the none-too-friendly soil. In the next the plant blossomed and spread so rapidly that serious observers thought it would cover the country within the century. Then came the blight of reaction as resurgent nationalism swept the land. Here, I felt, was a book which all students of the church in Japan should read. But this is not a dramatic narrative. That must be read elsewhere. This is a scholarly analysis of the period.

Dr. Thomas came to Japan as a missionary in 1933 just a half-century after the era of rapid advance got underway. Two years prior to his arrival Japan entered an era of tension. "Crisis" was on the lips of Japanese leaders throughout the eight years he was in the country. It was a time when Christianity faced criticism and suspicion from without and testing from within. His study ends in the same sort of atmosphere as prevailed throughout most of the period of his service here, so he is well qualified to understand the psychological situation which prevailed even though the church of the thirties, the level of general outlook, and the assumptions of the public had undergone great changes.

The Pacific phase of World War II was opening as Dr. Thomas was completing his thesis, and facilities for checking data were limited as all contact with Japan was cut off. Consequently, Dr. Thomas felt that prior to publication the material should be re-checked. Therefore, the assistance of The Reverend Frank Cary, a missionary of the American Board of Commissioners for Foreign Missions, was secured. Mr. Cary was born a year before the period covered by this study ended. His childhood and youth were spent in Japan. He has both childhood and adult memories of many, if not most, of the Christian leaders mentioned in this study. He has been a life-time student of this period and there is probably no better authority in the field. At considerable sacrifice he reviewed the work with painstaking care and made a number of corrections for which Dr. Thomas is very grateful.

My own contributions have been largely mechanical ones. Notes of substance have been left in the footnotes while those of reference have been transferred to the back of the volume. An index has been added and a few minor changes make the volume more suitable for the general public. It has been a great privilege to familiarize myself with many details previously unknown. I have benefited greatly and heartily commend this analysis of *Protestant Beginnings in Japan* to all those who wish to understand the church today, which in spite of many obstacles, past and present, is steadily becoming more firmly established.

WILLIAM P. WOODARD
International Institute for the
Study of Religions
Tokyo, Japan

January, 1959

PREFACE

Dr. Thomas has given us an extremely valuable study of a significant phase of the history of Christianity in Japan. As all students of Modern Japan have known, for a few years in the 1880's Christianity enjoyed an extraordinarily rapid numerical growth. After the centuries when it was denounced by the government as an evil religion and was driven underground and then, following the opening of diplomatic relations with the West, was cautiously and somewhat reluctantly tolerated, during part of the 1880's Christianity made striking gains. So phenomenal were they and so contrary to previous experience that even some normally sober observers believed that the conversion of the Japanese people might follow within a generation. But that prophecy was not fulfilled. A reaction came which was partly anti-foreign and anti-missionary. In the 1890's the hopeful dreams of the optimists were denied. Yet in retrospect the seemingly discouraging years which followed 1889 were perceived to have wholesome aspects. The churches emerged from the ordeal stronger in morale and with a more disciplined membership, better prepared to take a continuing part in the nation's life and to bear witness to their faith.

It is an account of the Protestant aspects of this story which Dr. Thomas has given us. He has gone diligently through the pertinent original sources, most of them in print and in English, but some in manuscript and in Japanese. He has shown discernment in analyzing them and the events which they depict. He has put the years in their historical perspective, pointing out the background in the record of Christianity in Japan from its introduction by Roman Catholics through the many years of persecution, telling of the coming of Protestantism, and analyzing the reasons both for the sudden popularity in the 1880's and for the reverses which followed. While the main emphasis is upon the years of prosperity, the sequel is summarized.

Here is an account which can be depended upon for accuracy and insight. To anyone interested in Christianity in Japan it will prove illuminating. All future historians of Christianity in Japan will find it indispensable, To those wishing to understand, whether now or later, the place of Christianity in the life of Japan, Dr. Thomas has opened vistas leading to deeper and broader comprehension.

KENNETH SCOTT LATOURETTE
Sterling Professor of Missions and Oriental History, Emeritus, Yale University

INTRODUCTION

The main purpose of this monograph is to record the principal features and analyze the progress of Protestantism in Japan between 1883 and 1889, the first years of rapid growth subsequent to Christianity's reintroduction. From 1859, when the pioneer Protestant missionaries first arrived, until 1872, but few effects of their presence were to be seen. In 1872 the first churches were organized, and a few months later the edict boards prohibiting Christianity were removed. Churches and schools were established and mass meetings conducted both in the treaty ports and in the interior during the ensuing decade of slow but certain progress.

Beginning in 1883 Japanese Christians and missionaries reported that the difficulties experienced by the pioneers had been overcome, popular antipathies had largely disappeared, and Christianity was being borne along with the popularity of western civilization. It was even discussed as a potential religion of the state. Missionaries were encouraged and aided by statesmen in founding churches. Confucianism lacked vitality, Buddhism was moribund, and Shintō, except for its concern with court rituals, was primarily occupied with the routine observance of traditional festivals, esoteric rites and the sale of charms. Priests became discouraged and some even entered the Christian ministry.

Crowds gathered to hear sermons and lectures. Religious books were sold in quantities. A Christian magazine became the leading interpreter of contemporary thought. With such a condition prevailing in a few cities it was assumed that similar success should follow elsewhere. Some missionaries predicted that the land might be Christianized within a decade or fifteen years. Many Japanese Christians, confident of immediate ecclesiastical independence, anticipated the day when the church, administered exclusively by nationals, would possess sufficient resources to displace the foreigners. The union of the different denominations into a single independent self-supporting church was regarded as a reasonable expectation.[1]

In the autumn of 1889 the national temper again changed. Christian school enrollments and church attendance declined. Anti-foreign and anti-Christian attitudes were voiced in the press and from the platform. Western nations became objects of scorn rather than of emulation. As Christianity previously had profited by its alliance with western culture, the reaction against occidental ideas and methods was accompanied by a retardation in the spread of Protestantism. It is our purpose to consider both the reasons for the rapid growth and for the recession. This will in turn presuppose a knowledge of the cultural background and associations of the missionaries as well as of the ecclesiastical, moral, ethical, political, social, and economic media in which the expansion of Protestantism took place.

He who would chart the course of history undertakes a delicate and dangerous chore. His is the responsibility for pointing out directions and routes which often are known to exist only by the fact that they alone can account for certain existing climaxes, developments, and conclusions. To construct from the letters, newspaper accounts, speeches of statesmen, and admittedly prejudiced reports, many of them mutually contradictory, the road that was followed and the reasons thereof, is the design for this study. If the way has been lost, or if the route we have delineated is not true to the facts, the fault is in the multiplicity of conflicting reports and opinions, as well as in the inexperience of the guide.

The problems include such queries as the following : Why did Christianity spread in Japan, and at a particularly phenomenal rate during the years 1883–1889 ? What correlation was there between the establishment of missionary outstations and the development of communications ? Did missions prosper or suffer because of the unequal treaties then in effect ? Did the processes employed for the spread of Christianity contribute to the reverses ? What part, if any, did the political forces which eradicated *Kirishitan* missions in the seventeenth century play in the reverses of 1889 ? How were other cultural institutions introduced from the west, such as education, affected during the same period ? To what extent were the methods of the west reproduced in Japan as the church sought to expand throughout the nation ? What trends towards indigenization were visible before 1890 ? Did these contribute to the reaction and to the retardation ? These are typical questions which perplex the student of the Protestant movement in Japan during the 1880's. Some of them can be answered with certainty. Others are capable of only a partial explanation. Final solutions for still others must await the discovery of materials which are as yet unavailable. Japanese Christians who have studied the thought-life and institutional changes of the Meiji era may be able to furnish information bearing on these points.

First among the sources referred to have been contemporary newspaper articles, editorials, and news items. The files of the *Japan Weekly Mail* have been examined both for background materials and for data concerning the Christian movement. As the foreign language newspapers in Kōbe and Yokohama were compiled largely of material adapted from local periodicals, they provide documentary evidence of the life and thought of the day. The scholarly editor of the *Japan Weekly Mail*, Captain F. Brinkley, gave to missionary problems and developments much consideration and space, a concern which may be attributed to the fact that the missionaries were a predominant element in the foreign communities in Yokohama, Tōkyō, Ōsaka, Kōbe and Kyōto, prior to the opening of the country in 1889 to residence outside specified areas.

The second most important source material has been correspondence reproduced at the time in the journals published by the mission boards of the Congregational and Presbyterian churches and in *The Missionary Review of the World*, an interdenominational organ. As fully three-fourths of the strength of Protestantism in Japan was included within the Kumiai Kyōkai (Congregational Church) and the Nippon Kirisuto Kyōkai (Presbyterian-Reformed Church), these sources have been adequate to delineate the main trends and movements. Sample checks have also been made of missionary literature published by the missions of several other denominations.

Manuscripts and letters from the missionaries to the home boards have constituted a further source. The Japan files of the American Baptist Missionary Union, and of the Board of Foreign Missions of the Presbyterian Church in the U. S. A. have been examined carefully for the decade 1880–1890. The correspondence, preserved in the Treasury Room of the Andover-Harvard Theological Seminary Library, dealing with the Japan Mission of the American Board of Commissioners for Foreign Missions proved too voluminous to examine in full, yet a cross section was studied, and numerous references have been made thereto.

Among published works in western languages the *Osaka Conference Report* (1883) and the *Report of the Tokyo Conference* (1900) have been most often cited. Particularly valuable has been the historical sketch prepared by G. F. Verbeck for the Ōsaka Conference, a collection of notes arranged chronologically according to missions. It is probably the most authoritative single document dealing with Protestantism in Japan prior to 1883.

The classic historical study of the Christian movement in Japan is that in two volumes by Dr. Otis Cary, the second of which traces the expansion of Protestantism to within a few years of the date of publication, 1909. Little reference has been made to it because we have drawn from Dr. Cary's main sources, those mentioned above.

Several allusions have been made to books in Japanese, particularly to treatises published by the *Nippon Kirisutokyō-shi Kenkyūkai* (The Society for Research in the History of Christianity in Japan). Many other valuable and suggestive books in Japanese are available which should be employed in tracing the spread of Christianity in Japan. However, for the period covered by this study, the main developments within the Christian movement were those with which the missionaries were closely associated, and concerning which they recorded their impressions at length, both for the information of the supporting constituency in America and for the sake of record.

The Hepburn system of romanization, with a few widely accepted modifications, has been followed in the transliteration of Japanese terms. Names are given in the conventional Japanese order with the family name preceding the given.

For their assistance to the author in his search for materials, he gratefully acknowledges his obligation to the Missionary Research, the Day Missions, the Yale University, the Union Theological Seminary, the Andover-Harvard Theological, and the College of Oriental Studies (Peking, China) libraries, and to the custodians of the archives of the Board of Foreign Missions of the Presbyterian Church in the United States of America, of the American Baptist Foreign Mission Society, and of the American Board of Commissioners for Foreign Missions.

The author is also indebted to the faculty of Yale University for the award of the George E. Hume Memorial Fellowship for two years, to the Presbyterian Board of Foreign Missions for the furlough study privileges generously extended, and to Dr. August Karl Reischauer* and Dr. Yuasa Hachiro† who read portions of the manuscript and offered important suggestions.

Especially desirous is the writer of expressing gratitude to Dr. Kenneth Scott Latourette for his invaluable aid in the preparation of this dissertation: it was he who originally suggested it, he who formulated the canons of selection[2] by which the chapters have been ordered, and he who rendered penetrating criticism and counsel in unstintingly proffered consultations.

For any errors, the writer alone is responsible.

W. T. T.

NEW HAVEN, CONNECTICUT
May 1, 1942

---

* Dr. A. K. Reischauer, an authority on Buddhism, was a Presbyterian missionary in Japan from 1905 to 1941.
† Dr. H. Yuasa, twice President of Doshisha University, is now (1958) President of International Christian University, Tokyo.

Part One

JAPAN IN THE
MID-NINETEENTH CENTURY

Chapter I

THE RELIGIOUS SITUATION

It was no empty nor static world to which Protestant Christianity was introduced in 1859. Japan was then a highly civilized country with a history that dated back to the dawn of the Christian era. The religions, art, literature, social institutions, written language, and ethical ideals of the nation, based on much of the best the other oriental lands had to offer, had been in process of development for over twelve centuries. Yet faced with an altered international situation following Commodore Perry's arrival, the nation as a whole demonstrated a true instinct and unprejudiced desire for progress.[1] The need for enlightenment conquered the two-century old dislike for what was foreign.[2] Christianity's re-introduction and advancement were expedited by the religious, social, political, and economic revolution in Japanese life no less than by the changes which had occurred in the west since the days when Japan adopted the policy of national isolation.

CONDITIONS IN GENERAL

Particularly significant for the spread of Protestantism were the developments derived from the Tokugawa period. The ethical standards, customs, institutions, and modes of life of the preceding age supplied the materials out of which the new Japan was shaped, although the west provided the patterns. Many of the forms of Japan's feudal past gradually disappeared, but the underlying sentiments and inclinations were not so easily effaced. The spirit, ideals, and principles of the occident but slowly made their way in Japan even after many of the cultural patterns and technology of Europe and America had been taken for granted. In the precipitous transition which was thus effected, the Protestant movement both prospered and suffered. Several of these aspects of change are of special importance.

The first had to do with social attitudes and civic responsibilities. The citizen of feudal Japan was constrained in outward conduct by obligations towards his family, guilds, and clan. Custom and ceremony dictated the course of his life. Social duties left little room for individual expression in the days before the principle of personal liberty was introduced. The previously fettered individual not only was free to act thereafter, but was incited to do so by pulpit, platform, press and school, during the period of ballot-box struggles, party agitations, and preparations for parliamentarianism. In the times of Oda Nobunaga and Toyotomi Hideyoshi, thousands of families had followed their lords in baptism. During the Meiji period the Japanese became individually responsible for their religious decisions.[3]

A second aspect of the change was that the life of the nation as a whole rather than the feudal domain became a focal point of attention. A constitution and new codes were devised which were designed for all classes and provinces. Local usage and individual caprice were replaced by principles national in scope. Courts which previously had settled cases according to custom and expediency now handed down judgments in the name of justice and equity. The political life of the nation during the '80's was shaping around principles which were applicable to all Japanese subjects alike.[4] The contribution of Christianity to this equalitarian concept was to be seen in the twenty-eighth article of the Constitution which provided that Japanese subjects, within limits not prejudicial to peace and order, and not antagonistic to their duties as subjects," should enjoy freedom of religious belief. At the time it appeared to be a praiseworthy gesture that a non-Christian land should grant freedom of religious belief to Christians.[5]

The vitalization of the latent energies of the nation constituted a third aspect of the transformation. Industries were started, commerce expanded, wealth accumulated* and a desire for knowledge awakened. To a limited extent a desire for the spiritual elements of Christianity was expressed, although the secondary values which were obtainable through the schools, hospitals and other philanthropic institutions were in greater demand. During the years of westernization the Japanese became a restless, active people moved by new impulses and strong ambitions. Their energies were divided towards the creation of material goods and the instruments of power.[6]

This increased motion placed an added burden upon the moral and intellectual resources of the nation. The precipitous nature of the transition, by removing many of the accepted restraints upon conduct,imposed a greater responsibility upon the individual conscience. Because conscience often was lacking, license tended to replace traditional discipline.[7] As the Japanese observed this change, they feared moral degradation had begun. The temporary undermining of the Confucian codes, the population shifts, the new science and education, and the development of commerce, created perplexing moral problems.[8]

A fifth characteristic of the transition was the failure of the existing religious and ethical systems. Confucianism,

---

* A Chinese student who has lived in Japan recently observed that Japan though actually poor had been able to develop as though it were a rich nation because of the concentration and conservation of wealth.

Buddhism and Shinto alike had played important functional roles in the agrarian, feudal life of Tokugawa Japan. The Restoration and its accompanying changes introduced new areas of human relations which necessitated great adaptation on the part of the nation's religious systems if they were to be ethically authoritative. So long had these religions been an accepted part of Japanese life that they did not readily adjust to the altered situation. Furthermore, existing creeds lacked the religious and ethical content needed for the guidance of life in a commercial, industrial society. For instance, what in the English and American legal system was known as equity, was far more important in Japanese institutions and life than common or codified law. Contract was more flexible in the east than in the west. These divergences between accepted customs in the occident and orient led to misunderstandings of Japanese morals and manners, which were extremely distasteful to the foreign merchants in Japan during the nineteenth century. As might be expected, the foreign traders in Hyōgo and Yokohama were strongest among the foreign residents in their opposition to the abandonment of extraterritorial privileges. One of the reasons for this situation was that existing religious and ethical teachings did not operate, or did so only inadequately, in the transition society. As the Japanese became aware of the ethical deficiency, they endeavored to rectify it. Some sought to modify existing codes and religious systems so as to render them applicable to the westernized areas of life; others advocated the acceptance of Christianity as the system best adapted to the new Japan. The confusion and the fact of transition constituted, in a sense, a vacuum which offered Christianity opportunity for expansion insofar as the new system possessed resources and was free to fill the void.

The essential elements of the situation which prevailed during the years of Protestantism's rapid growth were rooted largely in the nation's past. The Japanese are a religious

24

people. The earliest literary accounts treat nature and ancestors as the objects of reverence. This native inheritance they proved themselves able to supplement by successively adapting Confucianism, Buddhism and Christianity to their needs.

The Japanese mind is tolerant almost to the point of indifference. Being eclectic, it is receptive to contrasting religious systems.[9] Throughout most of their history the people have been open to outside influences.[10] The existence of one or more religions does not preclude a receptibility to innovations.[11] Rather, variations and new systems periodically are welcomed as the existing cults lose their vitality and freshness. Once established in Japan, the new religion becomes subject to the eclectic processes at work in the environment. Saichō, the founder of the Tendai sect in Japan, is credited with the simile of Buddhism, Confucianism and Shintō as the three legs of a tripod on which Japan's welfare depends.[12] Another common expression describes Shintō as the root, Confucianism the leaves, and Buddhism the flower and fruit of Japanese civilization.[13] Kyokutei Bakin,* Japan's greatest novelist, once declared, "Shinto reverences the way of the Sun; the Chinese philosophers honor Heaven; the teaching of the Buddha fails not to make the Sun a deity. Among differences of doctrine the fundamental principle is the same.[14] The three systems have become so interwoven during the centuries that to a certain degree in content, and to a greater extent in effects, they are indistinguishable. Shortly after the first Protestant church was established, both within and without its membership there were those who would adapt the Christian faith to its new environment. While the desire to indigenize the religion for the sake of making it more acceptable to the people was in most cases sincere, there were also persons who in the interests of

---

* Bakin (1767–1848) wrote two hundred ninety works much admired by Japanese readers; he has, however, proved less popular with foreigners.

patriotism would have made it secondary to the needs of the nation.

Despite the tendency towards syncretism, and its flexibility as to details, the Japanese religious consciousness is also intransigent. Successive waves of Chinese and western influence appeared to blot out the indigenous *kami* (Shintō deities) cult, yet it had repeatedly demonstrated the capacity for self-rejuvenation. *Ryōbu* (dual aspect) Shintō reduced Shintō's *kami* to a secondary position, and discarded much of its ceremony and ritual, yet pure Shintō has always retained functions and a status exclusively its own.[15] The ceremonies at Ise and other national shrines were continued even during the periods of Buddhist prosperity. At the time when the Tokugawa favored Buddhism for purposes of state, Shintō reappeared in the teachings of patriots, and finally played a significant role in demoting Buddhism from its position of prominence. Likewise, Buddhism suffered some hard blows during the age of civil wars and following the Restoration; yet despite the reverses experienced, ancient forms and beliefs which long since had disappeared from India and China were perpetuated in the temples of Japan.[16]

This tendency on the one hand to effect a synthesis, and on the other to preserve original traditions, has resulted in mass adaptation.[17] The form has been maintained, while the content and use have been varied according to local needs, *e. g.*, the Confucian ideas of virtue were borrowed, yet the incumbence of the Japanese emperor was left dependent upon his ancestry rather than upon the will of Heaven. The pride of the Japanese made them critical of the materials they borrowed. Even in the days when the Nara court was aping Chinese customs and manners. Prince Shōtoku recorded differences from the Chinese in interpreting Buddhist works.[18]

To become successful in Japan, a new religion must needs gain patronage among the ruling classes. Buddhism was recommended to the Japanese court by a Korean king and won the support of a powerful family. After the regent, Prince Shōtoku, undertook the task of rebuilding Japanese civilization upon the new religion, Buddhism became for all practical purposes the state church, which position it retained until the Restoration. Confucianism was introduced early into Japan, yet did not spread as a cult until the scholar, Hayashi Razan, persuaded Tokugawa Ieyasu to grant it official recognition. The rapid progress of Christianity in the southwestern provinces during the latter part of the sixteenth century was due in part to the Jesuit success among the local feudal lords *(daimyō)* who in turn were desirous of earning profits from trade.

Wide variations are included within the pattern of Japanese religions. Save for a hierarchy of priests and the department of government which handled Shintō affairs, the *kami* cult knew no organization prior to 1882 when the ethnic and religious differentiation was made.[19] Confucianism was perpetuated as a cultural force having neither system nor organization until the middle seventeenth century. The Jōdō sect of Buddhism was only a doctrinal system until decades after its founder's death. In each of these three cases, the lack of definite form and order facilitated the spread of the dominant ideas into other institutions. Having no organization, the teachings risked extermination; for instance, Taoism entered Japan as a doctrine about the time of Confucianism, yet its identity became merged into Shintō, Ō-yōmei philosophy, and Zen Buddhism.[20] The fluid condition of the ideas also made them susceptible to easy alterations. Thus Shintō took on the metaphysical girding of Buddhism and the ethics of Confucianism.

The Christian church as introduced by Xavier in the 16th century and by the Protestants again in the 19th century is unique in Japan. The term "church" has often been used in western writings to indicate local Buddhist temples, monasteries and sects. Actually it is a misnomer. Buddhist organization is far more vague and flexible than its Christian counterpart. Believers are enrolled at the temples, their support is solicited for local and missionary work, yet there is no Buddhist fellowship or communion worthy the name. The social aspect of religion in Japan is supplied by family, communal and group relationships. Worship at shrines and temples alike is perfunctory, with attendance usually voluntary. Prayers may be long or short, extemporaneous or written, pasted on the building or uttered by the priest on behalf of the believer. Credal statements are uncommon, and while there have been canons of scripture, the very variety has prevented them from attaining the importance attached within the Christian church to the Bible. The *Nihongi*, the *Kojiki*, and the classical written prayers *(Norito)* are treasured in Shintō circles but not to the same degree as the scriptures among the Christians. Sermons there are, especially in the popular sects founded during the Kamakura period. The services held in Shingon and Tendai temples are not presumed to have social value; the *sutras* (Buddhist scriptures) are usually chanted from the Chinese translations (most of them have never been reduced to Japanese) by priests who are quite often ignorant of the meaning of the sounds of the words. The services which are conducted several times daily are held to have value within themselves, and thereby resemble the Roman Catholic mass.

Japanese religion in its more indigenous expressions follows the genius of the people in being empiric and practical rather than metaphysical; ritualistic instead of abstruse.[21] Speculative philosophy is regarded as an amusement proper only for lazy monks. Such elements of speculation as are present are part of the borrowed philosophy and religion, the native cult being almost entirely lacking in metaphysics.[22] The original interest in Confucianism was not in its abstractions, but in the ethical relations it bore to Chinese governmental and political institutions.[23] Buddhism's chief attraction was that it was the vehicle of continental culture, and could be used to centralize the Japanese state. Roman Catholic Christianity was admitted in the later middle ages because the Japanese rulers believed they had to accept the Portuguese religion in order to engage them in commerce.

Religion in Japan is aesthetic, kindly and gracious. Originally nature and the universe were thought to be composed of myriads of sentient parts, all of which were or at least would become *kami*. This ascription of divinity to the powerful and awe-inspiring, the useful and the lovely, led to the worship of such varied objects as the sun, the cooking pot and the rocks on the hillside. Not fear but gratitude motivated their ritual.[24] Extremes of religious expression and fanaticism were unusual save in times of rapid social change. The persecution of religion was relatively rare. Oppression of religious groups was usually precipitated by their participation in politics, or engaging in activities which were regarded as harmful to the state.[25]

Although religious freedom existed in Japan to the extent that the welfare of the government was not endangered, in practice, the state has ordinarily kept religion under its control. There was no clear differentiation between religious and governmental functions in the earliest Japanese society. The polytheistic animism and ancestor worship as incorporated in ceremony, social practice and belief were constituent parts of the state system. Following the introduction of continental culture, Buddhism provided the moral and physical assistance whereby a central government was established in Nara.[26] The ecclesiastical hierarchy thereby became a dominant, political force. Even so, the "church" remained throughout the Nara period in theory, a department of the government.[27] In the Rescript of 749, Buddhism was spoken of as an instrument of government, "useful for protecting the state."[28] The provincial temples erected in the eighth century and earlier were constructed at the orders of the emperor because they were considered essential to the country's welfare.[29] Kūkai (Kōbō Daishi) and Saichō (Dengyō Daishi) in their age felt that the religious and political powers of the state should be coördinate. During the four centuries of the Heian era the Buddhist sects were so closely related to the governmental oligarchy that the politico-ecclesiastical rulers were able to dominate the important movements of the age.[30] The Kamakura period witnessed a reaction against the official formalism of the sects founded by Kūkai and Saichō and the growth of several popular religious movements. These were largely separated from the state though Nichiren, the founder of the school of Buddhism which bears his name, identified religion and the life of the nation.[31] Contemporaneous with the disintegration of the *bakufu* (feudal government) during the Ashikaga Shogunate, the monasteries and temples followed the pattern of the times by becoming small states unto themselves. They maintained armies which were used for offensive warfare as well as for defense; they made alliances with and against feudal lords who were striving for military supremacy; and in several instances they offered effective opposition to Nobunaga, the strongest power of the day. Hideyoshi and Ieyasu also had to contend against the warrior priests, but recognized that a pacified Buddhism could be an asset to the state. In order to destroy Christianity, the Yedo government elevated Buddhism once more to the position of a state cult, and for purposes of counterpoise established Confucianism as the religion of the *samurai* and scholars. This arrangement disappeared in 1868 after which date (until 1882) the government vacillated in its patronage, sometimes favoring Buddhism, sometimes Shintō.

The history of religion in Japan thus presents a variegated pattern. Shintō instilled a reverence for the universe and its parts, all of which were venerated as sentient beings. Confucianism provided standards of morality and philosophical ideals. Buddhism fostered notions of holiness, humanity and detachment.[32] The positive effect of Roman Catholicism on Japanese life and institutions was negligible.

SHINTŌ

Shintō, which means literally "the way of the gods," is the indigenous cult of the Japanese. Prior to the coining of the term in 555[33] there existed a reverence for sentient nature expressed through ritual.[34] All nature was thought to be alive, therefore such objects as the sun,* classes such as trees,* properties such as growth,* phenomena such as the wind and the practise of abstinence,* not to mention human beings* and possibly the spirits of the ancestors* were deified and worshipped. As the tribes were fused into larger units, the emperors, who were regarded as descendants of the kami that had created the nation, became objects of special reverence.[35] Even though Confucianism provided the dominant ethical norms for Japanese society and Buddhism pre-empted the leadership of many local shrines and assumed most of its emotional and intellectual functions, Shintō still continued to serve many of the primitive needs of folk faith and to provide rites for the imperial family and therefore acquired a political character.[36] Places of worship were simple and constructed so as to blend with the stern beauty of the landscape.[37] The most ancient ceremonies reflected

---

* (sun) Amaterasu Omikami.—*Nihongi*, Vol. I, p. 18; (trees) Kukunochi.— *Nihongi*, Vol. I, p. 22; (growth) Musubi no kami.—*Nihongi*, Vol. I, p. 5; (abstinence) Hirata and Tatsuta.—*Nihongi*, Vol. II, p. 416; (human beings), e.g. Koyane, ancestor of the Nakatomi house.—*Nihongi*, Vol. I, p. 82–83; (ancestors): References to the worship of ancestors are scarce in ancient Japanese literature. Aston believes it is an innovation from China.— *Shintō*, pp. 44ff.; Holtom, D. C., *The National Faith of Japan* (New York, E. P. Dutton & Co., 1938, pp. xiii, 329). p. 31, and Sansom, *Japan, a Short Cultural History*. p. 53 agree. Eliot, *Japanese Buddhism*, pp. 180–181, is inclined to recognize its indigenous origin. See *Nihongi*, Vol. I, p. 27 note.

the social needs of an agricultural folk; that is, they were designed to protect the food supply, secure prosperity, ward off calamities, continue the imperial reign, and effect ceremonial and moral purification.[38]

Shintō continued through most of Japan's history to be the cult of the imperial house, while Buddhism after the sixth or seventh century A. D. increasingly became the religion of the common people. It was inevitable that the primitive cult should largely have given way to a highly developed religion such as Buddhism, the cultural instrument whereby the national life was transformed.* The gradual shift from the native to the exotic religion was effected by interpreting the Japanese *kami* as avatars of corresponding Buddhist deities. *Ryōbu* (dual aspect) Shintō was the term whereby this synthetic system was known after the twelfth century, though its evolution had begun soon after the introduction of Buddhism.† Schools of "pure" Shintō were founded during the fifteenth century that sought to restore a reconstructed national cult to the position of official religion. In the eighteenth century a genuine renaissance was effected by several scholars who had concluded from a study of ancient documents that Shinto was the religion of the land, that the emperor as descendant of the Sun Goddess was the rightful head of the nation, and that the Tokugawa ruler,

---

* In Prince Shotoku's Seventeen Articles Buddhism is mentioned but not Shintō—*Nihongi*, Vol. II, pp. 129–133, yet the *kami* have been retained. —*Nihongi*, Vol. II, p. 135. Buddhist magic is regarded as superior to that of Shintō.—*Nihongi*, Vol. II, pp. 174–175. The victory of the Fujiwara clan over the Soga is also interpreted as the triumph of believers in the *kami* over the house which first accepted Buddhism.—*Nihongi*, Vol. II, pp. 184–194.

† 1. Holtom, *op. cit.*, pp. 34–35; Anesaki, *History of Japanese Religion*, pp. 111–122. See Aston, *Shintō*, pp. 360–362, who thinks the soul of Ryōbu was essentially Buddhist, some of its terminology alone being Shintō. Sansom, *op. cit.*, p. 223, contends that there is nothing in the writings of Kūkai and Saichō to prove they originated Ryōbu, and that the theory which regards the *kami* as manifestations of the Buddha was evolved at a later date.

the *shogun*, was therefore an usurper. This intellectual revival of Shintō contributed to the Restoration of 1868.[39] There is certain evidence that Hirata Atsutane, one of the scholars responsible for the revival, may have been influenced by Christianity. Imaizumi Genkichi and Muraoka Suketsugu have demonstrated that Atsutane's *Honkyō Gaigen* (Compendium of Fundamental Foreign Teachings) was patterned after one of Matteo Ricci's works, and that Hirata Tetsutane, his successor, had in his possession Chinese Old and New Testaments, and J. L. Nevius' Introduction to the Divine Way (*Shindō Sōron*) and Evidences of Christianity (*Tendō Sōgen*).[40]

Contemporaneous with the anti-Buddhist reaction that followed the Restoration Shintō became (1868) the official religion. In 1872 the government sought to improve the religious situation by replacing the *kami* cult with certain nationalistic principles, and by employing both Buddhist and Shintō ritual and personnel. Some device for uniting the supporters of the throne was also needed to assist in the substitution of a central government for the semi-independent principalities. Shintō, a perfect instrument for the purpose since it derived the emperor's authority directly from the *kami*, was thereupon made the official religion.[41] Five years later this experiment was abandoned, Buddhism and Shintō were granted their autonomy, and active steps were taken to transform Shintō into a civic institution divorced from religion.[42] As several newly organized cults combining nationalistic ideals and popular theism had identified themselves with Shintō, especially during the period when it was the state cult, the government in 1882 officially distinguished between Shrine (*Jinja*) and Sectarian (*Kyōha*) Shintō.[42] The former included those "characteristic ritualistic arrangements and their underlying beliefs by which the Japanese people celebrated, dramatized, interpreted and supported the chief values of their national life."[44] Sectarian Shintō finally consisted of thirteen sects which had developed from the instruction of popular teachers

during the nineteenth century. They were organized to con-
serve traditions and to emphasize such varying concepts as
nationalism, Confucianism, purification, and faith-healing.
Their ethical level was high. They emphasized purification
as a sound foundation for personal and social religion, and
pointed outwards towards universalism in contrast with the
earlier indigenous faiths of Japan.

CONFUCIANISM

Confucianism was introduced into Japan as early as the
fifth century,[45] and became intrinsic to the life of the nation
when the Chinese political institutions which it undergirded,
were borrowed, about the seventh century A. D.[46] It was not
recognized as a philosophical system, however, until the Tokugawa era. The tendency of the Japanese innovators to
adapt rather than copy from China was demonstrated in
their perpetuation of the theory of divine origin as the basis
for the emperor's status and authority rather than the Chinese
concept of virtue.* Confucianism in Japan prior to the time
of Tokugawa Ieyasu concerned itself primarily with government, history, politics and the formal facts of life rather
than with abstract philosophy. In 1608 the *Teishu* system
taught by the Hayashi family was made the official code of
the educated classes of Japan. This step was taken to
establish a counterpoise for the politically dangerous Buddhism which continued to be the religion of the common
people. As interpreted by Hayashi, Confucianism not only
taught the long honored virtues of loyalty, filial piety, brother-
ly love, humanity, righteousness, politeness and general tran-
quillity, but supplied them with metaphysical sanctions as
well. The *Teishu* system was granted official recognition

---

* The Chinese principle was well known and lip service given to it.—*Nihongi*,
Vol. II, pp. 223-238-239. The native principle was the one observed in
practise.—*Nihongi*, Vol. II, p. 226.

because its insistence that the five classic relations are counterparts of natural laws gave moral undergirding to the social and political *status quo*.[47] Of the rival schools which developed in spite of official prohibitions, the most influential was that of Wang Yang-ming (*Ō-yōmei*, in Japanese) in the teachings of Nakae Tōju. As it stressed the ultimate equality of all men, the Ō-yōmei system performed a revolutionary service for Japanese society. Tōju taught that man was created in the image of *Ryōchi*, the prime or universal conscience, that man's relation to it was filial, and that the moral life was spiritual exercise in devotion to the father of the universe.[48]

The tendency of Confucianism to become sectarian contributed to a reaction against foreign learning, and to a revival of interest in the Japanese classics, which was an integral part of the Shintō rennaissance mentioned above. Seeking to divorce Japanese religion from its Confucian connections, Motoori Norinaga, the noted Japanese scholar of the revival period, returned to the ancient mythology of early Japan and glorified even its absurdities. By recognizing and emphasizing the authority of those ancient accounts he supplied "pure" Shintō with an ideology, and post-Restoration Japan with a basis for patriotism.[49] Aston insists that Confucian teachings were abandoned in favor of the Japanese *kami* because the sophisticated abstractions of Chinese learning failed to satisfy Motoori's own religious longings.[50] Murdoch believes Motoori employed Confucianism as a scapegoat for his patriotic ideas; that is, he attributed the sad plight into which the national cult had fallen to foreigners, but left his readers to read between the lines the fact that the Tokugawa shōgun's usurpation of the emperor's position was the real crux of the matter.[51] Whatever Motoori's motivation, Confucianism played a prominent part in the Restoration and the revival of Shintō as the national cult.

Closely related to the Chinese system and to Zen Buddhism was Bushidō, the so-called "way of the warrior," which the feudal government, the so-called *bakufu*, adopted as an instrument of state towards the end of the seventeenth century. Bushidō had become a set of ideals for the whole of society, evolved from the disagreements of philosophers rather than by soldiers.[51] It survived after the Restoration as the code of the people. Bushidō was an amalgam of Buddhist endurance and scorn of death and danger, Shintō respect for country and sovereign, and Confucian loyalty and filial piety. It also insisted upon undivided attention to one master, and held a high regard for honor as over against life.[53]

Confucianism was a continuing force in the latter part of the nineteenth century through its influence upon ancestor worship, its inculcation of the five relationships, its insistence upon loyalty and filial piety within these relationships, and stoic discipline which through the influence of Bushidō had become a national trait.

TAOISM

Taoism, China's indigenous religion, while it sometimes has been identified with Shintō, did not survive in Japan as a system. It was appreciated during the Nara period for its magical claims. Some of the sects of Buddhism imported from China show the effects of Taoist environment. Zen Buddhism in particular reflects Taoist influence in its naturalism, quietism, and mysticism.[54]

BUDDHISM

The original offer of Buddhism in 545[55] and its acceptance by Japan in 552[56] were related to the facts that a certain Korean king was in military difficulties,[57] and that there were two contending factions in the Japanese court.[58] Buddhism's triumph was due to its dominant position within the Chinese civilization in vogue during the Nara period,[59] to the leadership of Prince, Shōtoku, Umayado, a personality capable of consolidating the religio-cultural movement,[60] and to the fact that the throne was twice occupied by a woman during the first century after its arrival.* Prince Shōtoku's initial act in 593 as regent was to establish Buddhism as the state religion.[61] Temples were erected at private and state expense.[62] Buddhist scriptures were expounded.[63] Professors were appointed to instruct the priests in the practise of the teachings of the Buddha.[64]

During the Nara period (710–732) Buddhism so dominated the court as to reduce the affairs of state to a secondary position. A Buddhist priest who was acting as advisor to one of the empresses was considered as a candidate for the throne. Temples were erected in such numbers as to absorb half the resources of the central government. The removal of the capital was the means finally adopted to break Buddhism's control of the nation's political life. Not only were monastic discipline, learning, customs and institutions introduced by the Nara rulers, but six separate schools of Mahayana Buddhism as well. Their common method of salvation, whether mystical, or rational, was to rid the mind of sensory illusions and to apprehend transcendental nature. The teachings of the sects were not regarded as exclusive dogmas but as prerequisites for profounder truth. Several of the different systems were often taught in the same monastery. Official encouragement of Buddhism had once been motivated in part by fear of disease. The final triumph of the Indian religion was due to a superiority in doctrine, ideals, and organization over the native *kami* cult, the missionary enthusiasm it engendered, its program of social work, its virtual mono-

---

* For an account of the reign of Suiko Tenno (593–628 A. D.) see *Nihongi*, Vol. II, pp. 121ff; for Kogyo Tenno (642–645 A.D.) see *Nihongi* Vol. II, pp. 171ff.

poly upon learning outside of court circles, and its tax-free lands.[65]

The Heian period witnessed a comprehensive interpretation of Buddhism suited to the expanding spiritual needs of the age. The essential teachings and method of salvation had needed to be made more available for the ordinary man without resorting to metaphysical and ritualistic extremes. Tendai and Shingon, two sects imported directly from China during the Heian era, fulfilled these requirements. The Nara groups had opposed the establishment of the two new orders especially since Saichō (Dengyō Daishi), who had been granted imperial permission in 805 to establish the Tendai Sect on Mt. Hiei, desired to set up a new ordination seat which would destroy their monopoly of priestly ordinations. The new religion taught that the absolute is present in all phenomena, and that enlightenment comes by combining the study of scriptures, religious practises and contemplation. The second innovator, Kukai (Kōbō Daishi) established the Shingon (true word sect), the cult of Dainichi Nyorai, on Mt. Kōya. His system was intellectual, magical, and symbolic rather than ethical; it held that the universe was both phenomenal and noumenal, and denied any ultimate separateness. This metaphysical concept lent itself in the 11th century to a blending of Buddhism and Shintō into *Ryōbu*, that is, dual aspect Shintō.[66]

Two varieties of Buddhism figured during the civil wars and military domination which marked the Kamakura period (1185–1338). Jōdo, Shin, and Nichiren were three popular doctrines and Zen a new type of intuitive, contemplative Buddhism initiated or introduced at this time. These divisions had a distinct national character due to the abnormal social conditions and needs which evoked them, and to the fact that Buddhism had by this time become indigenous. Jōdo and Shin taught that salvation was obtainable through the repetition of the nembutsu, the sacred formulae, *Namu*

Amida Butsu, that is, "Adoration to the Buddha Amida," in childlike trust in this Buddha's love and compassion. As this was a principle which could be practised in connection with other sects, its growth was thereafter rapid and constant. Shin differed from its parent Jodo in that it regarded a single repetition sufficient for personal salvation, and that the believer should live a normal life, dispensing with ascetic and monastic practises. The fact that Shin priests could marry resulted in the subsequent development of a hierarchical system and an inheritance of temples and privileges.[67] Popular in its appeal, national in its aims, and militantly critical of all other sects was Nichiren Buddhism, the sect founded by Nichiren, who more than any other religious leader might, because of his zeal for religious and political reform, be called a prophet.[68] Nichiren, who based his teachings solely on the Lotus Sutra, taught that salvation was achievable by the repetition of the formula *Namu Myōhō Rengekyō*, that is, "Adoration to the Lotus of Perfect Truth." Whereas the earlier speculative schools had appealed to the scholar, and the emotionalism of the three popular sects to the weary, illiterate, and oppressed, Zen became the religion of the warrior, suited as it was for camp life and conditions attendant upon war. Zen taught that enlightenment could be experienced in the absence of dogma, scriptures, ritual, teacher or images, that phenomenal existence was empty, vain and unreal, and that worldly cares could be transcended. While Zen's moral ideal was beyond good and bad, the attainment of intuitive assurance was measured by the quality of action and conduct. Justice, honor and courage were stimulated among the ruling classes, and from them filtered down to the common people. The emphasis upon things spiritual revealed man's affinity with nature. Aesthetic enjoyment became associated with commonplace things. These teachings and practices based upon them entered into the constitution of Bushidō.[69]

During Japan's dark ages (1338–1500) the Zen masters greatly influenced the *samurai*, the warrior class and the rulers, and kept learning alive outside the two main cities. The other sects assumed the traits of the warring age. They maintained armies, their monasteries became feudal castles, the priests terrified Kyōto (Miyako), the capital, and engaged each other and the feudal lords in war. During this age of conflict and destruction, architecture, painting and literature, being nurtured in the Zen monasteries, flourished as never before. In the civil war down to 1615 Buddhism was revealed as a threat to the rising military leaders. Nobunaga and Hideyoshi each in turn waged war against the Shin, Jōdo, Shingon, and Tendai sects. In 1571 Nobunaga destroyed 3,000 Tendai temples on Mt. Hiei and slaughtered the warrior priests. A ten year siege upon the Ishiyama monastery (Shin) in Ōsaka failed to overcome the Buddhist fighters. The emperor finally intervened to effect a compromise.[70] In 1585 Hideyoshi assailed and captured Negoro, a Shingon monastery, with its 2,700 temples and army of mercenaries, in retaliation for an attack the priests had previously made upon Ōsaka. Whereas Nobunaga had wished to crush Buddhism, Hideyoshi recognized that politically impotent, it would be a valuable instrument in the hands of the state. He therefore patronized it, and aided it financially to regain some of its former splendor.[71]

The Tokugawa rulers (1615–1868) continued Hideyoshi's policy. Buddhism was made the state religion for purposes of attacking the Christians (Kirishitans). Everyone was required to be registered at a local temple. Some of the temples destroyed during the wars were rebuilt. The edict of 1614 crystallized the then existing Buddhism and thereby perpetuated sects which might otherwise have disappeared. Whether because of its exploitation by the state, or because of its previous military defeats, Buddhism thenceforth manifested tendencies towards doctrinal refinement but little religious or cultural vitality. Dogmatic elaboration became common as the sects sought to oust heretics.[72] So enmeshed was Buddhism with the social and political *status quo*, it suffered persecution in the revolution which followed the reopening of Japan,[73] and the various sects were virtually disestablished by the decree of February 23, 1871.[74]

The contributions of Buddhism to Japanese life over the centuries have been numerous and profound. Buddhism was "the teacher under whose instruction the Japanese nation grew up." It was at one and the same time vehicle, inspiration, creator, and an essential element of continental civilization. The native *kami* cult became changed under its impact from a primitive mythology to a reasoned philosophy. The recording of history was introduced. The Japanese language became a cultural and educational device. Logic, psychology, and natural sciences were introduced. In short Japan became transformed under its influence from a collection of unorganized, uncultured tribes into a civilized nation. Japanese architecture, sculpture, and painting, and to a lesser degree music and poetry were created by Buddhism. In the area of religion, Buddhism enlarged the conception of divinity from an animistic polytheism to a lofty conception of the divine source, and deepened the sense of man's destiny by teaching that the universe is orderly and operated according to law, that morality is obedience to this law, and that religious sentiments can be induced by the proper religious stimuli.[75]

Such was the religious situation in Japan to which Christianity was first introduced. Scholars have set forth theories to the effect that Christianity made its entry into Japan through Shingon or other sects of Buddhism via China. Certain evidence has been adduced to relate Nestorianism and Gnosticism to Chinese Buddhism at the time cultural relations between Japan and China were in flux, These hypotheses offer interesting conjectures, but until additional proof is forthcoming, most western and Japanese scholars are agreed that they must be regarded solely as suggestions for research.[76]

CATHOLIC CHRISTIANITY—KIRISHITAN MISSIONS
(1549-1868)

Francis Xavier with a party of Jesuits and one Japanese convert reached the southwestern coast of Japan in 1549, bringing the first knowledge of what the Japanese called the Kirishitan religion. They were granted permission by the lord of Satsuma, in whose province they had landed, to preach their religion. Within a year one hundred fifty converts had been baptized and Xavier was ordered to desist. He determined at this juncture to make a trip to Kyōto, then known as Miyako, in an effort to interview the ruler of Japan. He stopped enroute at Hirado and Yamaguchi, and effected conversions at both places.[77] The trip was unsuccessful in that the missionaries were unable to present their credentials to either the emperor or the *shogun*. They deduced from their experiences, however, that their primary efforts should be directed toward the conversion of the ruler rather than the common people. They altered their methods accordingly. By the time Xavier sailed from Japan in 1551 several hundred persons had become Christians and the church was growing, particularly at points in Kyūshū and in Yamaguchi. Around 1560 a second effort in the Kyōto district resulted in the conversion of Takayama Ukon, one of the important persons to become a Roman Catholic during the era of Kirishitan missions.[78] After 1568 the missionaries were favored by Oda Nobunaga who had become the dominant political and military figure in the land.[79] Although the emperor had proscribed Yasokyō, another name for Kirishitan, Nobunaga recognized in it a convenient tool to use in his campaign against Buddhism, and in the missionaries men of learning and breeding who were socially agreeable. The ten years of his domination constituted the most unmolested period of Kirishitan activity. So successful were the missionaries in gaining the favor of the *daimyō* that by 1581 there were 150,000 baptized Christians though the foreign force number but fifty-five.[80] Toyotomi Hideyoshi, who succeeded Nobunaga as *de facto shōgun* in 1582, effected no change in policy towards the Kirishitans until 1587 when he posted an edict against Yasokyō and ordered the missionaries (but not the merchants) to evacuate.[81] The reason for the order was his fear that the powerful *daimyō* who were attracted to the foreign faith might combine against him or be used by the missionaries for subduing the land.[82] That he was more anxious to weaken than extirpate Yasokyō was demonstrated by the fact that the order remained virtually unenforced for ten years, during which time he weighed the relative advantages of promoting foreign trade and of suppressing Kirishitan missions. Meanwhile he organized the Korean expedition, and one of his two most important commanders was a Christian, who had under his command four Christian *daimyō* and 18,000 Christian soldiers.[83] The continued activities of the Jesuits resulted in thousands of baptisms including persons of high rank.

The reasons for this rapid success were numerous. Xavier arrived at a time when the country was decentralized, economically disturbed, and politically disorganized; the local *daimyō* were therefore free to accept or reject the faith according to their personal wishes.* The Ashikaga *shōgun* even during their period of dominance had been receptive to foreign ideas. The Japanese had long borrowed culture and religion from the Chinese and were thus open-minded about foreign ideas and religions. Buddhism had become aristocratic as well as military-minded; it lacked the ele-

---

* In Nagasaki, a territory belonging to the Kirishitans after 1513, virtually the entire city accepted the faith.—Matsura, *op. cit.*, pp. 129, 130.

ments of appeal in an age of anarchy. The resemblance to Buddhism led many to think they were embracing a new interpretation of the Indian Law.[83] The *daimyō* of the southwest were anxious to reap the profits which might accrue to their provinces from foreign trade, particularly in the import of firearms; they believed, with some reason, that they could attract trade best by patronizing the religion of the Portuguese. Having been adopted out of mixed motives, the faith was purified in the experience of many believers, giving them a missionary zeal and courage and stamina in the face of persecution.[85] The high moral character and sacrificial living of the Jesuits were in marked contrast with the life of the Buddhist priests.[86] These favorable conditions in Japan coincided with the wave of missionary impulse which followed upon the counter-Reformation and the imperialistic expansion of Spain and Portugal.

Competition from the Spanish priests complicated the position of the Jesuits. The Franciscans journeyed from the Philippines ostensibly to consult Hideyoshi concerning a trade agreement.[87] While quartered in Kyōto they erected a chapel and in 1594 began open preaching in the face of the anti-Kirishitan edicts. Two years later the Spanish pilot of the ill-fated *San Felipe* sought to intimidate the authorities by relating the geographical expansion of the European nations. Hideyoshi retaliated in 1597 by executing twenty-six missionaries and converts at Nagasaki, and by ordering all save a few designated missionaries to assemble at Nagasaki for deportation.[88] Many of them failed to obey the order, yet before great persecution could be inflicted Hideyoshi died in 1598. Tokugawa Ieyasu patronized the various orders for a time in an effort to develop a profitable foreign trade, being influenced in his attitude by the close relations which existed between certain Christian *daimyō* and the missionaries.[89] When the Spaniards proved more anxious to send missionaries than ships, Ieyasu grew wary. After Will

Adams, an English Protestant, became trade and navigation advisor, the *shōgun* began to consider methods of conducting foreign trade through some other power and without the presence of priests.[90] Perfunctory bans were published in 1607 and 1611, but not until 1614 was an ultimatum issued, for cumulative causes which were largely political. The Spaniards had taken coastal soundings. Christian officials had been detected in sharp practises. A *daimyō* sent an embassy to the Vatican and Kirishitan lands. Several believers were involved in a plot to overthrow the *shōgun*. News arrived of the presence of a fleet in Manila. Sectarianism and national jealousies had resulted in much quarreling and invective among the missionaries from the different countries. An aroused Buddhist priesthood brought to bear official pressure against the agents of the alien religion.[91] In 1614. therefore, an ultimatum was delivered ordering all missionaries to be gathered for deportation and all churches to be destroyed.[92] Many evaded the order, but were persecuted following the death of Ieyasu in 1616 even more vigorously than before. In 1629, the practise of trampling on the picture of Christ was instituted in Nagasaki.* During the thirty-nine years after the edict thirteen efforts involving seventy-nine Kirishitans were made to smuggle priests into the country.[93] The death blow to the movement was the suppression of the Shimabara rebellion in 1638, an insurrection among the Kirishitans and discontented agrarian elements.[94] Only 1,500 persons are known to have been martyred for their faith preceding this event; about 37,000 lost their

---

* Matsura, *op. cit.*, p. 134. In addition to the reasons for the extermination of the Kirishitan religion mentioned above it should also be noted that the missionaries and Christians had suffered various degrees of persecution from the beginning, that the patrons of the missionaries included *daimyō* who had been defeated in the civil wars, that the English and Dutch sought to prejudice the government of Japan against the Roman Catholics, and that the hostility of renegade Christians aggravated the plight of the missionaries.— Satow in *Transactions of the Asiatic Society of Japan*, Vol. VI, Part I, 1878, pp. 43–45; Matsura, *op. cit.*, p. 133.

lives in this defeat. Edicts were issued after the suppression of the rebellion forbidding all merchants save the Dutch from visiting the islands.[95] Ships which violated the order were burned and their passengers executed.[96] Thus did Japan isolate herself from the west in order to eradicate the Kirishitans and to escape the danger of becoming a foreign colony.

A Japanese scholar has said, " The Christianity of Japan outwardly perished but spiritually it lived. The Christian's faithfulness and sincerity and devotion, with all zeal and purity, were with few parallels in the history of world Christianity.[97] Yet, despite this fine sentiment, most of the effects of Kirishitan missions upon Japan were negative. The church won, then lost thousands of adherents, and persisted through the Tokugawa period only as a secret community. The experience endowed the Christian religion with a bad reputation which has never been completely expunged. The extended period of isolation prior to 1853 enabled Japan to become unified, and to make the transition from a feudal to a commercial economy without civil wars. This peace was secured by a rigidity which excluded all possibility for spontaneity or self-expression. The national consiousness was first aroused by fear of the foreign religion; the claims to absolute loyalty of the believer led the Japanese to reassert the principle of national loyalty. The moral ideal of chastity seemed to have gained currency from the Kirishitan example.[98] Other ethical and theistic ideas may have penetrated Japanese thought and religion. Certain placenames of Kirishitan origin were affixed to streets and mountains.[99] Kirishitan epitaphs were the first instances in which a mixed Japanese and Chinese script was employed. This type of writing became during the Meiji era a common practise.[100]

THE REINTRODUCTION OF CHRISTIANITY

The first missionaries to Japan in 1859 gradually learned that, as the religious situation was inseparable from the policies of the government, certain political problems had to be solved if Protestant missions were to make an impact upon Japan. The outstanding fact which confronted the missionary pioneers was the existence of the long-standing anti-Christian laws.*

For a Japanese to accept the hated religion of the west was punishable by death. Anti-Kirishitan propaganda had constituted the spear-head of the feudal government's, that is, the *bakufu's* isolationist policy since 1614. Fear and hatred were perpetuated among the common people by legends of infanticide by foreign priests, cannibalism, and attempts to subjugate the empire.[101] That the government had no intention of relaxing the ancestral laws was indicated by the imprisonment, persecution and scattering of thousands of Roman Catholics who declared their faith after they had contacted the newly arrived French priests in Nagasaki.[102]

Buddhism was in a state of decline. The years of official favor had not been salutary for the discipline of the monks and temples. Both Confucianism and Buddhism were persecuted while the mania for things foreign swept the land. They were accused of having retarded Japan's development and endangered her national safety by instilling patience, quiescence, and submission to superiors.[103] During the interval when Shintō was the official cult Buddhism survived by local patronage and by reason of its place in the undifferentiated religion of the common people, especially its monopoly of funerals.[104] The influence of Christian teachings and practises led to local reforms in Tōkyō and Kyōto,[105] but

---

* These were reissued as late as 1868.

not until after the conclusion of the period covered by this study did Buddhism experience an inner reformation. The Buddhist sects did seek to counter the advances of the Christian movement when it became evident that the former state religion was losing prestige and income.[106] By lectures, by publications, by subsidizing other periodicals to attack Christianity, and by bribing and threatening[107] converts to effect their return to Buddhism, the campaign was waged against the missionaries and the young church. The charge was made that to become a Christian was to be disloyal, and to destroy the constitution of the nation.[108] Buddhists sought to induce the inhabitants of interior villages to boycott their neighbors who embraced the new religion.[109] Buddhist and Shintō priests in Ōsaka sought an injunction against mass meetings held by Christians in theatres, but failed in their efforts.[110] During a slight reaction in the years 1878–1879 student evangelists from Dōshisha found that points around Kyōto, a Buddhist stronghold, which had previously been opened to Christian services were closed.[111] Niijima Jō experienced local difficulty in obtaining passports whereby alone could missionaries reside in Kyōto as teachers in the Dōshisha. After he had explained the purpose and organization of the institution to the vice-minister of Foreign Affairs in Tōkyō, the objections were removed.[112] The people of Kyōto were advised by the ward offices not to visit missionary homes or attend Christian preaching places.[113] A French Catholic missionary was beaten by one hundred twenty Kyōto Buddhist students in 1883.[114] In characterizing the Protestant denominations, a Buddhist periodical, the *Meikio Shinshi* referred to them as "wolves in sheep's clothing," "having money, they suffer from lack of learning," and "following ancient rules, they judge others who do not follow as foolish."[115] Yet so dangerous were the opponents, said the *Kaidō Shimbun*, the Buddhist priests were obligated to either drive away the missionaries or convert them to

Buddhism.[116] The *Meikio Shinshi* believed that to study the spirit of the times and adapt Buddhism to the changing needs of the nation would be a more effective method of opposition.[117] In practise both suggestions were followed. Insofar as the government would permit[118] during the ninth decade of the century, Buddhists sought to counter the advances of the Christians by both a positive program, and by direct attack.

In contrast with the decline of Buddhism, Shintō increased in prestige and status. The studies in Shintō made by Motoori Norinaga, Hirata Atsutane, and Rai Sanyō had contributed to the Restoration.[119] For a time Shintō was the state religion. European scholars had sought to induce Japanese statesmen studying on the continent to retain the *kami* cult in that capacity,[120] although even after the '80's Shintō had not become sufficiently powerful in the national life to justify its retention as the official religion.* Many new sects were organized during the nineteenth century which united nationalism with popular religious teachings. These were set apart in 1882 as the thirteen religious sects of Shintō.

Confucianism became a weakened ethical force. The notions of filial piety and loyalty were too deeply rooted to be permanently eradicated by new ethical ideals, though they were overlooked for a time. During the financial depression of 1883, popular resentment against the unfair treaties of the west resulted in an abortive attempt to revive Chinese learning and morality.[121]

---

* Verbeck says that in 1869 Shintō exerted little or no influence.—*Proceedings of the Ōsaka Conference*, p. 35. Down to 1905 Aston regarded it extinct as a national religion.—Aston, Shintō, p. 377.

Chapter II

THE SOCIAL SITUATION

THE POLITICAL SCENE

The commercial expansion of the western powers following the Napoleonic wars led to the stationing of fleets in the Far East. Whaling boats from New England were numerous in the northern Pacific. Ships needing repairs or supplies, and sailors wrecked off Japanese coasts were subject to the caprice of Japanese officials.[1] Several attempts by western nations were made to break the diplomatic, commercial and religious isolation of Japan but without success until Commodore Matthew C. Perry of the United States squadron in the Far East succeeded in 1853 and 1854 in concluding a treaty, which provided for the care of shipwrecked sailors, the provisioning and refitting of ships, the opening of two ports at one of which a consulate was to be established, and for trade in accordance with local regulations.[2] Townsend Harris, who was stationed at Shimoda in 1856 under the terms of this agreement, by the exercise of diplomacy, sympathy and persistence succeeded in negotiating additional treaties in 1857 and 1858 which granted citizens of the United States the right to reside in three open ports and to engage in commerce, subject only to the jurisdiction of their own consular courts.[3] Religious worship was permitted within the foreign settlements but the Japanese remained subject to the ancient restrictions against the Christian faith. Japan also concluded similar treaties with other powers of the west and China. Protestant missionaries entered Japan under the clause permitting nationals of the treaty powers to reside in the open ports.[4]

Perry's demonstration of strength had convinced the *shogun* and some of his ministers that Japan was in no position to refuse the demands of the western world. The imperial court at Kyōto and many of the *daimyō* believed that the exclusion policy should be maintained.[5] They insisted in their slogan *Sonnō Jōi* that the western barbarians should be expelled and the sovereign revered. For more than seven hundred years the *shogun* had paid slight attention to the political authority of the emperor, but under these circumstances he was compelled to temporize, weakened as his government was by class conflict, economic bankruptcy and social stagnation.[6] The *bakufu*'s finances could bear neither a civil nor a foreign war. Attention over many years had been focused by Japanese scholars upon the royal prerogatives of the Kyōto court. The Satsuma and Chōshū clans with political ambitions of their own had never been content with the dominance of the Tokugawa and were therefore in a mood to participate in any scheme likely to overthrow the Yedo rulers. The ministers of the *bakufu* began to refer matters to Kyōto, which unique procedure shook popular favor in the *shōgun*'s power. His position became even more precarious after foreigners began to reside in Japan. Minor armed clashes occurred between the Japanese and the foreign visitors and residents. The emperor issued an order expelling the occidentals. The Chōshū clan took action against vessels of the western powers passing through the straits of Shimonoseki. As the *bakufu* failed to give the aggrieved nations satisfaction, they combined their forces to destroy the fort at Shimonoseki, and then demanded an indemnity which the *shōgun* agreed to pay.[7] In November 1866, as a device to compel the emperor to ratify the treaties, a show of armed force was made off Hyōgo. The foreign powers succeeded in their plans.[8] The treaties were ratified. Conditions meanwhile pointed towards civil strife. The rapidly waning authority of the *shōgun* made it impossible for him to better conditions. He was memorialized on October 14, 1867 to restore the government to the emperor. He agreed, and on December 15, the shogunate was dissolved.[9] In March, 1869, the *daimyō* began surrendering their fiefs to the crown, thereby making possible a unified political state, with the authority vested in a single ruler[10]

So important had been the southern *daimyō* in effecting the Restoration it was feared that the leaders of the Satsuma and Chōshū clans might replace the Tokugawa at Yedo. To safeguard against such an eventuality the emperor in his coronation oath promised that a deliberative assembly would be called for the purpose of conducting public affairs in accord with public opinion.[11] When Ōkuma Shigenobu resigned from the cabinet in 1881 internal conditions forced the government to concede that a legislative assembly would be convened in 1890. The decade which elapsed before the first Diet was assembled was a period of agitation and political change. Itō Hirobumi headed a commission which studied the constitutional models of the west. Japan's was patterned after that of Germany as being a mean between the absolutism of feudal Japan and the republican systems of England and the United States. The Constitution was thus in process of formulation during the period covered by this study. The document and the Christian movement were alike influenced by the trend towards westernization then in process, though in somewhat different directions. Itō's problem was to utilize the constitutional principle, yet establish an imperialistic government which would be sufficiently strong to curb the individualism and socialism emerging because of Japan's contact with the west.[12]

The treaties the *shōgun* had signed furnished the basis

of an attack upon him by his enemies The party supporting the monarch criticised the *bakufu* for admitting the
westerners, but once the monarchists had obtained political
control, their isolationist pretensions were dropped and they
began to patronize the west. The emperor invited the foreign diplomatic representatives to Kyōto to be received in
audience. The people were ordered by official proclamation to
treat westerners with respect. Newspapers were penalized
for statements derogatory to the foreign powers.[13] As the
nation progressed in the assimilation of western culture the
inequality of the earlier treaties began to be felt.[14] The
matter of custom duties and the rights of extraterritoriality
enjoyed by foreign residents were especially irritating to the
Japanese, yet the western powers refused to alter the treaties,
questioning the adequacy of Japan's judicial system. The refusal was resented locally because of the west's basic assump-
tion that Japan's civilization was inferior, because of the loss
in revenue entailed, and because of complications in the
administration of justice, as, for instance, illegal practises
conducted under the protection of the settlements.[15] By way
of retaliating for the unequal treaties the interior was kept
closed to foreign commerce and residence. Save for holders
of passports issued for health reasons or for scientific investigation, the missionaries were confined to a few of the
larger port cities.* Repeated efforts were made by the
Japanese to secure a revision of these treaties,[16] but not until
1899 was Japan's judicial autonomy or the right to control
her own tariff's restored.

---

* During October, November and December 1883 the Kobe authorities issued
197 passports to foreigners for interior travel. It can safely be presumed
that many of them actually were for evangelistic purposes as these were not
vacation months.—*Yomiuri Shimbun* in *Japan Weekly Mail*, January 26, 1884,
p. 74.

ECONOMIC CONDITIONS

The basis of Japan's economy from ancient times was agriculture. Ninety percent of her people lived in villages. Industry was insignificant in quantity and was largely confined to handicrafts in the home.[17] Only during the Ashikaga period had foreign trade assumed quantitative proportions. Even after the treaties had been signed with the west, trade developed slowly. Tea and raw silk were the most important exports prior to 1887. Between 1872 and 1881 inclusively, the total unfavorable balance of trade was ¥49,262,283. By rigorously curtailing imports, a favorable balance of ¥19,652,729 for the next three years was registered, a fact which enabled the nation to store up a quantity of silver to buttress its depreciated currency. It was during the '80's that the weaknesses of Japan's economic system first showed the strain of the national transformation. Great expenditures, much of it in fixed investments which yielded small returns, exports increased in an effort to correct the unfavorable balance of trade, a decline of the value of exports to the west, reduced crops, a fall in prices due to the contraction of currency, and debt pressure were some of the reasons for the financial crisis. By 1885 many people had begun to wonder if the changes were worth their cost.[18] Yet the state was expected to take the leadership in all the innovations, so long had it maintained a paternalistic attitude toward the people.[19]

CULTURAL AND TECHNOLOGICAL DEVELOPMENTS

Japan's cultural development subsequent to the reopening of the country to the west was directed by two contradictory forces, one the movement towards a restoration of the ancient regime, the other towards a renovation of the national life along lines of western customs and usages. The former was conservative and nationalistic, emphasizing the Confucian ideas of loyalty and filial piety; it would maintain the ancient seclusion of the nation withal for the sake of progress. The latter would dispense with the institutions, customs, morals and religion in vogue during the Tokugawa era; it stressed individual rights as over against the claims of the family, and internationalism as opposed to nationalism.[20] The tension between the two was never completely resolved.

The anti-foreign sentiments of the emperor's party gave way immediately after 1868 to the spirit of reform, progress, and westernization. The restored sovereign proclaimed on March 14, 1868 that councils should be convoked for the settlement of state affairs by public discussion, that the government and social affairs should be conducted by the united spirit of the governing and the governed, that in national unification all the subjects should be given full opportunities for their aspirations and activities, that all absurd practises should be abolished, and that knowledge should be sought for throughout the world. In accord with these policies, students were sent abroad to study the industries, education, military organization, politics, art and culture of the west. Experts from France, America, England and Germany were engaged as teachers, advisors, and technicians.

Education in the new knowledge was regarded as the avenue to national renovation and personal accomplishment. *Bunmei Kaika* (Enlightenment and Civilization) was a popular slogan from the '74's down to the time of the reaction. Universal education based on French and American methods was adopted. Many western scholars after 1871 assisted in planning and putting into operation the educational program for the nation. By 1875 public primary schools had been erected not only in the cities but in many of the interior villages as well.[21] Mission schools inside the settlements grew out of classes originally started in private homes. Westerners, many of them missionaries, were invited to teach outside the treaty ports even though foreigners could not ordinarily reside in the interior. Thousands of Japanese books and magazines, and millions of copies of newspapers were sold or circulated annually.[22]

The physical sciences, ethics, sociology, and jurisprudence from the west undermined Chinese science and learning. The utilitarian ideas of Mill in combination with the ethic of the *samurai* produced an attitude that was sceptical of all religion.

In 1882 German philosophical productions and military achievements won high acclaim. After this date the prestige of things German was enhanced as officials and students returning from the continent gave glowing accounts of the important scientific and philosophical advances in progress there.*

Social reform made its appearance under both state and Christian auspices. Institutions for the care of the blind, deaf mutes and orphans, hospitals, and homes for the indigent were operated by provincial governments while reform movements were sponsored by the churches.

The removal of the capital from Kyōto to Tōkyō, then known as Yedo, symbolized the break with the 1000 year seclusion of the emperor. The feudal regime was replaced by a centrally controlled bureaucracy. The *samurai* class was abolished. The penal codes were revised in 1870. The substitution of a conscripted army in 1872 for the *samu-*

---

* From Germany Japan borrowed "the way of setting up western or representative government which should not actually infringe in any way upon the autocratic oligarchy of the Chōshū and Satsuma clan leaders . . . . They were sure that only a high degree of centralized power would permit the development of an army and navy, and a strong foreign policy which would save Japan from undergoing the same fate at the hands of western powers that the rest of Asia was undergoing."—Dewey, John, *Characters and Events* (New York, H. Holt, 2 vols., 1929), Vol. I, p. 156.

rai helped to weaken the military traditions of the ruling class.

The government which replaced the Tokugawa administration was composed of representatives from the clans that had participated in the Restoration. Popular efforts to alter clan control were inspired by the American and French Revolutions. Political parties made their appearance. There was much controversy over liberty and human rights.[23] The term *jiyū* (freedom) became attached to a newspaper, to a political party, and was one of the common terms of the era. When the government sought to suppress the assertion of individual rights as being dangerous, some use of arms and violence resulted. The imperial declaration of 1881 which promised a parliament led the agitators to divert their energies towards preparation for the event.

A national bank, specie bank and postal savings system were established to expedite trade, commerce and the westernization of social life. Transportation developed under private and government subsidized control. Steamboats, foreign-built at first, but later constructed in Japan, connected the port cities of the islands with the continent. A railroad was opened between Tokyo and Yokohama in 1872. In 1886 a telegraph system was established under the authority of the post office. In 1877 a Tōkyō telephone company was granted a charter.

Every aspect of life was expected to undergo reform. Dancing halls were sponsored by the government; English theatricals were given in higher schools; there was talk of adopting English as the national language; inter-racial marriage was discussed; Christianity was advocated as the national religion because it was the faith of the west. It was urged that the family of nations would adopt Japan only after it had conformed to the occidental pattern; that is, the unequal treaties would be revised only when the domestic reforms satisfied England, France, Germany, and America.

The Christian movement was conditioned not alone by the local environment but also by the type of culture with which it was contemporaneously introduced. It would therefore be well to summarize those components of western civilization, which, as will appear subsequently, were alternately responsible for the rapid advance and retardation of the church in the empire.[24]

Science, as an aspect of occidental culture, had come to the attention of the Japanese through their Dutch contacts.* The widespread ambition to acquire a knowledge of the physical universe provided openings for those missionaries who were versed in any of its branches, but on the other hand, the controversy and alleged conflict between science and religion served to undermine the influence of the latter. The supernatural Christianity which was taught in Japan discredited it among the intellectuals. The missionaries gave numerous lectures and published learned and popular discourses maintaining the compatibility of the faith with true science.

The progress man had made in the mastery of the universe through the application of science, was to Japan a second conspicuous and desirable feature of the west as well as the most telling indictment against her own culture. To supply the omissions of the past as well as to gain for the nation the material advantages of occidental civilization, a concentrated movement was launched under the auspices of the central government to modernize the nation by constructing railroads, steamships, telegraph, telephones and factories.

A closely related aspect of western culture that grew to

---

* "In Japan...Western Science was represented...by a few Hollander merchants and skippers...yet...there were always to be found Japanese of all classes intensely eager to learn, and if possible, to master the mysteries of the West ...Dutch books...were eagerly sought and purchased, often for literally their weight in gold, and translations of medical, military and scientific books were made with ever increasing frequency."—Boxer, C. R., *Jan Compagnie in Japan, 1600–1817* (The Hague, Martinus Nijhoff, 1936, pp. xvi, 190), p. xiv.

wide acceptance was the scientific method. The respect commanded by science, especially in the schools, extended its authority to all phases of life. One organization carried the enthusiasm for observing the procedure of science to the extreme of suggesting that a religion for Japan should be constructed on its principles, to the exclusion of all other religions.

A series of changes which grew out of the application of science was a fourth contribution of the west to react upon the Christian movement. The development of commerce and capitalism, which had preceded the reopening of the country, continued apace.[25] Factories were built. Population, which had been almost static during the entire Tokugawa period, began to increase. The cities of the Tokugawa period served as focal points for the activities incident to the process of westernization. Education, formerly in the hands of the Buddhist priest and following along lines of Chinese learning, was revolutionized according to the occidental pattern. Most of the educational responsibility was assumed by the government, although private and religious institutions had more scholars than accommodations. The esteem in which knowledge was held led to the installation of universal primary education. These changes caused a gradual decline in the family system, and the ethical and religious values it had fostered. The nation shrank in size as railways were extended, and coastal boats plied the shores.

A fifth set of changes in which Japan reproduced the western pattern was in the reorganization of society on the basis of a new ideology. The Confucian doctrines which the Tokugawas had established as orthodox made loyalty to superior and filial piety obligatory upon every Japanese, and thereby established a social pyramid with the *shōgun* at the top and the masses of the people at the base. The most novel of western ideas were those of democracy, liberalism, personal rights and individual freedom. These abstractions appealed partly because they were new and identified with the west, and partly because they offered release from the obligations of the system enforced by the Tokugawas. The competitive element of capitalism made its appearance as many of the ancient regulations were eliminated. The price exacted by the rising commercial classes for their support of the emperor as over against the *bakufu* was that ancient restrictions would be relaxed, and that Japanese trade and capital should be permitted to expand. They provided the financial support for the defeat of the *shōgun* in 1868 and for the establishment of the new government. Socialism and communism appeared in the west as a reaction against the extreme expressions of this spirit, yet they began to make their entry only towards the end of the '80's. A missionary, Dwight W. Learned at the Dōshisha in Kyōto, first expounded these economic theories in the classroom. It was the liberalism and freedom which was embodied in political platforms and in editorial policies, that made the greatest progress down through the year 1889, and culminated in the establishment of the national Diet.

Intellectual currents that were stirring the west were a sixth factor which soon found their way to Japan, thereby affecting education, religion, and other aspects of Japan's national life. Rationalism entered in the translations and original writings of Mill and Spencer. The theory of evolution was taught in the Tōkyō Imperial University. These doctrines were regarded by the missionaries as greater evils and worse opponents than the native religions against which Christianity had to contend.

Nationalism as a world-wide movement in the latter part of the nineteenth century was a seventh element reflected in Japanese events. It was a defensive and fragmentary nationalism which led the conservatives to oppose the admission of foreigners. It was an aggressive and unitary nationalism which featured in the reaction of 1889 and afterwards.

Peace was an eighth characteristic of occidental life which helped shape events in Japan during the early years of western intercourse. America was relatively pacific from the time of the Civil War to the turn of the century, and it was America which, more than any other single nation, was regarded as friendly to Japan between 1883 and 1889. During these years the other western nations which had long been empire-bound were relatively quiescent. Russia was a growing menace to Japan's security; China had not yet learned her military weakness; France drew dangerously near in annexing French Indo-China; the English seizure of Fort Hamilton in Korea caused Japan considerable worry; yet, relatively speaking, it was a peaceful period from the time of the opening of Japan to the end of the century. This fact enabled Japan to obtain needed materials and expert consultants which facilitated the nation's plans for westernization. Embassies were able to study the military and naval systems of the west without being regarded with undue suspicion. The state of international affairs facilitated in several respects the transformation which was undertaken during those years.

A ninth characteristic of the so-called Christian lands which influenced Japan was the abounding optimism of the age. In secular Japan and in the Christian movements there, confidence and hope were induced by changes effected with great rapidity. Particularly outside the church it was thought that education in sufficient quantities would eliminate the handicaps under which Japan as a nation was struggling. To obtain the material goods, and the secrets for their manufacture, the Japanese people were prepared to make any sacrifice. These secured, it was believed, the nation would then be able to take its place in the happy family of the countries of the world. The pace at which this process progressed led many westerners to believe that Japan would be forced to adopt the religion along with the culture of America and Europe. The possibility was cheering to most of the missionaries and religious workers, yet prior to the birth of this hope, the general tone of missionary correspondence was one of brave optimism as to the future. A balancing note was the occasional insistence that the changes were going too fast, that there was bound to be a reaction, and that the changes which really needed to be made were being sloughed over in the superficial transformation then taking place.

A tenth feature of the nineteenth century was that the western and northern European peoples were expanding, either as political powers or cultural forces, over most of the world, and that while this mass permeation of life and culture was in progress, western civilization itself was being modified. Thus the rapid changes which occurred after 1859 in Japan were doubly revolutionary, a fact which was retroactively unfortunate for Christianity. Many westerners in Japan and students returning after study abroad brought reports that the religions of Europe and America was not practised as the missionaries intimated, that not all the populations of those countries had accepted it, and that even among those who were nominal Christians many questioned all or part of the religion's tenets.

An eleventh observable aspect of nineteenth century occidentalism was that English speaking aliens predominated. There existed, it is true, a fondness of German culture, especially among the clans that had consummated the Restoration, where the conviction prevailed that Germany with her strong military tradition and minimum of democracy should provide the model for the nation's structural alterations. The close relationship between the languages and cultures of Germany and Holland, with which latter country alone Japan had continued intercourse during the age of seclusion, probably strengthened the attraction for things German. Much of Japan's science, her Constitution, and the national Diet were fashioned after the Prussian standards. Nevertheless, in many other respects Great Britain and the United States held the advantage. The staffs of foreign advisors included a plurality from England. Many American features were incorporated into the educational system. More significant than the guidance rendered by foreign experts with official status was the fact that the United States was the most friendly power, and that most numerous of the western professional residents were the American missionaries, who, having wide contacts with the former *samurai*, especially in the schools, assisted in an extensive transfer of the cultural and thought patterns from the United States to Japan.

Thus it seems clear that the cultural vehicle was indispensable to the entry and spread of Protestantism. To the extent that Christianity was credited with having supplied the western world with its moral attributes, it was appropriated by those patriots who assumed that foreign origin was proof of superiority. The position of Protestantism which was regarded now as created by, now as contributor to, now as component of, and now as identical with the culture of the United States and England, constituted one of its greatest assets.

The most obvious of the elements which marked the introduction and development of Christianity in Japan having been examined, it is evident that Christianity's spread must be attributed not to one fact alone, but to the character of the people, to their religious background, to the political and economic conditions which obtained in the nineteenth century, and to the impact of a totally new culture upon the ancient civilization of Japan. It was as true of Protestantism as of the entire historic development during the Meiji period, that, as Herbert Norman has stated,[26] " the design lay with the Meiji architects, but the material was largely at hand, a legacy of the preceding age." This generalization was particularly pertinent after 1889, and true also of the years 1883–1889.

The three religions of Japan proved much more virile and firmly rooted than the missionaries suspected. Buddhism appeared to be entirely out of harmony with the trends during the era of westernization, yet it demonstrated a surprising adaptability, taking over many of the teachings and methods employed by the missionaries. The *kami* cult had lost much of its hold on the people and thus was no menace to the progress of Christianity. Not until the months preceding the reaction did Shintō become a serious rival to the loyalties of the Japanese, and then primarily as a patriotic rather than a religious expression. Confucianism seemed of the three the least likely to survive, but the principles of loyalty and filial piety were embodied in the *Imperial Rescript on Education* issued during the first year of the reaction. Missionaries sought to counteract the influence of the older faiths by open attack and through positive presentations of their own religion.

The international and domestic circumstances interacted in various ways to affect the spread of Protestantism. Whereas the fear of Christianity as a political instrument had obstructed its progress during the introductory period, the importuning of the western powers to grant more favorable treaty terms, and the friendly popular sentiments towards America, directly aided the rapid expansion during the years 1883–1889. The social flux incident to the economic revolution produced an environment auspicious for new influences and exceptional opportunities for the Christian spirit to express itself through philanthropy and education.

Closely related to the three factors mentioned above, and more relevant, was the general cultural transition that provided a milieu for the spread of Protestantism. That things of the west were in demand, and that Christianity was the nominal religion of the occident, imparted to the missionaries and the faith they taught a prestige which furthered its reception and rapid growth.

This then was the general background against which the spread of Protestantism in Japan must be traced.

Part Two

THE FIRST THREE DECADES
1859-1889

Chapter III

CHRISTIANITY RE-ENTERS JAPAN

CATHOLIC, ORTHODOX AND PROTESTANT

Three major branches of the Christian church operated in Japan from the time the treaties granted to foreigners the right of residence. Rome entrusted the field to the Société des Missions Étrangeres de Paris.[1] The first missionary reached Japan proper, and was stationed at Yedo, September 6, 1859.[2] Later arrivals were located at Hakodate, Yokohama, and Nagasaki. Shortly after the Roman Catholic cathedral was dedicated at Nagasaki in 1865, many Japanese who claimed to be fellow believers were discovered nearby the city. Thousands of these subsequently were taken into the church, though many refused to enter into communion. The immediate growth of the Roman Catholic Church in the vicinity of its former stronghold brought the statistics into the thousands. The facts that the faith was still proscribed, and that the despised and feared Yasokyō was Roman Catholic, constituted a hindrance to the development of the church elsewhere. Much time elapsed before the popular mind was able to distinguish between the Roman and the two other varieties of Christianity.

The Greek* Orthodox Mission was founded by Ivan Kasatkin, ordained as Nicholai, who was stationed as Consular Chaplain at Hakodate in June 1861. Churches were subsequently established in that city and in Sendai and Tōkyō.[3] The progress of this faith was hindered by the paucity of foreign workers[4] and the fact that the subsidy received by the mission from the Russian government gave it a political aspect which made the people dubious of its true purposes.[5] The striking features of this church's development was that the instruments of its spread were almost exclusively Japanese pastors and laymen. This fact was effective compensation for the scarcity of foreign missionaries and funds. The national character of the Greek Orthodox Church made its appeal to the patriotic Japanese of the nineteenth century. The Protestant missionaries looked with more favor upon its congregations that upon those of the Roman Catholic Church. Numerous instances are cited in which evangelists and church members changed from the Greek Orthodox to one of the Protestant churches.

We are concerned henceforth primarily with Protestant missions in Japan save as the activities of, or popular attitudes towards Roman Catholic and Greek Orthodox agents and agencies reacted upon the total Christian movement. The Protestant representatives were natives of England, Canada, Germany, Scotland, and the United States, and of differing denominations within those countries. Differences of theology were, prior to 1890, of less significance than divergencies of ecclesiastical order and church government.

---

* The term "Greek Orthodox" is retained in this text because it is generally, though incorrectly, used in most of the references discussing this subject. The term "Eastern Orthodox" or simply "Orthodox" would be more appropriate since out of sixteen or more Orthodox churches only five are Greek, seven are Slavic, two are Rumanian and two Arabic. (See Hastings, *Encyclopedia of Religion and Ethics*" VI. 428b.) The Japan Orthodox Church is one of the latest members of the Orthodox communion. All the above are independent bodies.

Overlapping there was, and competition between the different denominational groups obtained in some areas, but Japan was a populous country with opportunities adequate to challenge the energies and talents of every protestant missionary. The fact that the foreign communities were confined to a few open ports was both an asset and a liability for the development of inter-mission relationships. Ill feelings were engendered among the missionaries in the few instances in which converts and trained evangelists transferred from one to another of the Protestant denominations. The sense of a unique possession of the truth among the representatives of the missions occasionally led to claims and complaints which confused the infant churches. On the other hand, the proximity of the foreign residents in the port cities resulted in the evolution of types of cooperation which accelerated the development of each of the several sectarian churches. Among the missionaries who were early on the scene and who continued their activities over an extended period there was a spirit of tolerance and fraternity which cut across denominational lines. In such matters as projected church union, the translation of the Bible, the compilation of the hymnal, the preparation of Christian literature, the holding of mass meetings, and the promotion of conferences for joint sharing of experience and fellowship, the common problems and dangers faced by the missionaries had made most of them mutually tolerant, and interested primarily not in the spread of their own doctrinaire positions but in the Christianizing of the nation.

The efforts of certain groups were met with greater response than others. The growth of the Kumiai churches, which were Congregational in polity and were connected with the Japan mission of the American Board of Commissioners for Foreign Missions, was most phenomenal of all, the membership increasing from approximately 1,000 to 10,000 in the course of the years 1883–1889. The Nippon Kirisuto Kyōkai

(Church of Christ in Japan) associated with the Presbyterian-Reformed missions had almost the same numerical membership. The Methodist groups, while not organized into a single family, came third in order of numbers, with approximately 5,000 by the end of the decade. The Nippon Seikōkai (Holy Catholic Church), established by the Anglican and American Episcopal missions, had a thousand members less. The Baptists were fifth with only a thousand communicants.

The most effective missions were also the strongest numerically and financially. The American Board of Commissioners for Foreign Missions had in Japan by 1889 eighty-nine representatives, the largest foreign staff during its history.[6] Likewise in the case of the other missions, the size of the affiliated Japanese churches was roughly proportional to the size of the foreign personnel and the financial resources at their disposal.

The policies of the several missions relative to the concentration of forces likewise affected the growth of the churches associated with them. The Japan mission of the American Board of Commissioners for Missions first occupied Kōbe, Ōsaka and Kyōto. Later Okayama, Tōkyō, Sendai and a few other points were assigned representatives, in most of which cities there was a sufficiently large staff to undertake a relatively thorough and continuous task. The degree of concentration was less in the case of the other missions, although the policy of the Presbyterian mission was to allocate the foreign staff to a few centers so as to engage in comprehensive teaching and preaching. The Presbyterians recognized their inability to hold more than two or three stations if they were to have regard for efficiency.[7] The scattering of forces meant that during furloughs and illnesses the church and educational projects were suspended temporarily or terminated. Representatives of the Domestic and Foreign Missionary Society of the Protestant

Episcopal Church in the United States were the first to reach Japan in 1859, yet the dividing of the supervising bishop's time between China and Japan, and the subsequent widespread location of the missionaries, caused the growth of the church to be slower than that of the Methodists who, while they had arrived much later, decided that no central station should have less than two missionaries, and that operations in Tōkyō demanded a corps approximately commensurate with the magnitude of the church's task and their denominational proportion of responsibility for its accomplishment.[8]

A third decisive factor was the kind of Japanese taken into the church and the extent to which administration was transferred to national leadership. Again it was the Kumiai churches which attracted the largest number of outstanding Japanese. Without Niijima Jo,* Sawayama Paul, and the Kumamoto Band, the history of Christianity and of the Japan mission of the American Board of Commissioners for Foreign Missions would read quite differently. The connection of these persons with the church gave it prestige and zealous and capable leadership. They in turn attracted men of their own type, *samurai*, many of whom were prominent in the affairs of new Japan. The results were therefore cumulative. Uemura Masahisa as the dominant personality within the Nippon Kirisuto Kyōkai helped shape not only his own congregations, seminary and denomination, but the entire Christian structure in Japan. His emphasis upon the strengthen-

---

* Niijima was named *Shimeta* by his parents but after his return from America he always wrote his name as *Jo*. He romanized his family name as Neesima and called himself Joseph Hardy Neesima. He was a graduate of Amherst College (1870) and Andover Theological Seminary (1874). Fifteen years later Niijima was responsible for arranging for Uchimura's attending Amherst and graduating in 1887. For an unusual chapter in the development of Japanese Christian leaders through connection with a small New England college, see Cary, O., *Uchimura Kanzo no Ketsudan no Natsu, 1885* nen (Uchimura Kanzo's Summer of Decision) *Jinbungaku* Vol. xxiv April 1956 pp 95–131. Also Cary, O., *Uchimura Neesima and Amherst—Recently Discovered* Correspondence, Japan Quarterly, Vol. III No. 4 pp. 439–459.

ing of the church institution influenced not only his own denomination but other groups as well. The Baptists on the other hand admitted towards the end of the period they had not a single outstanding leader or scholar among the Japanese. The converts had been won individually largely through the efforts of the missionaries. While deprecating this method of growth and recognizing the need for leadership they were unable during this period, save for the translator and evangelist associated with Dr. Nathan Brown, to attract those with such qualifications. Had the dominant personalities who constituted the Sapporo Band, and Uchimura Kanzō in particular, remained within the Methodist Church, the evolution of that denomination during the years 1883–1889 probably would have been attended by greater success.

To ascertain why certain of the denominations attracted Japanese leadership is difficult. The national character of the two largest churches was more obvious than in the case of the others by virtue of their names. Instead of employing the western terms " Presbyterian " or " Congregational " they selected the presumptive but ecumenical title " The Church of Christ in Japan." Later when the churches connected with the Japan mission of the American Board of Commissioners for Foreign Missions assumed the name *Kumiai*, that is, " associated together," they borrowed a term which had been applied to them by others. Indigenous titles were one less obstacle against which the Kumiai Kyōkai and Nippon Kirisuto Kyōkai had to contend. More important as a means of attracting potential leadership was the fact that education was stressed by the missions of the first four mentioned denominations. Within the Kumiai Kyōkai, Niijima's conviction that what had been done in New England by way of providing religious education should be reproduced in Japan, became almost a dogma. The largest single concentration in Japan of missionaries under the American

Board of Commissioners for Foreign Missions was at the Dōshisha. This was the school which led the Kumamoto Band into the Kumiai Kyōkai. Individuals connected with the other three missions, in order to secure residence outside the treaty ports, founded a number of schools, many of which in time became ranking educational institutions. The American Baptist Missionary Union learned only towards the end of the period the importance of education in Japan. Its missionaries had believed that by preaching and by the distribution of the Bible alone the church could be established most firmly. They had not reckoned with the desire for education among Japanese youth. However, the Baptists concluded by 1889 that in order to attract Japanese to the church in numbers and to train them for leadership it also would be necessary to establish and maintain educational institutions.

The Japanese were drawn into the two largest denominations also by the opportunities within the ecclesiastical systems for national leadership. The hierarchical polity of the Methodist and Episcopal churches, and the reluctance of the Baptist missionaries to concede authority handicapped these denominations during the years 1883–1889.

The degrees of local autonomy extended by the supporting boards to the missions conditioned the activities of the latter. The changing conditions in Japan necessitated a flexible policy if the missionaries were to keep pace with the needs and desires of the national churches. Again it was the Congregational Church in the United States which took the most liberal view of the situation. The American Board of Commissioners for Foreign Missions was said to have had no policy when the missionaries wished to transfer powers and responsibilities to the church, and fortunately, for *a priori* methods invented in America would Christianize no Oriental lands.[9]

Thus the expansion of Protestantism in Japan during the

years 1883–1889 was best facilitated by intense cultivation rather than by widespread activities, by gathering individuals into communities for nurture and growth, and through the employment of a variety of methods including education, rather than by concentration upon single line of approach. In general, the techniques employed by the pioneers were continued by their successors throughout the remainder of the century. Likewise the kinds of Protestantism which spread in Japan during the period under review were those which had been introduced into the nation prior to 1883.

THE FIRST MISSIONARIES
1859–1882

Protestant missionaries made their entry into Japan under the terms of the treaty of 1858 which provided that westerners were at liberty to reside and to observe their religion within the treaty ports.[10] Townsend Harris, in negotiating the treaty for the United States which served as a pattern for those signed by other western nations, sought to introduce a clause permitting the preaching of Christianity to the Japanese, but without success.* Interested visitors to Japan, however, concluded that judicious missionaries should be able to make some progress despite the handicaps under which they would be working. Recommendations that missionaries be appointed to Japan were therefore sent to the boards of foreign missions of the American Episcopal Church, the Presbyterian Church in the United States of America, and the (Dutch) Reformed Church in America.[11]

In each case the suggestion was favorably received, with the result that in 1859 representatives of all three churches reached Japan. J. Liggins and C. M. Williams, for three

---

* *Home and Foreign Record*, July 1860, p. 208. The treaty with the Netherlands forbade the importation of Christian books, prints, and images.— Gubbins, *op. cit.*, p. 266.

years missionaries in China under the Domestic and Foreign Missionary Society of the Protestant Episcopal Church in the United States, were transferred to Nagasaki. They reached their post shortly before the port was opened to foreign residence. J. C. Hepburn, M. D. and wife, who had formerly served under the American Board at Singapore and Amoy, came to Japan as a Presbyterian missionary and arrived from America at Kanagawa in October of the same year. S. R. Brown, D. B. Simmons, M. D., and G. F. Verbeck of the (Dutch) Reformed Church in America reached Nagasaki via Shanghai in November. The following month their wives and families followed them from China. Verbeck was chosen for the position because it was thought his origins would enable him to take advantage of the long background of Dutch influence in Japan.[12] The only other mission to enter Japan during the first decade following the opening of the country was the American Baptist Free Mission Society, under which auspices Jonathan Goble and his wife arrived at Kanagawa April 1, 1860. Goble had accompanied Perry on his expeditions to Japan for the express purpose of surveying its mission possibilities, and had continued his studies until the time of his appointment as a missionary.[13]

Although changes occurred in the personnel the number of reinforcements was not large the first ten years. The Episcopal mission had been first to get its missionaries into Japan but because of the division of Williams' responsibilities between Japan and China, subsequent to his consecration as bishop, and the misfortunes of other members, the work was thinly dispersed and the field vacant during three of the first ten years. By 1872 the mission consisted of Bishop Williams and A. R. Morris at Ōsaka.[14] At the end of 1872 the Presbyterian missionaries in Japan were J. C. and Mrs. Hepburn, Henry Loomis and wife, and E. R. Miller at Yokohama, and David Thompson, Christopher Carrothers and families at Tokyo.[15] Changes and shifts in the Reformed

mission placed Brown, J. H. Ballagh and family and Mary
E. Kidder in Yokohama, G. F. Verbeck in Tōkyō, and Henry
Stout in Nagasaki by the end of 1872.[16] A special gift to the
Church Mission Society following the special appeal for prayer
made by the missionaries in Japan in 1866 led to the sending
of George Ensor and H. Burnside and wives in 1869 and 1871
respectively.* Representatives of the American Board of
Commissioners for Foreign Missions first reached Japan in
1869. By the end of 1872 the Kōbe station was occupied
by D. C. Greene, J. D. Davis, and J. C. Berry, M. D., and the
Ōsaka station by O. H. Gulick and M. L. Gordon, M. D., and
wives.[17] Mrs. Mary Pruyn, Mrs. L. H. Pierson, Miss J. N.
Crosby, and Miss L. M. Guthrie were delegated by the
Woman's Union Mission Society of America for Heathen
Lands to Yokohama where they established in September
1872 the Kyōritsu Jogakkō (American Mission Home).[18] Thus
concludes the list of the missionary personnel on the field
at the end of the interval sometimes referred to as the
period of preparation.

Seven missionary organizations were working in Japan
in 1872. During the next decade, thirteen new ones made
their entry. The American Baptist Missionary Union replaced
the American Baptist Free Missionary Society in 1873 when
its seven missionaries landed and settled in Yokohama.[19] The
General Missionary Committee of the Methodist Episcopal
Church, U. S. A., having decided to begin work in Japan in
1873, sent ten representatives who took up residence in
Hakodate, Yokohama, and Nagasaki.[20] Four missionaries of
the Methodist Church of Canada located in Yokohama, and
two men representing the Society for the Propagation of the
Gospel in Foreign Parts, arrived in Tōkyō 1873, and made

---

* *Proceedings of the Osaka Conference,* pp. 29, 46. Their work as well as that
of representatives of the Society for the Propagation of the Gospel who arrived in 1873 was until 1883 nominally under the jurisdiction of the Bishop
at Victoria, who was resident in Hongkong.—*Tokyo Missionary Conference
Report,* p. 879.

their headquarters in Mita, some distance from the foreign concession.[21] The following year missionaries of two Scottish organizations established missions in Tōkyō. Two represented the Edinburgh Medical Mission, and five the United Presbyterian Church of Scotland.[22] Four under the Evangelical Association of North America settled in Yokohama in 1876.[23] The Society for Promoting Female Education in the East sent out two women in 1877.[24] In the same year two appointees of the Cumberland Presbyterian Church took up residence in Ōsaka.[25] Work was begun by the London Baptist Missionary Society in 1879 by a representative who had resigned from a secular teaching position to become a missionary.[26] The Board of Commissioners for Foreign Missions of the (German) Reformed Church in the United States made its initial effort in sending two persons to Yokohama the same year.[27] The Methodist Protestant Church. which for several years prior to 1880 supported a number of girls at the Kyōritsu Jogakkō, during that year sent to Yokohama a worker to undertake a new educational project.[28]

Thus by the end of the introductory period, a total of eighteen missions had been established in Japan. American organizations led the list with nine societies. Of the 226 missionaries (including wives), the English, Scotch, and Canadian missions included slightly more than one-fourth.[29] The type of Protestantism propagated in Japan during the period was therefore dominantly American and secondly British. The main point of difference between the two types was that most of the English missionaries were Anglicans, whose religion was liturgical, employed the Prayer Book, and by tradition was more closely identified with the state than was American Protestantism.

TYPES OF PROTESTANTISM WHICH SPREAD FROM
1883–1889

The Edinburgh Medical Mission, the United Presbyterian Church of Scotland, and the Society for the Promotion of Female Education in the East either discontinued activities or transferred their projects to other agencies during the seven year period covered by this dissertation. Fifteen of the societies continued, however, and their numbers were supplemented by one English, one continental, one Canadian, and eight American missions. The British society known in many lands as Christian Missions (commonly called the Plymouth Brethren) sent one family to Japan in 1888.[30] The Allgemeine Evangeliche-protestantischer Missionsverein (General Evangelical Protestant Missionary Society) of Switzerland and Germany was established at Tōkyō in 1885.[31] J. Cooper Robinson of the Episcopal Church of Canada arrived in Japan in 1888 and located at Nagoya. J. G. Waller, who was sent out by the same mission the following year, was stationed at Nagano and Matsumoto for work about those centers.[32] The Church of Christ Mission, consisting of four ordained missionaries, began at Akita in 1883.[33] The Society of Friends was founded in Japan by the Women's Committee of Friends in Philadelphia in 1885, when Mr. and Mrs. J. Cosand settled in Tōkyō.[34] The Methodist Episcopal Church, South, entered Japan in 1886 and concentrated in Hiroshima and Kōbe.[35] The American Christian Convention Mission was founded by D. F. Jones at Ishinomaki in 1887, and moved the following year to Tokyo.[36] The Presbyterian Board of Foreign Missions in the United States commissioned two persons who reached Japan in 1885. At the request of the Nippon Kirisuto Itchi Kyōkai, they located at Kōchi in Shikoku. The American Unitarian Association sent A. M. Knapp to Japan as its representative in 1877, who came not as a missionary, but as an envoy to "express the sympathy of the Unitarians of America for progressive religious movements in Japan.[37] The Southern Baptist Convention first appointed missionaries to Japan in 1860. Their loss on a ship which was never heard from after its departure from New York, and the American Civil War, delayed the arrival of workers from this Church until November 1889, when J. W. Mc Collum and J. A. Brunson and their wives reached Yokohama.[38]

Relative to the Protestant bodies engaged in Japan by the end of 1889, several general statements may be made. There were twenty-six different foreign mission agencies, two of which, the (German) Reformed Church in the United States, and the Methodist Protestant Church, maintained representatives only in Japan.[39] It would appear that either the unusual opportunity, or the challenge presented by Japan, was especially attractive to the churches of the United States. Among the societies which entered after 1882, only those which affiliated with established national churches or mission families were in a position to make noteworthy contributions prior to 1890. Since the groups which entered between the years 1883 and 1889 were for the most part limited as to personnel and financial resources, and the missionaries necessarily were obliged to study the language and establish institutional foundations, it may be concluded and rightly so that the accomplishments of this seven year period were achieved primarily by the older mission agencies and churches. The most dissident elements among the Protestents made their entry during the years of easy growth. With the Allgemeine Evangelische-protestantischer Missionsverein society came a liberal theology. The Unitarians flattered and sought to supplement the Japanese religions whereas the older missions had attacked local religious beliefs and practises. The Plymouth Brethren, themselves factious, were a divisive influence among the older churches. The missionaries of the German-Swiss agency were not so intent upon making converts as upon impressing the minds of the Japanese in favor of Christianity and of imbuing Japanese society with the Christian spirit.[40] Several scholars were among their number, who quite apart from their liberal oblique slant did especially valuable historical research and theological instruction.

As has been indicated, the greatest number of Protestant missionaries was from America. The Protestantism which spread in Japan was therefore primarily American, and only secondarily British, and thirdly German.* A number of the characteristics[41] of nineteenth century western Christianity were reproduced in the Christian movement of Japan.

As propagated in Japan Protestantism was first of all an individual rather than a community faith. Buddhism had been for centuries the religion of the state. Confucianism had constituted the ethical and moral code of the *samurai* during the later Tokugawa period. Roman Catholicism had spread during the period of Kirishitan missions as a mass movement. Protestant missionaries preached a message of individual repentance and salvation. It is doubtful if many of those who listened to sermons comprehended this radically different note,[42] yet it was in line with the increased emphasis upon personal rights and individual liberty which were then the objects of political struggle. There was in the nation a limited amount of agitation for its nominal conversion, but the missionaries in general were opposed to such a step.

In the second place, revivals occurred in connection with the Christian services. The emotional element is integral in the drama, art, and literature of the Japanese people, but

---

* Liemar Hennig, missionary under the aforementioned German-Swiss agency, made application at the close of his first term of missionary service in 1939 for a scholarship at an American theological seminary. He stated as a reason for his desire to study in the United States the fact that Protestantism in Japan was American, and that any missionary who hoped to contribute to the development of the church in Japan should familiarize himself with the Protestantism of the United States.

individuals do not as a rule give public expression to their feelings. During the prayer meeting which led to the organization of the first Protestant church, however, the prayers offered by the Japanese in attendance were said to be eager and intense.[43] The nation-wide revival reported in 1883[44] was referred to by a Tōkyō pastor as a new Pentecost.[45] In a rural community to which the revival interest had spread, common forms of greeting adopted by the Christians were, "Have you received the Holy Ghost?" and "Is Christ with you?"[46] The English word revival transliterated into Japanese as *rebaiburu* became a common term in 1884.[47] Revivals, which had been instrumental in the growth of the church in America, were likewise serviceable in the establishment of the Christian movement in Japan.

A third characteristic of Protestantism in the West was its multiplication of organizations to augment the work of the churches. Many of these were borrowed by or adapted to Japan. Some of these, such as Sunday Schools, will be discussed in connection with the methods employed. Others that might be mentioned here were the Nippon Seisho no Tomo (Scripture Union of Japan) which was organized as a branch of the Children's Special Service Mission for work among adults, November 12, 1883,[48] city and student YMCAs,[49] and Christian Endeavor societies.[50]

A fourth typical Protestant manifestation of the age was schism. By 1883 there were two independent Japanese congregations which had broken loose from foreign support and denominational influences. The writings of Uchimura Kanzō and Kanamori Tsūrin evidenced that there was within Japanese Protestantism an intransigence which would in the future manifest itself in independent institutions and indigenous ideas.

Certain aspects of the Evangelical Movement made their appearance in Japan during these years as a fifth reflection of western Protestantism. The emphasis upon individual rather than mass conversion has already been mentioned. Save in the Episcopal congregations ceremony was minimized. This fact may be attributed to two influences, first, the strength of Congregational and Presbyterian simplicity among the missionaries, and second a reaction against ornate Buddhist ceremonies. The importance of the second cannot be measured with any degree of certainty, but it rightly may be claimed that this contributed in part to the slow growth of the liturgical churches. Instead of presenting showy services, most of the missionaries and Japanese evangelists sought to win the people to an intellectual and emotional experience which could be maintained by cultivating the spiritual life. The Bible and hymnal were used widely by converts, and publishing houses printed various types of tracts and books calculated to strengthen the believer's inner resources. Even more important than private devotion was the emphasis made upon right doctrine, if the list of works published on the subject during the years 1883–1889 is a criterion. Efforts to Christianize the whole of the empire were made by several of the societies, and the workers expended their activities over a maximum area in order to achieve their goal within a minimum space of time.

Shortly after the establishment of the first congregations, the spirit of philanthropy and sharing, common to western Protestantism, began to be demonstrated among the Japanese church members. Their first impulse was to make available for others of their countrymen the Christian message. Following in the footsteps of the missionary doctors, they soon began to engage in social service among dependent groups. Orphanages and temperance societies were commenced as expressions of this humanitarian spirit. The bulk of these Protestant projects were founded after 1889, however.

A seventh aspect of nineteenth century western Protestantism was its tendency towards unity in the face of its variety. The fact that this characteristic was reproduced in

Japan was both a reason for and means whereby Protestant-ism expanded between 1883 and 1889. The tension between these conflicting trends will be treated in detail below.

The kind of Protestantism which spread was determined by the denominational affiliations and nationalities of the missionaries who occupied Japan. Of the twenty-six societies represented in the empire during the years 1883–1889, the largest proportion of the missionaries were connected with the non-liturgical denominations of the United States. The missions that profited most from the unusual opportunities between 1883 and 1889 were those which during the intro-ductory period had trained large staffs of able missionaries and evangelists, and established self-sustaining, independent, national churches.

The Christianity which spread, reproduced in general the types which prevailed in America during the nineteenth century. It now remains to be seen where and among what classes of people Protestantism was disseminated.

AN URBAN UPPER CLASS MOVEMENT

The travel restrictions, the popular antipathy against Christianity, and the language handicaps in large measure confined the activities of the missionaries to the foreign settlements until the treaties were revised in the '90's. Kanagawa and Yokohama, Nagasaki and Hakodate were the initial points of missionary operation. Yedo (Tōkyō), Hyōgo (Kōbe), Ōsaka, and Niigata were next to be occupied. It was in these centers that the first chapels were erected, either for use of the foreign populations or as evangelistic centers. Schools and dispensaries begun in missionary homes, in connection with the churches, or even in specially con-structed buildings, were located within the areas where treaty-power aliens were subject solely to the consular juris-diction of the foreign powers.

The concentration of missionary and church activities in the cities, and particularly in Tōkyō, continued even after the limitations given above decreased in importance. The urban aspect of Protestantism in Japan was dictated by several reasons. First, missionaries could not leave the foreign settlement without passports. Second, the movement of the Japanese, particularly the students and former *samurai*, to the cities afforded a means of approach even within the terms of the treaties. Third, the metropolitan districts were intellectually more emancipated than the rural areas in which latter Buddhism was especially strong. Fourth, the demands made upon the Protestant agencies to provide educational facilities afforded ample contacts for the staff members without their leaving the cities. Save for a few exceptions the schools were instituted because they afforded the one large opening for missionary activity. They were continued that they might provide a Christian education for church members and adequate educational facilities for the Christian ministry. Throughout the period, the number of teachers was inadequate to staff the mission schools. There was consequently little necessity for missionaries going outside the limits imposed by the treaties in order to find contacts.

A second reason for the urban concentration of Christian churches and schools was that missionaries could obtain permits for living outside the settlements only in event that they were in Japanese employ. Few of them were willing to engage in tasks other than direct teaching. Most of the interior schools being located in population centers, the missionaries who resided outside the settlements were still located in cities. Kanazawa, Kyōto, Sapporo, Hiroshima, Nagoya, Shimonoseki, and Sendai became points of flourishing church growth through the establishment of educational institutions.

Protestantism also spread, though slowly, into the rural districts. So widely had it been disseminated that by 1889 every important city on the main island, Kyūshū, and Shikoku had been visited by missionaries or evangelists. Foreigners were able to travel outside the settlements on passports issued for purposes of scientific research and health. Some of the missionaries availed themselves of this privilege for preaching purposes, rationalizing their conduct by a variety of arguments. First, the government though aware of the practice, raised no objections to it. The regulations were political rather than religious in intent, being aimed not against Christianity, but against an *imperium in imperio*. Second, the fact that the government was seeking to maintain an attitude of religious neutrality forbade the granting of passports which would authorize the bearers to preach Christian doctrines. . . .Third, no deception was practised in the use of passports by missionaries since the authorities were aware of the existence of Christian churches in the interior and the visits made by the missionaries to them. Public religious services were conducted only after permission had been granted by local officials in accord with the rules for public meetings. Fourth, since immediate revision of the system was not to be expected, to refuse to use the limited passports was to postpone the time for extending the message beyond the treaty ports. Meanwhile anti-Christian ideas were spreading, "erroneous ideas of liberty, progress and civilization" were "exerting a misleading and demoralizing influence" on many who were seeking for knowledge.[51] Several missionaries periodically visited outstations to preach and supervise the activities of Japanese evangelists. In some instances the missionaries and associates or city pastors traveled together. By various methods, therefore, Protestantism was widely spread outside the treaty ports.

Protestantism took deepest root in the cities, however, because of the concentration of missionaries there, because the largest number of converts, the students, remained in the cities rather than returning to the provinces, and because there was more money in the urban areas to maintain an exotic religion. Most of the missionaries were anxious that the church in Japan support itself. The natural poverty of the land was such that rural districts could effect this much less easily than the cities. Pastors who sought to effect self-support and missionaries with limited funds at their disposal, inevitably concentrated upon population centers.

A second characteristic of the Protestant movement in Japan was that the most rapid progress was achieved among the upper levels of the population. The evidence is contradictory as to the strata of the church membership. Some critics allege that the Protestant church in Japan appealed only to the outcasts and the poorer classes. It is true that the lepers, the blind, the sick, and the poverty-stricken were attracted by Christian teachings and philanthropy, but the largest part of the membership came from the upper middle class. There were several explanations for this phenomenon. First, the desire of the Japanese workers and missionaries alike to achieve self-support necessitated drawing a class of people into the church which was able to pay local expenses. Second, the large percentage of persons who joined the church *via* the Christian educational institutions either before entering school were, or shortly after graduation became, economically self-sufficient. Third, thirty percent of the church membership came from the *samurai* class, although it constituted but five percent of the total population. The relatively large ratios of Christians in the local assemblies, in the first Diet, and in government and educational posts, were additional evidence that the Christian church permeated the upper middle level of the population.[52] The fact that the churches are today almost exclusively made of such people confirms this supposition.

Protestant Christianity spread then primarily in the urban population centers, and only secondarily in the rural areas; and its greatest strength was among the educated, upper middle classes of the population.

CHARACTERISTICS OF PROTESTANTISM'S GROWTH[53]

The processes whereby Protestantism made its way in Japan differed in several aspects from those which characterized the spread of the Roman Catholic and the Greek Orthodox faiths, as well as from those of all previous religions which had been introduced into Japan. Many of these processes persisted from 1859 through the period covered by this study, and in a measure determined the impact of the religion upon the nation.

The first characteristic of Protestantism to be noted is that it relied primarily upon personal rather than upon governmental resources. Buddhism came recommended by a Korean king. The worship of the Buddha was adopted experimentally by one of the powerful families. Xavier and his Jesuit colleagues had royal backing when they sought to establish the church in Japan. Roman Catholic missionaries were assisted by the French government. The Greek Orthodox mission received a subsidy from the Russian Government. The Anglican missionaries were members of the Church of England, though the missionary subscriptions by which they were supported were voluntary. Some few schools were inaugurated through the joint efforts of local governments and certain missionary agencies, but for one reason or another, they were discontinued within a relatively short time. The largest part of the funds which were utilized in the propagation of Protestantism in Japan, however, were voluntary contributions from churches and individuals in the United States.

Missionaries did enjoy the privileges extended to the nations under the terms of the treaties. They were exempt, through the period covered by this essay, from Japanese judicial processes. Once during the early years western gunboats waited in Yokohama harbor ready to evacuate the foreign residents in event of anti-foreign riots.[54] In 1871 the missionaries entreated their governments, on grounds of humanity rather than religion,[55] to bring pressure to bear upon the *bakufu* in the interests of the Kirishitans who had been persecuted, arrested and exiled. The next year a committee of American missionaries prepared a memorial to the President and Secretary of State requesting that the United States government cooperate with the other treaty powers in judicious and friendly endeavors to secure by treaty stipulations the right of religious conscience, freedom to travel and live in the interior, permission to teach the Christian religion, to employ servants, translators and teachers, and to gather the Japanese believers into churches.[56] All these excursions into politics, in which opposition was offered by the missionaries to the Japanese government, occurred during the period when Christianity was being introduced into Japan. Yet the missionaries also petitioned their governments in 1884 to restore to Japan her national integrity, by revising the treaties in her favor.[57] This new departure in the separation of Protestant workers from the imperialistic policies of their nations, made an important contribution to the removal of the political suspicions against them. During the years 1883–1889, the missionaries enjoyed official favors in their efforts and their attitude towards the government underwent a pro-Japanese change.

A second characteristic of the spread of Protestantism in Japan was the participation in the movement by women, a development made possible by the improvement in travel facilities, by the orderly conditions which prevailed in Japan, by the leadership which women gradually assumed within the church in the West, by the establishment of women's boards for the support of single women as foreign missionaries, and by the emerging feminist movement in the Occident. The direct activities of the single women missionaries were teaching and administering day and boarding schools and kindergartens, and visiting the country churches;[58] indirectly their approach was by teaching the home arts, training and superintending Bible women[59] and colporteurs and translating and publishing tracts.[60]

Mary E. Kidder (Mrs. E. R. Miller), a member of the (Dutch) Reformed Church was the first unmarried female missionary assigned to Japan. She arrived in the autumn of 1869, a full decade after the landing of the pioneer missionary families. Following a period of language study in Niigata, Miss Kidder began teaching in a day school in Yokohama,[61] which by 1875 developed into the Isaac Ferris Seminary.[62] The Kyōritsu Jogakkō, a girls' boarding school, was opened at Yokohama in 1871 by three persons who had come to Japan under the Woman's Union Missionary Society.[63] Three unmarried women reinforcements for the Presbyterian mission and two for the American Board mission arrived in 1873. After that time the personnel of most of the other missions at work in Japan was likewise augmented.[64] The demand for girls' schools led to the establishment of such institutions in many places where women were located. A large number of the female educational institutions were started in this fashion.

By the end of 1882 there were fifty-six single women as well as eighty-one wives on the foreign staffs of the various missions located in Japan. There were thus 137 women as compared with eight-nine married and single men.[65] At the end of 1889 the number of unmarried women had increased to 103, making a total of 251 women as compared to only 148 men missionaries.[66] Thus, whatever success was achieved by the missionaries was due in no small measure to the activities of the women. They contributed chiefly to schools for girls and women, in which field they had a virtual monopoly. Whereas competition from the government institutions in the field of men's education forced the mission ary schools to improve the curriculum and teaching facilities, little effort was made by the state or other private agencies to provide for the education of women.

In some missions women missionaries proved their merit and demonstrated their qualifications in the face of strong opposition. In most cases women had no vote in mission councils even concerning matters relating to their own activities.* Wives were usually not computed as *bona fide* missionaries. Towards the end of his missiohary career, J. C. Hepburn, who had been moderate in his prejudices and liberal in his views, wrote that a work seemingly peculiar to his day which he had regarded from the beginning with doubt and mistrust was that of women; that women were nevertheless coming to the front, breaking the bonds which held them, asserting their rights and displaying a real ability.[67] A not uncommon allegation by male missionaries was that for women to assume such positions of leadership was heretical and unscriptural. The pressure was in some few instances so strong that individuals were forced to leave the field. In justice to the missionaries it should be indicated that these attitudes were not essentially different from those which prevailed in the churches of the west at the same time.

In contrast to the situation which obtained within the missions, men outnumbered the women in the national church. In 1883 the percentage was seventy-four to twenty-six. By 1886 the ratio had dropped to sixty-three men for each thirty-seven women.[68] One reason for the masculine predominance was that the strong barriers separating women from public life made them subject to criticism for attending public meetings.[69]

A third feature of the spread of Protestantism in Japan was the high standard set by the missions and the Japanese

---

* The American Board group at its first session following the arrival of requested "lady associates" amended its constitution to grant them vote concerning their work. F.C.

evangelists for admission into the church. While the amount of pre-baptismal instruction varied according to the individual missionary or evangelist, the requirements for acceptance into the church were high. The methods employed by the Jesuits in the sixteenth and seventeenth centuries had resulted in mass conversions. During the rule of the Tokugawa, a Japanese subject was required to register at a local Buddhist temple irrespective of his religious convictions or practises. Protestants set a high standard for admission into the church, although the restrictions were relaxed somewhat during the years 1883–1889. The rate of increase was for a short while after 1882 so rapid that the standards fell, yet many of the untutored converts separated from the church during the reaction. The condition of admission to the church remained a personal religious experience, however, even during the era of rapid increase. Only in connection with the revivals was there anything resembling the earlier mass movements.

A fourth feature of Protestant missions in Japan was the disproportionate influence of the church in relation to its size. Mass permeation was the effect as Christianity, an integral element of western life, helped to fashion Japan's emerging culture. The influence of Protestantism was greater than that of the other two branches of Christianity. Roman Catholicism concentrated upon the task of strengthening the Church rather than seeking to mould the nation's culture. Russian civilization was not as highly regarded as that of America and Britain, nor were the resources of Greek Orthodox Church in Japan sufficient to affect the total life of the nation. The effects of Protestantism, as will be indicated, were to be seen in various phases of the cultural development of the new nation.

A fifth point of importance was the decreasing missionary control. While there were exceptions within certain of the missions, the general policy was to pass the administration into the hands of the national leaders. There were certain conditions which necessitated this shift, and which accelerated the process following the reaction. The first of these was that Japanese Christian leadership came rapidly to the fore. Niijima Jō[70] achieved prominence both as a preacher and as founder of the Doshisha. He was regarded in some quarters as the head of Christianity in Japan.[71] His influence in official circles enabled him to take the initiative in numerous matters connected with the work of the Japan mission of American Board of Commissioners for Foreign Missions, of which he was an associate member. Sawayama Paul became known as the ministers' minister. The self-sacrifice on his part which enabled his congregation to begin as a self-supporting institution furnished the churches of the American Board Mission with a pattern which was widely followed.[72] The Kumamoto Band provided churchmen in the personalities of such Japanese as Ebina Danjō, Kanamori Tsūrin, Miyagawa Tsuneteru, and Kozaki Hiromichi,* pastors, educators, editors, and evangelists. Many of the Japanese who gathered in Tōkyō in May 1883 for the Triennial Conference were already outstanding figures in the religious life of the nation.[73] The school founded in 1876 at Tōkyō for the daughters of Japanese officials by Sakurai Chika was the earliest instance of a Japanese pioneering in the field of Christian education.[74] This institution later became merged with the Tōkyō Joshi Gakuin, the Presbyterian girl's school. A second reason for the decreasing control of the missionaries was the early realization of self-support and independence by many groups of Japanese Christians.[75] The growing consciousness that to the national church belonged the responsibility for evangelizing the land was traceable to the instruction of the missionaries,[76] to the anti-foreign feelings which were part of the

---

* Though a fellow student at Kumamoto and Doshisha, Kozaki Hiromichi was not technically a member of the Kumamoto Band.

heritage of the past, to the restrictions upon missionary travel which forced upon the native Christians the burden of expanding the church into the interior, to the fact that many missionaries were engaged in educational institutions,[77] and to the proved ability of the Japanese leadership.[78]

The processes whereby Protestantism spread in Japan differed then but little from those which were effective in other mission lands during the same period. The missionaries relied upon personal rather than upon governmental resources. An important role was played by women missionaries. High standards for church admission were set and maintained. Instead of mass movements into the church, there was mass permeation of the national life with Christian ideals and customs, so that the influence of Protestantism was much greater than its numerical growth would indicate. From the time of the founding of the first churches, the missionaries' authority over local congregations was on the wane. These generalizations are pertinent to most of the missions although truer of some than of others. They are also relevant in varying degrees to the different methods used, to which study we now turn our attention.

Chapter   IV

EDUCATION

The methods employed in the spread of Protestantism in Japan both prior to and following 1882 were essentially identical. Those techniques which had been effective in the first instance, were usually continued as a matter of course.

The methods were the logical outgrowth of the missionary's conception of his purpose[1] and the nature of the environment in which that purpose was implemented. With the exception of a few liberal sects which entered during the latter half of the eighties, the missionaries sought to induce a particular type of Christian experience, obtain assent to a certain theological statement, stimulate the growth of certain attitudes and behavior, and organize the believers into churches that within a minimum length of time would become self-supporting. The nature of the environment in which the pioneers sought to effect these aims has already been outlined. Schools were, in the case of the more influential missions, the means whereby the initial contacts were secured. Even while the anti-Christian edicts remained unrepealed, English day schools for boys and girls, and religious meetings and Bible classes for young men and adults were being conducted in missionary homes.[2] The results of these efforts led to the establishment of churches which were missionary in purpose. As public sentiment permitted, public lectures for the discussion of moral science, the Japanese religions, and philosophy were promoted, first in Tōkyō and then in the various cities and towns. Dispensaries were common during the early years, but the decreased emphasis upon medical missions after 1883 marked the main difference between the methods of the latter years from those of the introductory period. The literary output prior to the time the translation of the Bible was begun was primarily for the purpose of facilitating the missionaries' study of the language. The years of our special study witnessed a rapid multiplication of periodicals, books, and tracts on Christian subjects, prepared in large measure by the missionaries but increasingly by the Japanese Christians. Evidences of the fact that Protestantism was to become famous in the twentieth century for its social mindedness and works of philanthropy, were hardly to be seen by the end of 1889. A single orphanage was the one important social welfare institution founded by Japanese Protestants during the so-called period of rapid growth. Efforts to unify the activities of the Protestant agencies had been made during the years before 1883. Some of them were successful, notably the merger of the work of the Presbyterian and Reformed missions into a single Japanese church. While even greater attempts were made between 1883 and 1889 the only success was achieved along lines laid down during the earlier period, that is, through merging of some of the activities within families of missions.

Schools were opened by the first Protestant missionaries for the training of Japanese youth. Nor were the Japanese slow to respond. Few of those who matriculated did so from any desire to become Christians. Rather they were motivated by a desire to study foreign languages under skilled instructors, and to master the occidental learning which loomed so important in the transition the state was undergoing. Thus, the students were easily recruited, and they in turn acquired a knowledge of foreign languages and western education. The mission schools were staffed by better educated men than were many of the state schools which hired foreign instructors indiscriminately. The former acquired a reputation for scholarship which attracted the more serious students.[3]

The manner in which many of the mission schools were founded was a very natural one. After a group started in the missionary home had attained sufficient size to necessitate moving to more ample quarters, the "school" might meet for a time in a rented building. As the native style structures were unsuited for school rooms, a site would then be selected and purchased, inexpensive buildings erected, a library and apparatus provided, a staff of Japanese teachers and one or more missionaries installed, and fixed courses followed. The running expenses amounted to about one-third the cost of maintaining similar institutions in America, yet such schools were not self-supporting. The difference between tuitions and costs of operation was supplied by mission boards, churches, and a few interested Japanese citizens. Self-support could not be realized in the mission schools because of the low standards set by the state schools as to tuition charges, and because of the general indifference to higher education among the wealthier classes. Competition depressed the tuition fees, and philanthropic indifference made it difficult if not impossible to secure endowments locally. It was among the *samurai* that the desire for learning was strongest, yet these former warriors manifested little ability for business and were thus in no financial position to grant substantial aid to the schools. Although the mission educational institutions were not self-supporting, few of the students were dependent upon their charity.[4]

Some kindergartens and primary schools there were, but the bulk of the educational facilities was designed for youths between the ages of twelve and eighteen, that is, the Christian institutions catered primarily to the high school age, the final stage of training for nine-tenths of those who entered. The curriculum included science, literature, language and religion, but not technical subjects. There were some missionaries who were averse to Christian educational institutions, but the concensus of opinion held that Christianity in Japan could not rest content with simple experiences and implicit faith. The church also was obliged to give a clear and explicit answer to the disputed questions of the unsettled period. Most of the schools included distinctly Christian elements in the curriculum as well as daily chapel, weekly prayer-meeting, and Sunday services. Many of the teachers and students engaged in Sunday school and summer vacation religious activities outside the school. The Bible was not universally taught.[5]

In 1883 there were nine mission schools for boys with a total attendance of 454, or an average of fifty-one to each school. The fifteen girls' schools had a combined attendance of 566 which averaged thirty-seven per school.[6] During a similar period in China after more than seventy-five years of Protestant efforts[7] the mission schools averaged fifty-four per institution, and in the United States where secondary education was much older and better established, the average attendance was 158 per school.[8]

Hundreds of young men and women thus given the advantage of a Christian education went forth into Japanese society carrying with them the impression of the classroom and chapel, and many as church members. A number of them entered the ministry or became helpers and lay-preachers, some became in their villages and communities the centers about which new churches were formed, and a few joined the faculties of schools of which they were graduates. Others entered Japanese or foreign firms, edited periodicals, and entered the law and diplomatic service. They were excluded from no sphere of life, though in some localities prejudices blocked their way. While the direct influence could not be measured, their presence had a definite leavening power in society. Commentators have remarked that abstract Christian principles acquired a wider circulation and produced a larger influence in the lives of the students than could be estimated by a mere tabulation of the number who became members of the churches.[9]

Mission schools were criticised in Japan as engaging in education not for its own sake but for collateral purposes, that is, for the spread of Christianity.[10] This was a justifiable criticism in that the missionaries included within their view of education concepts which were not demonstrable according to the quantitative methods of science. On the other hand gratifying pedagogical results were achieved with respect to the development and discipline of the students enrolled.[11]

The missions were not unanimous in their views as to the advisability of founding and supporting schools to provide a secular training. Christian education was expensive.[12] Some of the missions preferred to spend their budgets and energies for other purposes,[13] although the denominations which became numerically largest and of greatest influence were those with affiliated schools. The first distinctly missionary institution was founded by Christopher Carrothers of the Presbyterian mission in 1869.[14] A class for boys begun in Yokohama in 1875 was moved to Tōkyō in 1880. Union College and the Union Theological School combined in June 1886 to form Meiji Gakuin.[15] Mr. Wycoff opened a boys' school under the auspices of the (Dutch) Reformed Church mission in October 1881. This was moved to Tōkyō and merged with the Presbyterian school in the summer of 1883.[16] A boys' school, St. Timothy's, was organized in Ōsaka in 1872 by a missionary of the American Episcopal Church.[17] and two years later another, Rikkyō (St. Paul's), was founded in Tōkyō.[18] The latter was conducted jointly by the English and American Episcopal societies after 1881.[19] The for-

I͏ͷO͏Z5

mer was amalgamated with Rikkyō in Tōkyō in 1887, and then raised to the status of a college.[20]

In any consideration of mission schools in Japan, the Dōshisha comes first. It was the largest, the most inclusive, and the only one to have attained university status by 1890.[21] It was not, strictly speaking, a mission school. The missionaries connected with the American Board of Commissioners for Foreign Missions merged their plans for a theological school with those of Niijima Jō, who had visions of an institution which would be to Japan what some of the leading Christian colleges of New England were to America. A goodly number of the missionary staff joined with him in building up the Dōshisha in Kyōto. Yet from its inception, November 1875, it was a Japanese institution.[22] It necessarily assumed the status of a Japanese rather than a mission school in order to secure permits for the American teachers to live outside the treaty ports. In support as well as in administration it also differed from other mission institutions. It must be admitted, however, that Niijima was a salaried associate member of the Japan mission. In the administration of the institution, D. C. Greene, M. L. Gordon, J. D. Davis, and D. W. Learned were important personalities during the years prior to 1890. The strength of Dōshisha was attributable in part to its numerous foreign faculty which offered a superior type of education, much of it in English. But in other respects, the Dōshisha was a Japanese institution. Niijima was the founder.* It was he who negotiated with the officials for a location, and permission to establish a Christian school in a Buddhist stronghold. It was his reputation and ability which enabled the institution to bear

---

* Without detracting from the credit due to President Niijima as founder, honesty requires the coupling with his two other names as cofounders, Yamamoto Kakuma and J. D. Davis. The blind Yamamoto's consistently sympathetic backing and timely gift of land made possible location in Kyōto. Most of the initial Dōshisha students were pupils of Davis who brought them up from Kōbe. F.C. LINCOLN BIBLE INSTITUTE

up under strong opposition. In addition to tuition fees which provided a major part of the operating expenses, large donations were solicited and obtained from Japanese patrons. The alumni association assumed a measure of responsibility for supporting the institution. The property was held by a Japanese company, known as the Dōshisha, and the management of the school was entrusted to the whole body of teachers.[23] The Board of Directors was entirely Japanese. Niijima was followed as president of the institution by Kozaki Hiromichi. The leadership of the institution has been, therefore, from the day of its establishment, in Japanese hands.

The course of study in the English and Scientific department of the Dōshisha extended over six years, the first two of which were preparatory, devoted chiefly to English study, and the latter four to instruction in advanced English or science. Bible study was voluntary. A theological department offered a three year course for those who had studied English, and a vernacular course for those without the language background.

In 1882 the American Methodist Mission moved the Theological and Training School connected with their denomination from Yokohama, where it had been conducted since before 1879, to Tsukiji, Tōkyō. In the autumn of 1886 the school was relocated on the newly purchased campus of the Anglo-Japanese University of Tōkyō, better known by its Japanese designation, Aoyama Gakuin.[24]

Missions figured more prominently in women's than in men's education. Whereas the government made increasingly larger provision for the training of the male portion of the population, the field of girls' and women's education was abandoned, at least until 1890, to private and religious agencies. Mrs. Hepburn started a class for girls in Yokohama in 1867, which she continued to teach until 1870 when it was transferred to Mary E. Kidder. Shortly afterwards, with the patronage of the governor of Kanagawa prefecture, a girls' school was opened, which by the end of 1872 had a student body numbering twenty-two. In 1875 this became the Isaac Ferris Seminary, a boarding school with an initial enrollment of fourteen.[25] In October 1872 representatives of the Woman's Union Missionary Society of America for Heathen Lands founded a school for Eurasian girls in Yokohama, which was known as the Kyōritsu Jogakkō. Three-fourths of the students were always native-born Japanese.[26] Mrs. Christopher Carrothers and Hara Taneaki began a Presbyterian girls' school in Tsukiji, Tōkyō, in the spring of 1874 which was subsequently known as the Hara Jogakkō or Ginza School.[27] On January 5, 1874 The Graham Seminary was opened in Tōkyō by Miss Youngman and Miss Parks.[28] In September 1878 the two schools were united.[29] In 1876 Sakurai Chika, the wife of a Japanese evangelist, started an independent school at Banchō, Tōkyō, with nine students. The institution came under the care and aid of the Presbyterian mission in 1878 and control in 1881.[30] Henry Stout had sought to establish a school in Nagasaki in 1869, but abandoned the project shortly afterwards until December 1878, when it was reopened.[31] A girls' boarding school was started in Tōkyō in 1872 by Dora Schoonmaker of the Methodist Episcopal mission.[32] In 1875 Ellen Eddy commenced for the American Episcopal mission, St. Agnes in Ōsaka, and two years later Miss Pittman (Mrs. J. Mc D. Gardiner) took over the Tōkyō school for girls Mrs. C. T. Blanchet had begun in 1873 (or 1874) in her home.[33] By 1883 the Japan mission of the American Board of Commissioners for Foreign Missions had three prosperous institutions for the education of girls under its care. First in point of establishment was the Kōbe Jogakkō in 1875, which offered three years of preparatory and five years of seminary training. Most of the graduates were Christians, and a number returned to enter the faculty. The second school was the Dōshisha Jogakkō opened at Kyōto in 1877 for both day and boarding students. Some of the members of the first graduating class (1882) continued as faculty. The Namba Jogakkō in Ōsaka was established in January 1878. The city Kumiai churches raised the funds necessary for the erection of the buildings and, save for the salaries of the missionary teachers, the maintenance. In the curriculum of all three of these Congregational institutions as well as in most other mission schools, English studies were central.[34]

Such were examples of the institutions founded during the introductory period, which prospered along with the many others that sprang up after 1883. They had been founded, first, as a method of approaching the Japanese people in view of the anti-Christian edicts and prejudices, and second, as the most expedient course offering itself at a time when permits to reside in the interior were difficult to obtain. As these reasons gradually lost their validity the schools were perpetuated and improved inasmuch as there arose the inevitable necessity of having an educated church membership and leadership, inasmuch as the governmental educational system was non-Christian and to a certain extent anti-Christian,[35] and inasmuch as an increasingly larger proportion of the church membership came through the mission schools.

Several references have been made already to the training of Christian leaders. Almost all the missions established theological seminaries and many of them schools for the training of Bible women. These were not large institutions. Indeed, the first theological students of the three Episcopal societies after 1898 lived with Bishop Williams and were instructed by the missionaries.[36] Pastors and missionaries cooperated during the earlier years for the purpose of training persons locally who were desirous of entering the ministry.[37] Only later was there a centralization of instruction. It seemed advisable that local candidates be trained near home; otherwise boys who had entered the church in say Kanazawa, if sent to Tōkyō for preparation would be tempted to accept a church in or near the capital rather than return to the rural or isolated areas.[38] To avoid the danger of losing their own picked men, as well as to obviate the expenses incident to sending students to the metropolitan areas for training, more than one school was started sometimes by the same mission. Only gradually were seminaries developed to give specialized instruction, although there were exceptions to this general principle. The mission of the American Board of Commissioners for Foreign Missions merged its desires for a seminary with Niijima's plans for a Christian college, and opened the Dōshisha in November 1875. The first graduates were trained in theology.[39] The matter of joint theological education was proposed to the Council of the Missions of the Presbyterian Church in the United States of America, the United Presbyterian Church of Scotland and the Reformed Church in America, September 17, 1877, that is, even prior to the consummation of the union of the work of these three bodies in the Nippon Kirisuto Itchi Kyōkai, which occurred October 3, 1877. It was recommended that there be a single theological school under the general oversight of the Council of the Three Missions Cooperating with the Union Church of Christ in Japan bearing the name the Union Theological School. Starting out with three missionary instructors, one Japanese graduate had been added to the faculty by the end of 1882.[40] The first theological class under the Reformed Church of America mission was organized and taught by S. R. Brown at Yokohama in 1874.[41] The work was transferred to Tōkyō, as part of the union school in 1877.[42] A theological seminary having been proposed in 1878 for the instruction of ministerial candidates of the three Episcopal societies, the Divinity Training School was established with five students and by December 1878 had enrolled a total of thirteen.[43] In

1880 the missions of the Evangelical Association and the Methodist Church of Canada entered into an agreement for conducting a joint theological college.[44] In 1880, A. A. Bennett of the American Baptist mission was given charge over a small group of students preparing for the ministry.[45] The American Methodist Theological and Training School which had been conducted at Yokohama was removed in 1882 to Tōkyō.[46] The Cumberland Presbyterian Church Mission entrusted the training of its ministerial candidates to the Dōshisha seminary.[47] By the end of 1882 there were seven such schools with a combined enrollment of seventy-one students, the Church Missionary Society alone having two seminaries.[48]

The number of persons preparing for the ministry increased from seventy-one in 1882 to 287 in 1885. Changes took place in the training facilities of the several missions and churches. The Union Theological Seminary of the Nippon Kirisuto Itchi Kyōkai was merged with the theological department of Meiji Gakuin. The mission of the (German) Reformed Church in the United States, having located at Sendai, opened a theological seminary in connection with its school, the Tōhoku Gakuin.[49] The preachers' classes which had been begun by A. A. Bennett of the Japan mission in 1879, of the American Baptist Missionary Union, were organized in October 1884 into a theological seminary with three professors and five students.[50] The Methodist schools including the theological department were merged at Tōkyō during the year 1883 in the Aoyama Gakuin. The department of divinity was raised to the status of a seminary in 1887.[51] A theological school was opened in 1887 at Tōkyō by missionaries of the Allgemeine Evangelische-protestantischer Missionsverein.[52] The purpose in starting and the method of conducting these institutions was primarily practical. Students were usually assigned to particular evangelistic responsibilities during the vacation months and holidays.[53]

Mention has already been made of the important role played by women as missionaries in Japan. Yet they no less than the men owed many of their accomplishments to Japanese associates. The Bible woman was the female equivalent of the male evangelist. Chronologically her evolution in Japan paralleled a similar development in China.[54] She acquired the reputation of being a personal servant to the woman missionary, so closely did her efforts supplement those of the foreigner. The Bible woman evolved later than the evangelist because of the relatively lower position of women in oriental society. It was first necessary partially to effect the woman's emancipation before her services could be available, or before the Japanese community would respect her professionally. The types of activity in which female missionaries were engaged, for instance, the holding of Sunday Schools, neighborhood prayer-meetings and Bible-readings, house to house visitation, and Bible instruction in Japanese day schools[55] necessitated the assistance of trained Japanese women, though there was a sentiment within some of the mission against hiring them.

The earliest known reference to the existence of a body of Japanese women trained for specific Christian tasks was that in 1878 in connection with the Presbyterian mission.[56] Yet, since in 1883 there were thirty-seven of these women employed by seven missions,[57] it is probable that they trace back to an earlier date. Clara A. Sands of the American Baptist Missionary Union mission, was teaching a number of her students in 1882 to become Bible women.[58] Through the instruction of female missionaries connected with the American Board of Commissioners for Foreign Missions, a number of Japanese had been prepared to engage in personal and home evangelism.[59] Among the students and alumni of the Kyōritsu Jogakkō, twelve had served by 1883 in the capacity of Bible readers.[60] Likewise the Evangelical Association mission trained some of its women church members for female evangelism.[61] The Cumberland Presbyterian mission made use of women for these purposes but granted them no foreign subsidy.[62]

Women were often supported either partially or fully for specific Christian tasks by the local churches. Of many it was said that their services were no less indispensable than those of the pastors. Some of them became so well known that their names were household words.[63] During the early years they were instructed directly by the missionaries. In 1881, Mrs. Louise H. Pierson, of the Women's Union Missionary Society established the first training institution, the Bible School for Women, at Yokohama, in connection with the Kyōritsu Jogakkō.[64]

Prior to 1883 female language teachers assisted with women's meetings and accompanied the wives and unmarried lady missionaries when they visited Japanese homes. Some, employed as Bible readers, mixed with the illiterate classes, teaching them or reading to them from the Bible. By the time of the Ōsaka Conference in 1883 " Bible woman " had become a common term and during the same year several of the missions opened special schools, such as the Kōbe Training School,[65] for their instruction. The curriculum included Biblical and theological courses, Church history and apologetics as well as secular subjects for those who were lacking in educational background.[66]

In addition to conducting schools for young men and women which prepared the former for the Imperial University and theological studies, and the latter for educated womanhood, and the theological schools for ministerial students and training schools for Bible women, the missionaries engaged in various other types of educational efforts.

In the field of primary education the missions were most delinquent. Stray references to such schools may be found,[67] but no concerted effort was made to supply a Christian education to boys and girls entering school for the first time.

This omission is not beyond understanding : education was not deliberately selected as a means of reaching the Japanese people. The earliest students who presented themselves to the missionaries were usually persons of maturity and previous training. The educational institutions which developed from these opportunistic beginnings spread in various directions. The personnel and resources were never sufficiently adequate to provide a complete education from the earliest stages through university. Many of the missionaries of necessity used English as the medium of instruction. The language handicap limited the range of communication to those students who had already been studying long enough to learn in a foreign tongue. The point at which this subject was introduced into the curriculum was the first year of middle school (which corresponds to the seventh grade in the American school system), and it was this same point that, except for the kindergartens, marked the lower terminus of the mission school curriculum. The resources, and perhaps the will, were lacking to enlarge the curriculum to include those ages with which the missionaries could have had but limited or no contacts.*

Kindergartens were also commenced by missions and churches as means of extending the influence of the Christian movement. The dates of this work for pre-school age children are obscure yet the first of its kind was begun at Tōkyō in connection with the Girls' Higher Normal School on November 14, 1876, that is, thirty-six years after the opening of Froebel's kindergarten in Blankenburg.[68] The

---

* The failure to assume responsibilities within the primary school field ultimately meant abandoning it to the government. Yuasa Hachirō, former president of the Dōshisha, regards this as a serious oversight on the part of the mission boards and churches, since Christian influences have been omitted from the child's life during the impressionable years. The program of nationalistic education which has developed in connection with the six-year period of compulsory education has given the state a firm hold upon the patriotic and religious attitudes of Japanese youth.

first Christian kindergarten was started by Francina E. Porter at Kanazawa in 1886. As it was a pioneer institution, officials visited it from long distances to study the methods employed. Not until 1889 did another mission follow suit when the mission of the American Board of Commissioners for Foreign Missions started the *Hikari* (Light) Kindergarten, which was later renamed *Shoei* (Glory), at Kobe, and an affiliated school for the training of kindergarten teachers.*

Sunday schools were in operation from as early as 1871 when Mrs. E. R. Miller assembled the children of the English soldiers stationed at Yokohama for Sunday Bible study.† Among them were some Japanese boys and girls, who after 1874 were separated into a Sunday School of their own.[69] John C. Berry began in December 1873 the first such school conducted in the Japanese language.[70] From that time onward Sunday Schools became a common feature of the programs of missionary extension and of the local churches.[71] Methods which were employed in teaching these schools were one or a combination of the following: concert recitations, familiar talks and story-telling, class conversation, and *rinki-kō* (circle talks) in which each of the students took his turn in interpreting the lesson.[72] By 1882 the Methodist Episcopal Church mission had begun the preparation in Japanese of Sunday School lessons based on an American series.[73]

---

* *Japan Christian Yearbook*, 1909, pp. 292ff.; *Japan Christian Yearbook*, 1910, p. 217. Yet the Evangelical Association of the North American Mission claims to have had "a kindergarten school" in 1882 at Tokyo. This was dissolved when the church with which it was connected disbanded.—*Proceedings of the Osaka Conference*, pp. 167*, 170*.

† *Mission News* Vol. XII No. 5 p 92. Mrs. D.C. Greene writing of first days in Japan (Nov.–Dec. 1869) said, "The first church service we attended in Japan, was at Dr. Hepburn's dispensary in Yokohama, which, on Sunday, was used as a chapel. Mrs. Hepburn had a Sunday school for Japanese children and young people, before the service, and she asked me to help about the singing, as they sang only English hymns. I taught them 'Jesus Loves Me,' which was just getting popular in America." F.C.

The informal study group was one of the earliest and, because of its adaptability, widely used means of reaching the Japanese people. When Hepburn explained to an inquisitive *gendarme* the significance of a picture of the crucifixion, he was employing this method.[74] Some of the early missionary efforts to translate the Bible in conjunction with the Japanese teachers were equally pointed, and admittedly designed to influence the assistant as much as to prepare a finished translation.* The interest excited by the Bible, first in Chinese and English, and later in Japanese, led to the organization of Bible classes.[75] There was hardly any limit to the number a missionary could conduct. The type of teaching was adapted to the size and kind of the group as well as to the linguistic capacity of the missionary instructor. In some instances students of English or morals were willing that the English Bible be used as a text.

The spread of Protestantism in Japan was also expedited by missionary and non-missionary relations with government and private schools. These positions enhanced the status and influence of the missionaries. Opportunities often afforded for religious instruction outside the classrooms in several notable instances resulted in a strengthening of the Christian movement. A number of teaching hours was sometimes undertaken in schools outside the treaty areas, as a means of obtaining permission to reside in the interior. G. F. Verbeck became an educational advisor to the Tōkyō government in 1869 after having taught in a government school in Nagasaki for five years.[76] A. C. Shaw of the Society for the Propagation of the Gospel in Foreign Parts

---

* The only Protestant "martyr" was Ichikawa Einosuke, language teacher to O. H. Gulick, who was arrested in 1871 because he had been a student of the Bible while aiding in translating portions of it.—*Proceedings of the Osaka Conference*, pp. 33–34. The first person to accept baptism was an ex-language instructor, Yano Riu, October 1864.—*Proceedings of the Osaka Conference*, p. 51.

taught for some time in Keiō Gijuku, the school of Fukuzawa Yukichi* in Tōkyō.[77] George Cochran of the Canadian
Methodist mission began in 1874 to teach in the Dōninsha
in Tōkyō,[78] one of the then outstanding schools in Japan.[79]
C. F. Wolf resigned from the same mission in order to assume a similar position in 1876.[80] George W. Knox of the
Presbyterian mission substituted at the Imperial University
for E. Fenellosa in 1886.[81] The missionaries who were able
to move into the interior prior to and during the period
1883–1889 did so by accepting teaching obligations. Presbyterian missionaries occupied Kanazawa in 1879 because interested persons were then desirous of opening a school in
the city. Christian services were opened almost immediately
after their arrival.[82] By 1883 they had made plans for the
organization of their own school which would allow their

---

* The name of Fukuzawa Yukichi will occur frequently in this study in part
because of the two-contrasting attitudes he assumed towards Christianity and
its development in Japan, but primarily because of the influence which he
had upon the scholarship and political events of the Meiji period. He and
Nakamura Masanao were the two most illustrious members of the Meirokusha (The Meiji Six). Fukuzawa, born a *samurai*, educated after the Confucian traditions, began the study of European languages when he was twenty.
His attitude towards the old learning changed but not that towards religion.
He did not care to examine religious systems, though he was anxious that
the best prosper in Japan and devoted his life to the improvement of education in Japan. His Keiō Gijuku (later Keiō Gijuku Daigaku) was the
training school for many of the democratic and liberal leaders of the age.
He inculcated an appreciation of utility in contradistinction to the prevailing
notions of inherited position. Skilled as a writer, both his ideas and his
style were aped by less able men. His newspaper, the *Jiji Shimpo*, which is
quoted frequently herein, was one of the leading Tōkyō dailies. Fukuzawa
was known as the "Sage of Mita" after his democratic manners, his scholarship, and the part of Tōkyō in which he lived and taught.—Oshimo, *op. cit.*,
pp. 66–68; Anesaki, *History of Japanese Religion*, pp. 350–352; *Japan Weekly
Mail*, March 16, 1890, pp. 260–261; *Chrysanthemum*, October 1881, pp. 392–
396. Fukuzawa was voted the most popular man in the nation in a *Konnichi
Shimbun* poll in 1884.—*Japan Weekly Mail*, May 23, 1884, p. 480. Two of
Fukuzawa's sons studied at Oberlin about the same date. Apropos of their
matriculation it was said, "this hitherto prominent opponent of Christianity
is at heart nearer the truth...than he has credit for."—Missionary Herald,
January 1884, p. 3.

residence, and yet admit religious elements into the curri-culum.[83] It was on this basis that residence in Tōkyō out-side the foreign settlement was permitted.[84] While most of the arrangements mentioned above were continued during the period 1883–1889, the expansion into these areas had taken place during the introductory period. The exception was in the case of those missions, which, perceiving the opportunities offered in Japan, entered during the wave of prosperity; likewise some of the older missions expanded in these years into hitherto untouched parts of Japan by em-ploying similar techniques.

Two non-missionary personalities who served as instruc-tors in government schools to the strengthening of the Christian spread in Japan were Colonel William S. Clark and Captain L. L. Janes. Both made their contributions in the introductory period, about 1876, but the results of their work were most in evidence after 1882. Clark, a graduate of Amherst College and then President of the Massachusetts Agricultural College, spent only part of a year in Sapporo organizing a school which subsequently gained the status of an imperial university. He insisted upon the right of teach-ing ethics from the Bible and preached on Sundays to stu-dents who visited his house.[85] The students who became converts under his influence were organized into a denomi-national church, which in 1883 was made an independent body. The outstanding figure within the group which or-ganized this church was Uchimura, Kanzō, one of Japan's greatest Christians.[86] Uchimura entered the college the sec-ond semester and so was not one of the Clark disciples, but he was greatly influenced by Clark's teachings. Janes, a West Point graduate, while teaching in Kumamoto so influ-enced two score of his *samurai* students that they formed a band, named after the city where their school was located, and entered the Dōshisha in the autumn of 1876. Their contributions to this institution, to the newly organized churches in Kyōtō, and to the leadership of what became the Kumiai Kyōkai, explain in large measure why the mission of the American Board of Commissioners for Foreign Missions, which arrived on the field relatively late, was almost immediately able to become one of the dominant missions.[87]

In several instances the missionaries entered into agreements with local groups for the establishment and maintenance of schools, in which all funds were provided by the government or patrons.[88] Complications often developed in these schools, because of the conflict in motivation, the missionaries being interested primarily in the opportunities for evangelism, and the patrons and students in receiving the maximum educational benefits.[89] Tōka Gakkō in Sendai was representative of the type. A native of the city, Tomita Tetsunosuke, took the lead in this effort. In 1874 while Japanese consul in New York, he had been impressed by the wide influence of New England colleges. In 1886, as vice-president of the National Bank in Tōkyō, he decided Japan should have a similar college system to instruct the nation in morality. His plan was to erect buildings and equip the school with Japanese instructors, provided a mission would supply the foreign staff. In May 1886, Niijima Jō and J. H. DeForest went to Sendai to confer with the promoters, a committee of influential persons including the governor and mayor, who reported that ¥5,000 had been subscribed to establish the school. The Dōshisha representatives were assured that morning prayers and the teaching of the Bible would be permitted in the institution.

The school was opened in October in a temporary building with 118 students. The enrollment increased rapidly and more permanent quarters were gradually provided. Tomita made a personal gift of ¥10,000. Appeals came in from other cities requesting the same mission to cooperate in the establishment of similar institutions.[90] In March 1892, after five and a half years of operation, the school closed. The termination of the experiment was necessitated by a series of factors, which will be dealt with more in detail in the concluding chapter. Anti-foreign and anti-Christian sentiment was directed against the school. Niijima, who had been acting as principal, died in 1890. The non-Christian trustees advocated the removal of the Bible from the curriculum. The missionary teachers resigned because of the feeling of hostility against them. The establishment of a government school of the same grade was the event which sealed the doom of Tōka Gakkō.[91] Uchimura Kanzō, commenting upon the difficulties of such an arrangement, concluded that the tension between non-Christians who were desirous of making the institution primarily academic, and the missionaries, who were interested chiefly in Christian propaganda, created an impasse conducive neither to effective education nor Christianization.[92]

In summary of this seemingly confusing detail, it might be stated that schools were first in time of origin, and possibly of importance, among the methods employed by the missionaries for spreading Protestantism in Japan. The possibilities for educational work appeared limitless. Even after government provisions obviated the need for certain types of schools, the openings which were still available for missionary teaching were sufficient to absorb the time and talents of the foreign staffs. Many of the institutions sought to comply with the growing government requirements. Others were maintained exclusively for the purpose of enabling the missionaries to retain permission to reside outside the treaty ports. The larger institutions adhered to a formal program of studies which prepared the students for entrance into higher government schools and for professional careers. With a few outstanding exceptions, the mission schools were inferior in equipment and buildings to the government schools of the same rank. Only in the quality of foreign teachers and English instruction were the former superior to the latter institutions. It was in the sphere of women's education that the mission schools were offered least competition.

Most of the societies maintained one or more schools. Even those which were engaged solely in direct evangelism found it necessary to maintain theological seminaries and training schools for Bible women, or cooperate with the schools of other denominations. Sunday Schools, informal study groups, night classes in churches and missionary homes, as well as the more advanced and formal schools were among the means whereby Protestantism spread and the church was strengthened. Missionaries also accepted employment in secular and government institutions for the purpose of reaching students who would otherwise be beyond the range of Christian influence. Schools then were of primary importance in the policies and programs of the mission agencies and churches. The history of Protestantism in Japan would have read quite differently but for the universal desire for knowledge on the one hand, and on the other the willingness and the competency of the missionaries to avail themselves of the opportunity which Japan's zeal for education afforded.

Chapter   V

CHRISTIAN LITERATURE

Another method whereby the missionaries sought to satisfy the eagerness of the Japanese to learn was by the production of Christian literature.

Even before missionaries to Japan were free to preach, they circulated literature. The desire for knowledge, to which this approach was designed to appeal, led to the rapid production and wide circulation of tracts, papers and books. When the missionaries first arrived, the only available writings for the dissemination of Christianity were in Chinese and English. As books and newspapers were being widely read throughout the empire, missionaries by 1872 recognized the need for Christian pamphlets and tracts in the vernacular and many accordingly endeavored to supply it.[1]

The translation of the Bible was felt to be the first great need. When J. C. Hepburn published his dictionary in 1867 on which he had been working for eight years, he determined that the time had arrived to undertake the translation of the scriptures.[2] He recognized that the translation should be not the product of one man's labors, but a joint undertaking which should be recommended to the Bible Societies by most or all of the missionaries engaged in Japan.[3] K. F. A. Gutzlaff, B. J. Bettelheim, and S. Wells Williams earlier had seen the need for and had made elementary translations of some of the gospels into Japanese. Jonathan Goble, S. R. Brown, and J. C. Hepburn had made private translations, but the first important step towards a cooperative version was taken at the General Convention of Protestant Missionaries, held at Yokohama in September of 1872 when it was agreed to form what subsequently was known as the Yokohama Translation Committee consisting of one representative from each mission. This body concentrated upon the preparation and printing of the New Testament.[4] On October 30, 1876 a council of missionaries at Tōkyō similarly undertook the translation of the Old Testament. A general council meeting at Tōkyō in May 1878 agreed that a Permanent Translation Committee should be established, that the missions should be represented proportionally, that this committee would appoint sub-committees on translation and revision according to localities, and should superintend the joint work so as to insure uniformity of text. As the Yokohama Translation Committee manifested a desire to place itself under the guidance of the Permanent Committee, both the Tōkyō and Yokohama committees were dissolved. On October 23, 1878 the first meeting of the Permanent Translation Committee was held in Tōkyō at which time the local translation and revision committees were selected.

The New Testament translation was completed in November 1879 and published the following April. The Old Testament was published in 1888. The bulk of the New Testament was translated by J. C. Hepburn and revised by D. C. Greene and S. R. Brown. D. C. Greene and L. H. Gulick saw the book through the press. While the Old Testament was apportioned out to groups of missionaries, most of the actual translation was completed by J. C. Hepburn, Guido F. Verbeck, and P. K. Fyson. J. C. Hepburn and J. A. Thompson supervised the printing. The missionaries were assisted by Japanese scholars, particularly in respect to the composition and style of the translation. Matsuyama Takayoshi,* Okuno Masatsuna, Miura Tōru, and Takahashi Gorō rendered most assistance with the New Testament, and Matsuyama Takayoshi and Uemura Masahisa with the Old Testament. The style was classical language (*gagen*) mixed with popular language which avoided the difficult and abstruse style of the literati and the vulgar expressions of the colloquial (*zokugo*).† The translation and publication of the New Testament was subsidized by the American Bible Society, and the Old Testament by the British and Foreign Bible Society and the National Bible Society of Scotland. The completion of the former was celebrated at the Shinsakaebashi Church (Nippon Kirisuto Kyōkai), Tōkyō, April 19, 1880. On February 3, 1888, a similar event marked the publication of the entire Bible.[5] The work was not without defects. Inaccurate renditions, paraphrases, and private interpretations were sometimes inserted instead of faithful translations. There was a lack of uniformity in the style and the translation of terms. Unnecessarily difficult Chinese characters were employed. The ideographs and the syllabary (*Kana*) did not always correspond. An absence of honorifics made the wording often insufficiently reverent. These, plus a too slavish adherence to the Chinese version were some of the marked faults.[6] In spite of these imperfections, this, the authorized version, was a great asset to the Christian movement in Japan.

The first Bibles were imported from China and sold by the missionaries. The first agency in Japan was established in 1875 by the National Bible Society of Scotland. The American Bible Society followed in 1876 and the British and Foreign Bible Society in 1881.[7] The three agencies effected a union as of July 1, 1890.[8] The method of colporteurage

---

* Hepburn said that if the New Testament translation had any merit it was attributable to the contributions of Matsuyama, who had been Greene's teacher at Kōbe.—*Home and Foreign Record*, March 1880, pp. 80–81.

† Some thought the translation a failure for this reason. See *The Chrysanthemum*, May 1882, pp. 207–213.

was tried for a time but finally abandoned since it did not effect a widespread distribution. As men of the requisite training and culture were unobtainable for colporteurs, they were largely replaced after 1872 by depots and agencies for the sale of Bibles and other forms of Christian literature.[7]

In addition to the version prepared by the Permanent Translation Committee which became standard throughout the nation even within the Baptist churches, Nathan Brown, senior member of the Japan mission of the American Baptist Missionary Union, prepared a colloquial New Testament that was published in 1884. For a time Nathan Brown had cooperated with the Yokohama Translation Committee, but because of differences with the American Bible Society, as well as because of definite ideas of his own as to the type of translation which was needed, he withdrew from the cooperative venture. The two versions differed in that Brown made little use of Chinese characters, and departed from the formal written style of the day. The very fact of the simplicity of the Baptist version, both as to the use of the Japanese syllabary rather than Chinese ideographs, and as to style, made it generally unacceptable.* Brown had sought to put the Bible into the terminology of the common people, but it was not this level of the population which was attracted to Christianity. The colloquial version wielded its greatest influence in the revision of the New Testament over thirty years later. Mention should also be made of an edition which was made in the eighties by W. J. White, the manager of the Christian Tract Society. While White had proposed following Brown's translation, but adding Chinese characters in order to make the version acceptable to the learned classes, the text was actually changed in the revision

---

* " Unfortunately, the Japanese language, intricate and impersonal, is singularly ill-fitted to reproduce the rugged sublimity of Hebrew thought. Chinese lends itself somewhat better to the task."—Chamberlain, Basil Hall, *Things Japanese* (Japan, J. L. Thompson, 1939, pp. xiv, 584), p. 355 note.

process so as to constitute a third version. It will suffice to mention in this connection that the Japanese language was in process of changes no less revolutionary than those in the social and political spheres. The translation of the scriptures was greatly complicated by the divergent beliefs as to the more acceptable form of writing and printing.* The style which finally prevailed at the time of the revision of the New Testament, a semi-colloquial yet stately Japanese, with Japanese syllabary printed alongside the Chinese characters, was in use but did not predominate prior to 1890.

Tracts were a second type of Christian literature employed in the spread of Protestantism in Japan. The first, a translation from a Chinese pamphlet entitled *Shinri Ekichi* (The True Doctrine Made Plain) by D. B. McCartee was prepared in 1863 (or 1864) and printed the following year by J. C. Hepburn. The blocks were cut secretly by a Japanese who was in the employ of a Jewish merchant in Yokohama.[10] The next publication did not appear until 1872 when the *Sanyōbun* (Three Essential Documents) consisting of the Ten Commandments, the Lord's Prayer and the Apostles' Creed was translated and printed by Hepburn, Nathan Brown and Okuno Masatsuna. To it was appended *Yasokyō Seido Nyūmon* (Introduction to the Righteous Way of Christianity).[11] Kate M. Youngman superintended the translation and publication of *Kami no Ōinaru Ai* (The Great Love of God) in 1873. These three had been undertaken by missionaries in eastern Japan. J. D. Davis of Western Japan in 1873 wrote in colloquial Japanese and published what was probably the first original tract, *Makoto no Michi wo Shiru no Chikamichi* (A Short Cut to an Understanding of the True Way). By 1883, 100,000 copies of this booklet had been circulated.[12] The

---

* The material for this paragraph was abstracted from numerous letters of Nathan Brown and F. G. Harrington to the American Baptist Missionary Union.

American Tract Society assisted with several publication efforts of the missions from 1874 until 1878. The London Religious Tract Society subsidized the missionary literary output from 1876, until after the conclusion of the period covered by this study,[13] publishing tracts for inquirers, children and various professions on Sabbath observance, the devotional life and other subjects.[14] While the books and tracts varied in quality and effectiveness, one of the prominent missionaries of the period said that the much good which had been accomplished by the scattered leaves was not to be measured merely by the number who ascribed their conversion to these tracts, but also by the fact that such publications were one of the means by which Christian truth increasingly affected the thought of the Japanese people.[15]

Third among the types of Christian literature which contributed to the spread of Christianity in Japan were original works and translations in oriental languages treating Biblical and devotional subjects. Most of the volumes published in Japanese during the ninth decade of the nineteenth century on Christian themes were written by, with the assistance of, or under the direction of missionaries. They were greater in number than had been those written throughout the entire introductory period. Although some Japanese Christians did produce books by their own initiative, most of the competent nationals were obliged for financial reasons to engage in self-supporting teaching, preaching, and editorial work. Missionaries alone among the Christians were able to give themselves to extensive literary work, assured at the same time of an income.[16]

According to available bibliographies of oriental works read by Japanese Christians, 432 titles had been published by the end of 1882. Some of these were in the language of the Loo Choo Islands and a few were in Chinese, but most had been written in Japanese. The list includes Bibles and portions, commentaries, translations, tracts, song-books, apologetic works, devotional aids and attacks upon Christianity including a revision of such works as Arai Hakuseki's *Seiyō Kibun* (Strange Stories of the Occident).* Of these 432 works, ten were published prior to 1855, and another seventy before 1872. The remaining 352 were issued during the period from 1872, the time of the founding of the first church, to 1883, the beginning of our special study, During the seven years, 1883 through 1889, 453 additional titles appeared. The general types of works remained almost unchanged, although the names of Miura Tōru, Ibuka Kajinosuke, Uemura Masahisa, Sawayama Paul, and Kanamori Tsūrin, outstanding figures in the Christian movement, appeared increasingly as the authors of original works. Missionaries continued to revise, dictate, and cooperate in the translations. D. W. Learned's New Testament commentaries and texts in church history, doctrine, and homiletics were prepared primarily for the student and evangelist rather than for the lay public.[17] Uchimura Kanzō was able to effect the conversion of his father by inducing him to read a commentary in Chinese on the Gospel of Mark; but such instances were rare.[18]

A fourth, and more indigenous, form of Christian literature was the periodical. During the period prior to 1883 four important religious journals were founded. The oldest was the *Shichi Ichi Zappō* (Weekly Miscellany) which appeared first in Kobe December 27, 1875. The publisher was Imamura Kenkichi of the Zappōsha, the editor Murakami Shunkichi, and the missionary associate editor O. H. Gulick. It was an eight page journal intended to meet the religious needs of Christian families, and to bring knowledge to inquirers concerning Christianity. By 1883 the *Shichi Ichi Zappō* had a subscription list of 760. The laws forbade

---

* An account of the examination of Sidotti who was arrested and brought to Yedo in 1709.—See Aston, Japanese Literature, pp. 253–256.

foreign residents to publish periodicals in the Japanese language, hence the necessity for nominal Japanese management, although the work was carried on under the auspices of the Japan mission of the American Board of Commissioners for Foreign Missions. During the summer of 1883 the paper and establishment were transferred to the Keisei-sha Publishing Company, in Tōkyō, under the auspices of the *Fukuin Dōmei Kai* (The Japan Evangelical Alliance), for the purpose of printing an interdenominational journal. The editors of the *Fukuin Shimpō* (Gospel News), as the successor to the *Shichi Ichi Zappō* was called, were Kozaki Hiromichi, Uemura Masahisa, and Ukita Kazutami. Within a short while it became exclusively the organ of the Kumiai Kyōkai. In 1889 the name was changed to the *Kirisutokyō Shimbun* (Christian News).[19]

The *Yorokobi no Otozure* (Good Tidings), a monthly newspaper for women and children, was begun in 1877 by Miss S. B. McNeal of the Woman's Union Missionary Society, with Miura Tōru as associate editor. In 1882 Mrs. E. R. Miller replaced Miss McNeal as editor. The circulation had reached 3,100 copies monthly in 1883, a record which it maintained throughout the period. In 1883 a supplement was begun for young people with a circulation of five hundred.[20]

The oldest of the monthly magazines was the *Rikugō Zasshi* (The Cosmos) which was established for the Young Men's Christian Association by Kozaki Hiromichi and Uemura Masahisa in 1880. The first number appeared on October 11th. The editions were about sixty pages each. The stated aims were, first, to improve the morals, customs, and manners of the middle and upper classes of the people, second, to hold up religious views to the people, and third, to set forth correct views and interpretations of Christianity.[21]

The *Maishū Shimpō* (Weekly News) was a fourth periodical under Japanese auspices with a weekly circulation of about 800 copies, started shortly prior to 1883.[22]

The *Kyokai Shimbun* (Church Newspaper) was published in February 1874 by the Taikyōin Shimbunka.[23] The mission of the American Episcopal Church inaugurated the *Dendō Zasshi* (The Evangelist) in 1881.[24]

No information as to the multiplication of publications during the years 1883–1889 is available, although it is recorded that by 1894 there were forty periodicals dealing for the most part with distinctively Christian subjects.[25]

It was in this area of literary production that the Japanese Christians reached their maximum effectiveness. Whereas most of the Christian books had been written by or with the aid of missionaries, the reverse was true in the case of Christian journalism. Pastors Uemura Masahisa, Kozaki Hiromichi, and Ibuka Kajinosuke and laymen such as Uchimura Kanzō, Iwamoto Zenji, Takahashi Gorō (editor for several years during the '80's of the *Rikugo Zasshi*), Shimada Saburō (editor of the Tōkyō *Mainichi Shimbun*), and Tokutomi Soho (editor of the Tōkyō *Kokumin Shimbun*) did much through the religious and secular press to bring a knowledge of the Christian faith before the people.[26]

A fifth type of literature which contributed to the spread of Christianity especially among the educated classes was that which was written in English. Pastors, officials and many of the professional men who had been abroad, studied under the missionaries, or had passed through the mission schools and government university, were students of English. It was to books published in Great Britain and America that they turned for much of their secular and religious knowledge.[27] Not only in the cities but in rural areas as well pastors and teachers read books and magazines which were published abroad.[28] School libraries were stocked with Japanese books but with a larger percentage of foreign works.*

---

* One of the assistants in the Kyōto Imperial University Library informed the writer that only one out of every seventeen books in the library in 1940 was Japanese, all others being works in foreign languages.

A sixth literary expression of Christianity which accelerated its spread was hymnology. Western music was so unlike that of Japan, that J. C. Hepburn but stated an accepted belief in 1861 when he declared that no Japanese was capable of singing a hymn.[29] Events demonstrated that the Christians could learn to sing, yet even towards the end of the '80's the congregational music in most of the churches left much to be desired.* Missionaries encouraged the use of hymns in connection with worship services but not at the public lecture meetings. Collections of words which had been translated and fitted to western sacred music appeared as early as 1873.[30] Prior to 1882 hymnals had been published by several denominations, the first to contain the staff, notation, and music in four parts being the Methodist Hymnal of 1879. The first complete hymn and tune book appeared in 1882, the revision of which in 1886 contained 247 hymns and the first music fitted to indigenous Japanese poetry. George Allchin edited a union hymnal, the *Shinsen Sanbika*, which was published in 1890.[31]

The thirst of the Japanese people for knowledge, and their ability to read, facilitated the presentation of the Christian message through the written word. The translation of the scriptures influenced the Japanese language and made possible a Bible reading church. Tracts were designed to reach non-believers. In an effort to educate church members and to provide pastors with homiletic aids Christian

---

* The singing in native churches is frequently deplorable, a travesty on the melody that is thought to constitute the high-water mark of Christian devotion. But everything must have a beginning...the conservatism...which leads missions to introduce a system of worship, in a totally unaltered form, into a strange country, may in the end justify itself by events. The Christian services as at present rendered in Japanese may tend to excite the opposite of reverential feelings in the breasts of critical onlookers;...but...modifications must come from the Japanese themselves and not from abroad."— *Japan Weekly Mail*, August 6, 1887, pp. 132–133.

books were written. Save for a few original productions, most of them were translated from foreign language publications by Japanese associates with missionary supervision or cooperation. Periodicals constituted another type of Christian literature in the production of which the Japanese proved themselves especially competent. Pastors and laymen, teachers and professional journalists assumed editorial responsibilities. Hymnology, though somewhat retarded, played a distinctive role in the expansion of Protestantism. These six forms of Christian literature were thus among the means whereby the spread of Protestantism in Japan was expedited during the years 1883–1889.

Chapter   VI

SOCIAL WELFARE ACTIVITIES

Since the turn of the century, Protestantism in Japan has been popularly equated with social work, yet only the beginnings of a welfare program had been made by Japanese Christians prior to 1890.   The explanations for these phenomena are several.   The government itself took the initiative in meeting certain types of social need.   Japan by 1883 had made more progress in medical science than along any other line of western learning,* there being in almost every town at least one Japanese physician using modern medical methods.†   The fact that there was little demand for foreign physicians was in striking contrast with the evolution of the Christian movement in other eastern lands.   Again, during the years when the missionaries were handicapped by prejudice and anti-Christian legislation, the greatest demand

---

* One reason for the rapid development of medical science in Japan was that during the Tokugawa period medicine was the one foreign subject Japanese were allowed to study.   Many of the political and educational leaders of the Meiji period had studied Dutch medical science, not to become doctors, but that they might obtain an education along other than conventional Chinese lines.

† *Japan Weekly Mail*, March 15, 1884, pp. 258–259.   As early as 1879 there were 1817 licensed physicians, 939 of whom had passed the medical examinations, and 5230 medical students.—*Japan Weekly Mail*, February 16, 1884, pp. 156–157.

was for schools, which one channel largely absorbed the energy and talents of available foreign workers and the resources of the supporting mission boards. The relative absence of philanthropic institutions may also be attributed to the fact that the younger churches took their lead from the west, where Christians did not adopt the social settlement approach to any considerable degree until towards the close of the century. The aim of self-support was a fourth reason which hampered the development of welfare projects. The missionaries in seeking to establish congregations which within a minimum space of time could become independent and self-supporting, concentrated upon the classes which were financially able to support the Christian institutions. The Quakers alone went first to the poorer classes.* Despite these factors which retarded the application of Christianity to social needs, evidences of a growing conscience within the church were not totally lacking.

Several medical practitioners were among the early missionary arrivals, who by demonstrating that the missionaries sought no political or economic results, but only the physical and spiritual good of the people, prepared the way for the teachers and preachers. Many of the patients treated in the dispensaries and hospitals and by the traveling physicians were led to an acceptance of the Christian faith.† The earliest efforts along these lines were made by Dr. J. C. Hepburn in 1860 at Kanagawa, whose clinic continued a bare five months before it was closed by the authorities.[1] Following his removal to Yokohama in 1862 the dispensary

---

* One writer claims this was a mistake in judgment. "The Quakers ought to have begun with the intellectual classes, for every movement in Japan is from the top."—Scott, Robertson, *The Foundations of Japan* (London, John Murray, 1933), p. 204.

† *Tokyo Missionary Conterence Report*, p. 539; Bishop Williams of the American Episcopal Church stated that in one particular year one-half of these baptized over that period were led into the Church through connection with a dispensary.—Tucker, *op. cit.*, p. 95.

was reopened, and continued in operation until 1877 when personal illness and pressing literary responsibilities forced its discontinuance.[2] On the walls of the waiting room hung translations in Japanese of the Ten Commandments and Biblical verses.[3] As the doctor's reputation spread, he was visited not alone by hundreds of patients but by Japanese physicians as well.[4]

John C. Berry reached Kobe in 1872. The following year he started teaching a class of ten students at the Hyogo Prefectural Hospital.[5] By 1875 with the assistance of two Japanese doctors a medical course was being offered. By invitation a hospital was opened at Himeji, fifty miles away. In cooperation with rural physicians, consulting rooms were opened at a half dozen points, which Berry visited monthly, treating from 500 to 700 patients, but permitting the Japanese doctors to assist him and to collect the fees.[6] In April 1879 Berry began an association with the prefectural hospital in Okayama where 14,000 patients were treated annually.[7] He also opened clinics throughout the countryside, where he not only treated medical cases, but gave practical experience to Japanese physicians.[8]

Dr. Arthur H. Adams, under the American Board of Commissioners for Foreign Missions, by opening a dispensary in conjunction with a group of Japanese doctors introduced medical missions to Ōsaka in 1874. Five years later Dr. W. Taylor in replacing Adams opened a hospital.[9]

Dr. H. Laning of the American Episcopal mission who entered Ōsaka shortly after Dr. Adams, treated 1,000 patients in his first half year and 2,500 patients during the twelve months of 1878. St. Barnabas Hospital, the outgrowth of Laning's clinics, was erected in 1883, and continues to this day.[10]

Dr. Henry Faulds of the United Presbyterian Church of Scotland, began the treatment of outpatients and gathered around him a group of medical students in Tsukiji, the foreign concession of Tōkyō, in May 1874. The following year he established the Tsukiji Hospital.[11] During the year 1881, 14,000 persons were treated, but due to the increase in the number of free dispensaries, as well as to the fee required at the Tsukiji hospital, the number of patients decreased during 1882.[12]

The earliest references to services performed by the Edinburgh Medical Mission which arrived in 1874 was a clinic operated in connection with the evangelistic activity of Theobald A. Palm at Niigata.[13] During 1882, 2,950 in-patients and 151 out-patients were treated.[14]

The Akasaka Hospital, interdenominational and independent, was organized in 1886, an outgrowth of a dispensary which had been established in 1884.[15]

As the schools of medicine in Japan each year graduated hundreds of doctors, trained in German methods, the occasion for foreign practitioners tended to disappear. Medical missions had become by the '80s primarily a benevolent service for the poor, rather than an auxiliary to the general Christian approach.* By 1883 municipal and private hospitals with Japanese physicians had been built in most of the cities. As the Japanese doctors were generally reluctant to minister to the foreign residents, some few western physicians and surgeons remained in Japan for this purpose.[16] Following the Ōsaka Conference, save for the Episcopal missions, medical work was gradually terminated.[17]

One of the medical projects which flourished was the Nurses' Training School in Kyōto, established by John C. Berry in 1887. He first sought to obtain support in America to make the school and clinic interdenominational, but failing, he established the school as an adjunct of the Doshisha. At

---

* *Tokyo Missionary Conference Report*, p. 541; see *Tokyo Missionary Conference Report*, pp. 548ff., for a dissenting expression of opinion. There were five hospitals and eight dispensaries under the several missions, which treated 25,000 patients in 1882.—Tucker, *op. cit.*, p. 116.

the dedication of the wards and dormitories in November 1887, the governor of Kyōto was among the dignitaries on the program.[18] The Presbyterian mission refused to join with Berry on the ground that private nurses were not suited to Japanese life and customs, governmental hospitals with wide facilities had been established in every city, and medical services were no longer a major field for missionaries.[19] Berry's projected Christian medical college did not materialize.[20]

The visit of George Müller, the English social worker, to Japan in 1886 stirred the Christian conscience to make provision for orphans. A Baptist missionary in Shimonoseki intimated a desire to found a home for those in his city, but a return to America forestalled his plans. Ishii Jūji, a convert from the Roman Catholic to the Kumiai Church who was studying medicine in Okayama, was led the following year to give aid to a beggar woman and her children. He adopted one of the children, found other homeless waifs, and rented a Buddhist temple in which to house them. This institution became known as the Okayama Orphanage. Friends assisted with funds and by 1889 fifty-five children were being cared for, with many others, victims of a flood in Kishu, seeking admission.*

In a report, which John C. Berry submitted after having obtained permission in 1875 to inspect the national prisons, he suggested the reformatory value of Christianity[21] and shortly afterwards a Christian was appointed by the governor of Kōbe to be a teacher in the prefectural prison. A number of Christian books sent by Niijima Jō to the Ōtsu prison in 1877 directly led to conversions.[22] The Kumiai church

---

* *Japan Weekly Mail*, October 26, 1889, p. 379; Cary, *op. cit.*, Vol. II, p. 196; *Missionary Herald*. August 1892, pp. 343–348. That the state was not entirely negligent along these lines was indicated by the fact that of the 4,958 known foundlings, as of June 1882, 4,243 were being reared at public expense.— *Japan Weekly Mail*, November 7, 1893, p. 686.

in Matsuyama, Shikoku, in the year 1888 arranged with the authorities to conduct daily services at the local prison which were attended by about fifty inmates. The warden himself was among those who became interested and was baptized, an event which led to radical changes in the prison discipline.[23] About the same time Christians were appointed teachers of morality to the five penitentairies where long time criminals were confined and they continued to serve in this role until the superintendent of prisons was changed in 1895. Two of the teachers, Hara Taneaki in Hokkaidō and Tomeoka Kōsuke at Wakamatsu, became famous for their efforts to reform criminals.[24] As the missionaries were not permitted to visit the prisons, Japanese Christians were responsible for initiating and maintaining these projects.[25] The greatest development in Christian prison reform came after 1890.*

The prevalence of moral evil was one of the favorite correspondence subjects of the early western residents in Japan. The Christian conscience soon lent itself to attacks upon licensed prostitution, concubinage, intemperance, and smoking.[26] Secular periodicals joined in the chorus against commercialized vice and thereby advertised the reformatory cause.[27]

The first temperence society in Japan was organized November 10, 1886 at Yokohama in the Kaigan Church. On November 17, 1888 a badge was decided upon, and the society voted to publish a periodical, the *Yokohama Temperance Magazine.**

The first continuing Japanese society to function along these several lines was the Fujin Kyōfūkai (Women's Christian Temperance Union) which was organized December

---

* The Katei Gakkō, a reform school, was founded in the '90's by Tomeoka, Arima Shinnosuke, teacher of morality at the Hyōgo Prison after 1884, where the warden was a Christian, was inspired by Berry, and baptized by Tomeoka.—Hiyane Antei, *Kirisutokyo Jimbutsushi*, pp. 315–320. Deforest, J. H., *Sunrise in the Sunrise Kingdom*, pp. 140–141.

6, 1886, with twenty charter members at a Tōkyō Presbyterian Church. The officers included some prominent names among the Japanese Christian community. Yajima Kajiko (president), Miura Riu, Hattori Chiyo, Sasaki Toyoju, and Ebina Miya were all wives of prominent men or famous in their own rights. The organization of the society was stimulated by the visit in that year of Mrs. Mary Clement Leavitt representing the Women's Christian Temperance Union. In 1888 a periodical was started, of which Mrs. Sasaki Toyoju, Mrs. Takeo Tadao and Mrs. Takeoshi Yosaburō were successive editors.[29] The following year the society presented a memorial to the government requesting that the criminal law relating to concubinage be altered so as to give the wife as well as the husband the right to seek a divorce on the grounds of breach of marriage contract.[30]

The Sapporo Temperance Society of sixty-five members was organized November 21, 1887 through the joint efforts of Iwai Shinrou, a shoe manufacturer who although a Christian had been unable to renounce *sake* drinking, and Rev. Takenouchi Tanetarō, an evangelist in the Sapporo Dokuritsu (Independent) Kyōkai. The president was Itō Kazutaka. On December 5, 1887, the movement enlarged to become the Hokkaidō Temperance Society.[31]

Efforts along similar lines in Tōkyō resulted in 1890 in the organization of the Tōkyō Temperance Society. although it was directly precipitated by the arrival of Miss Jessie Ackerman, a representative of the International Women's Christian Temperance Union.[32]

These beginnings along lines of social reform between 1883 and 1889, inauspicious though they were, were destined to feature subsequently in the spread of Christianity in Japan. By the end of the period of rapid growth medical missions had decreased to a position of small quantitative importance, but Christians were developing a conscience and sense of obligation with special reference to the care of orphans, prison conditions, and public morality. There was doubtless a connection between the effort being made to prove Japan's parity with the great powers and the sensitivity of the Japanese Christians to social evil. The leadership in these movements was national from their inception.

Chapter VII

THE CHURCHES AND EVANGELISM

Most if not all the Protestant missionaries in Japan were dominated by a desire to win individuals to the Christian faith and to organize them into congregations. The local communities of believers which were thus established, in turn became a means whereby the efforts of the missionaries and their Japanese associates were extended into the surrounding communities. Affiliated day schools and dispensaries were opened often in connection with the churches. Many of the Japanese members and officers devoted their spare time to personal evangelism and preaching, in numerous instances starting branch churches in different parts of the same city or locality. Home mission agencies were inaugurated to superintend and finance these and other younger projects in əvangelism. Thus the local congregation served a strategic purpose in the spread and establishment of Protestantism in Japan. The strengthening of Christianity's institutional forms was secondary only to the missionary's desire to convert individuals to Christianity.

The first congregations having been founded, the missionaries faced the problem of organizing them into nationwide units. During the years that the pioneers had shared life together in the treaty ports, unable to engage in direct religious work, their denominationalism had lost much of its edge. Many of the foreign representatives had cooperated in the preparation of language study materials, and in the translation of the Bible. The dangers inherent in breaking down the anti-Christian prejudices they had shared together. Among them were some who had concluded it was unnecessary to perpetuate the denominational differences which separated Christians in the west.* Not all were so minded, and the younger recruits in particular were of a different opinion. The tension which developed between these two groups, was to characterize the Christian movement in Japan through the years 1883-1889. The minority sought to build a unified, interdenominational, national body of Christians, the majority to perpetuate the denominational forms and differences of the western sects. A third type professed a desire for unity and were able to agree upon matters of name and creed, yet ultimately demonstrated their wish to fashion the government of the united church according to the polity of their own denominations. The influence of the third type was sufficiently powerful to effect either the merging or a close cooperation between the missions of some of the churches of similar polities. It was not until later that some of these " families of missions " were to become a single national church, and it was only in 1941 that the minority view mentioned above prevailed.

THE EARLIEST CHURCHES, 1872-1882

Previous to 1872 a total of only ten persons had been baptized by the Protestant missionaries, and not all of them were then alive.[1] As the result of a series of prayer meetings held in Yokohama in which some Japanese joined, the

---

* For the sake of uniformity with the churches started in Yokohama by the Reformed and Presbyterian, the Congregational missionaries in Kōbe, Osaka and Sanda arranged for the election of elders in their earliest churches. Perhaps a feudalistic type of loyalty on the part of the samurai-trained early pastors was as important a factor as any in denominational development.

first Protestant church in Japan was organized March 10, 1872. It consisted of eleven members, nine of whom had been baptized that day.[2] The name adopted was the Iesu Kōkai (Jesus Church). It was later changed to the Kaigan Nippon Kirisuto Kōkai (Kaigan[3] Church of Christ in Japan). The rule of faith was the Bible. The congregation refused to identify itself with any division of the church in the west.* Both the name and faith of this first church was prophetic of an organic union which was not to be realized for almost three-quarters of a century. While catholic in nomenclature and creed, the government of the body was presbyterian. J. H. Ballagh, a member of the (Dutch) Reformed Church mission, who had been instrumental in the formation of the congregation, was called to become its first pastor.[4] A sister church, later known as the Shinsakaebashi Nippon Kirisuto Kōkai was organized the following September 20th at Tōkyō under the supervision of a Presbyterian missionary, David Thompson. The membership was eight, including one woman, Mrs. Ogawa Kin, seven of whom were transfers from the Kaigan Nippon Kirisuto Kōkai in Yokohama.[5] The catholic aim of these two congregations, the minority desire mentioned above, was endorsed at the General Convention of Protestant Missionaries in Japan which met during the days September 20–25, 1872 at Yokohama. Twenty-one missionaries attended one or more of its sessions.[6] The convention drafted a document which stated that the diversities in Protestantism obscured the unity of the church, that the missionaries in attendance were desirous of unifying their methods of evangelism, and that they would seek to secure as far as possible an identity of name and organization in the Japanese congregations they would be instrumental in establishing.[7]

---

* The term adopted for church was 公 (catholic, or public association). On October 3, 1877 the combination 教会 (teaching association) was substituted for it.—Imbrie, Wm., *Church Unity in Japan* (Tokyo, Kyobun-kan, 1914) pp. 42, 11.

Despite these professions, with few exceptions, the churches formed after this convention perpetuated the denominational features of the superintending missionaries. From Sapporo and Hakodate in Hokkaidō, throughout the cities of the main island and Shikoku, to Kagoshima and Nagasaki in Kyūshū, most of the local congregations which came into being adopted either then or later the sectarian title of some existing church, and reproduced in creed, constitution, and church government the prototypes introduced by the missionaries. By the end of 1883 there were ninety-one such congregations and two independent churches. Thus was thwarted for the time being the aspiration of many missionaries and Japanese Christians that the Protestant church throughout the empire be catholic in name and in fact. Save for groups with common polities and creeds, the movement towards unity, though not towards form of cooperation, was, as we shall see, premature.

The original Yokohama and Tōkyō congregations set the pattern for churches established by the (Dutch) Reformed Church missionaries at Ueda and Nagasaki.[8] The Chōrō Kōkai founded by Presbyterians, save the one at Shinsakaebashi in Tōkyō, became affiliated with the Presbytery Chūkai of Japan which was organized December 30, 1873 under the Synod of China.[9] On May 29, 1874 and again in July of the same year, the mission of the American Board of Commissioners for Foreign Missions reaffirmed a desire for union and the intention of adhering to the basis adopted in 1872.[10] Subsequent to the organization of local churches in Kōbe and Ōsaka in 1874,[11] however, it was learned that while they were identical in name and creed with the Nippon Kirisuto Kōkai, the rules for church government written in part by J. D. Davis, were congregational rather than presbyterian.[12] Organic union thereby for the time being became impossible.[13]

Action on an overture dated April 1, 1876 by the mission

of the Reformed Church of America to the Presbyterian mission, proposing that the two cooperate in matters of education, was temporarily postponed by the latter body.[14] The next month, the Presbyterian mission, pursuant to an opinion submitted by the Board of Foreign Missions to the General Assembly of the Presbyterian Church in the United States of America,* proposed a conference with the mission of the Reformed Church to discuss the formation of a common presbytery.[15] The meeting was held May 18, 1876 at which what became known as the Council of the Three Missions was formed. The United Presbyterian Church of Scotland was invited to join.[16] The Women's Union Missionary Society cooperated from the time of the Council's inception.[17] A committee appointed by the Council to confer and prepare standards of government and doctrine presented its report June 21, 1876, which covered name, creed, and the relation of the missionaries to the presbytery. The name adopted was the Nippon Kirisuto Itchi Kyōkai (Union Church of Christ in Japan).[18] It was determined that missionaries should retain their ecclesiastical connections with their homelands and also become members of the presbytery.[19] The Westminister Confession of Faith, the Canons of the Synod of Dort, and the Shorter and Heidelberg Catechisms, despite serious opposition, were made the standards of doctrine.[20] These remained standard until a new creed, constitution, and canons were adopted December 1890.[21] The Church was officially organized on October 3, 1877.[22]

The three missions resolved on June 21, 1877 to organize all the existing Japanese churches under their respective care into a single body.[23] The congregations which affiliated

---

* "Missionary Presbyteries and Synods which hold the same faith and order should be encouraged to enter into common church relations with each other in any country in which the missions of more than one Presbyterian body are concerned.—Appendix to the *Annual Report of the Board of Foreign Missions*, 1877, pp. 137–140.

were the four constituting the Nippon Kirisuto Kōkai, and the five affiliated with the presbytery of the Chōrō Kōkai (Presbyterian Church.[24] April 5, 1881, the field covered by the cooperating missions was divided into three presbyteries, the Eastern with eight churches, the Northern composed of twelve churches, and the Western comprising five congregations in Kyūshū and the western provinces. The General Assembly (*Daikai*) which met November 1, 1881, was coterminous with the former single presbytery.[25] Several experiments were tried with reference to evangelistic cooperation within this framework. In 1879 a Board of Home Missions (*Dendō Kyoku*) was formed consisting of three ministers and three elders which administered funds contributed by the congregations. This was replaced in 1883 by a system of mission control and Japanese counsel. A third development was effected in 1886 when the General Assembly again established a Board of Home Missions in which representatives of the missions cooperated with an equal number of the pastors in matters of finance and control.[26] These last mentioned steps according to chronology belong below, but to bring the Presbyterian-Reformed experiment in church union through the period covered by this study, it has been completed at this point.

The only other step towards organic union of subsequent significance was a joint conference of the several Episcopal missions held in May 1878 when it was agreed to use but one book of common prayer, and to form a joint theological school.[27]

ERA OF RAPID ADVANCE, 1883-1889

Between 1883 and 1889 the process of church establishment continued in much the same manner as during the introductory period. Local congregations were formed in connection with schools, by graduates, by theological students while itinerating during vacations and holidays, by groups of interested individuals who after self-study invited a minister or missionary to meet with them, and in numerous other ways. The tension between the desire for church unity and the necessity for perpetuating denominationalism was maintained. While the local congregations usually bore the sectarian stamp of the founding group, there were several characteristics common to the work of the missions, most of which derived from the earlier period.

The aims of the various missions were similar, particularly with respect to the establishment of an independent, self-supporting church in Japan. As was discovered at the Ōsaka Conference in 1883, differences in opinion concerning the best means of achieving the end did not obviate the general agreement as to the importance of setting up local congregations which would ultimately stand alone. At one extreme were the missionaries of the American Board of Commissioners for Foreign Missions who, having founded thirteen independent churches, believed that organization should be denied a local congregation until it could subsist without foreign assistance. Others, apprehensive lest the Japanese assume the responsibilities for independence before they were prepared, advocated a policy which would extend aid in the early stages of development. They reasoned that material assistance was necessary among a people so poor, and that this would give the missionaries contact with and right of supervision over the churches during the formative period. A special committee which dealt with the matter urged the danger of dependence upon foreign subsidy.[28] The Episcopal missions departed from this policy deliberately because they thought that better and more permanent results could be obtained by a more liberal extension of assistance.[29] Kanamori Tsūrin urged that the evangelistic undertakings of the church be made entirely self-supporting, and that foreign money be used only for indirect work such as the training of ministers and the preparation of Christian literature.[30] The Naniwa Church, established in Ōsaka, January 20, 1878 by Sawayama Paul, became self-supporting from the start despite the poverty of the small congregation, because of the pastor's determination to accept only what the members could pay him. This church inspired the first home missionary society, sponsored the first Christian self-supporting school for girls, started another independent church in Ōsaka, and made beginnings in nine other places.[31] While the example illustrates what was possible among the Japanese Christians, it should be pointed out that the pastor and his wife died at an early age, very probably of the physical sacrifices entailed by the demonstration.

The zeal of the converts should be mentioned in this connection as one of the factors in the spread of Protestantism in Japan. A considerable proportion of the graduates of Christian schools entered the ministry or remained as instructors in the institutions. They did this for a fraction of the salary they could have earned in government service. Church officers made extended preaching tours into the unchurched interior, oftentimes paying their own expenses. The church placed heavy financial responsibilities upon converts as contrasted with Buddhism, which made few monetary exactions save for special masses and funerals. The small Protestant congregations, in seeking to become independent, demanded large amounts from the believers not only for local expenses but for home and foreign missions as well. The spirit in which such obligations were assumed was instanced by an incident in a Tōkyō church. Following the pastor's anouncement that the time to despatch an evangelist to the provinces was near at hand, the members rose one by one and promised to contribute according to their means. The editor of the *Japan Mail* commented on the event, saying, " these churchgoers...regarded their faith as a very real factor of their daily lives...it...bound them together in a brotherhood of most practical benevolence.[32]

The above mentioned characteristics were especially operative during the years 1883-1889. In 1883 self-support seemed within easy reach. The growing size of the churches as well as the desire of the Japanese to spread the Christian message and to finance the expenses, underlay the optimism that the nation would within a short while become independent of missionary aid and support. The reaction so cooled the zeal of the converts, decreased the size of the congregations, and retarded the spread of Protestantism that to the above mentioned factors leading to self-support less significance was attributed after 1889 than previously.[33]

A third characteristic of the spread of Christianity through the churches prior to 1890 was the continuing interest in organic union. Several moves in that direction were partially successful, though the failures contributed to the reaction and subsequent retardation in the expansion of the Christian movement. The growth of the five "families" of missions illustrates the presence of the will to unity and concerted action.

Cooperation between the Episcopal missions in the matter of the *Book of Common Prayer* has been mentioned previously. The organization of the Nippon Seikōkai (Holy Catholic Church in Japan) in later years was facilitated by the favorable manner in which this experiment eventuated.[34] The jurisdiction of the American and English bishops constituted a matter of friction until 1883 when the American bishop was assigned to Tokyo, the English bishop to Ōsaka and Nagasaki, and Kyōto was made "common ground."[35] The three missions continued their activities separately until the arrival of the Rt. Rev. Edward Bickersteth who had been appointed to superintend the English societies in Japan. In conjunction with Bishop C. M. Williams he called a conference of missionaries to meet at Tokyo May 21, 1886 to consider a resolution passed at a Church Mission Society conference held at Ōsaka May 3, 1886 proposing the unification of the scattered congregations of the three missions. A second conference met in Tōkyō the ensuing July 8th at which a constitution and canons (drafted during the interval by the two bishops assisted by nine American and English presbyters) were amended and adopted. The first synod of clerical and lay delegates of the English and American missions was convened at Ōsaka on February 8, 1887. The Nippon Seikōkai, in communion with the Episcopal churches of America and England, was then organized and the constitution and canons accepted. The Constitution was based on the Bible, the Nicene Creed, the Sacraments, and the Three Orders. The translation of the prayer book was continued. A Japanese missionary society was organized.[36] No dioceses were fixed, so that respective jurisdictions of the bishops constituted until 1894 a source of confusion.[37]

The story of the organization of the Nippon Kirisuto Itchi Kyōkai came within the introductory period. During the years 1883-1889 the mission council and church alike were strengthened by the addition of the missions of the Presbyterian Church in the United States in 1885, the (German) Reformed Church in the United States in 1886, and the Cumberland Presbyterian Church in 1889. The "Council of the Three Missions" became "The Council of Missions Cooperating with the Church of Christ in Japan.[38] During the years 1883-1885 the establishment and care of the churches was almost wholly the domain of the several missions in the areas to which they had been assigned. As the joint conferences afforded the Japanese opportunity for counsel but settled on them little obligation, their interest was slight. In 1886 a new plan of financial cooperation and coordinate control of evangelism was inaugurated according to which the General Assembly elected a board and each of the presbyteries a committee consisting of equal numbers of missionaries and Japanese ministers or elders. The General Assembly board collected funds which were administered by the presbytery committees. To each *yen* raised locally the Council of Missions added three *yen*. The liberal gifts of the churches to this fund aided the process of expansion during the years of rapid growth. Some of the evangelism nominally under the separate missions was actually directed by the presbytery committees. The weakness of the plan was its over-organization.[39]

The first congregations established under the auspices of missionaries of the American Board of Commissioners for Foreign Mission bore the same title as did the first two Protestant Churches namely, Nippon Kirisuto Kōkai. They were organized according to the Congregational pattern, hence needed some distinguishing title. In 1885 the name Kumiai Kyōkai (Associated Churches) was chosen.[40] Missionaries became by invitation corresponding members of the General Conference (Sōkai) and of the advisory councils, but had no control over local churches.[41] This loosely knit federated type of church enjoying a maximum of Japanese control appealed to the national consciousness of the people especially since it was in harmony with the then popular conceptions of freedom, personal liberty and individual expression. Strong Japanese leadership such as was wielded by Niijima Jō and Sawayama Paul was given greater opportunity for expression than under the presbyterian and episcopal types of organization. These reasons partially explain the strength and leadership of the Kumiai Kyōkai during the years 1883–1889.* Likewise important was the fact that the American Board of Commissioners for Foreign Missions,

---

* In the instructions given the first American Board of Commissioners for Foreign Missions' Japan missionary was the exhortation to strive to develop self-supporting, self-governing churches. F.C.

more than any other western agency, answered the appeal from the field for an enlarged personnel. By 1889 there were eighty-nine Congregational missionaries in Japan. Their effectiveness was enhanced by the fact that in 1883 there were but four stations, and that most of the work thereafter was concentrated around Kyōto and the eastern shore of the Inland Sea. It might also be stated that among these many missionaries were several who were outstanding in ability, both as scholars and teachers, and as preachers and organizers of churches.

The representatives of the American Baptist Convention, the English Baptist Mission and the Southern Baptist Convention cooperated in the formation of local churches on the congregational plan. The members of the last named mission did not arrive until the year our period closes, and the one English Baptist family transferred its work to the American Baptists the following year. Thus, most of the evangelistic activities were under the first mentioned of the Baptist groups. City evangelism, itineration, summer tours by missionary teachers, and the establishment of a school in Sendai in order to secure a passport for purposes of evangelizaton were some of the methods followed by their representatives.[42] Some of their interior efforts were transferred to the Church of Christ (Disciples) mission after its arrival in 1883.[43] There was no national organization of the churches though the congregations were encouraged to form regional associations for mutual encouragement. An annual conference of missionaries was held from 1877 onward to take advisory actions on church and mission matters. While the congregational polity of the mission left the churches practically independent, unity of policy was secured through the conferences.[44]

Clearest evidence of cooperation between missions in the absence of a unifying framework was seen in the case of the Methodist group. Missionaries of the Methodist Episcopal Church concentrated in Tokyo and northward and in Nagoya; those of the Methodist Church of Canada in Tōkyō and on the central west coast; the workers of the Evangelical Association were located in Tōkyō; Methodist Protestant Church missionaries were centered in Yokohama; those of the Methodist Episcopal Church, South, located in southwestern Japan on the Inland Sea. Save for duplication in Tokyo where the needs were extensive, the constituent missions of the Methodist "family" were well distributed for purposes of extending the Methodist communion throughout the nation. The Japan Conference of the Methodist Episcopal Church was organized in 1884; that of the Methodist Church of Canada during 1889; the mission of the Evangelical Association was organized during the first episcopal visit of a bishop in 1885.[45] Despite the absence of a centralizing superstructure, the degree of cooperation by the several bodies was so thorough they were really not divided.[46]

In addition to these five mission families, which account for the larger part of the local congregations as of 1889, the other agencies with missionaries in Japan concentrated upon the areas where they were located. Only the Unitarians did not seek to organize congregations.

In connection with the steps which led to the formation of the Nippon Seikōkai occurred an abortive effort to unite the several Protestant missions and churches. At the time of the meeting of the first synod in 1877, Bishop Bickersteth proposed a resolution favoring the establishment of a church in Japan which should impose no non-essential conditions of communion. A memorandum to this effect was submitted to the non-Roman mission agencies and churches together with a letter from the English bishop requesting them to communicate with the foreign members of the missions.

Bickersteth also enclosed two of his own recent sermons in which he claimed that the Anglican Communion unites the endowments and characteristics which have been granted to others separately and that by degrees members of the various denominations would find a rallying point in "the only Communion which ... has touch and contact with them all.[47] Considerable controversy was provoked between missionaries of the Nippon Seikōkai and members of the Council of Missions cooperating with the Nippon Kirisuto Itchi Kyōkai over alleged claims of the Episcopal Church to an exclusive position. These and other replies to the suggestion indicated that the missions were unwilling to accept the conditions involved in Bickersteth's plan for securing unity.[48]

Scarcely had the above negotiations been terminated when a move was made towards uniting the two bodies which embraced over two-thirds of the total Protestant church membership and self-supporting churches, over half the ordained ministers and the source of almost four-fifths of the contributions. These were the Nippon Kirisuto Itchi Kyōkai and the Nippon Kumiai Kyōkai (Japan Congregational Church).[49] In May 1887 the General Assembly of the former and the General Conference of the latter met separately in Tokyo. Each appointed a committee to confer and report concerning a basis of union. A statement of doctrine and polity for a proposed Nippon Rengō Kirisuto Kyōkai (United Church of Christ in Japan) was drafted and adopted by both the General Assembly and the General Conference. The churches appointed ten members each to a joint committee to prepare standards of government and doctrine in accordance with the plan of union.[50] After conferring for nearly a year, the group unanimously adopted a "Constitution and By-laws and Appendix," which was presented to the General Assenbly and the General Conference in 1888.[51] As some of the ministers of the Nippon Kirisuto Itchi Kyōkai regarded the doctrinal statement as inadequate, congregational meetings

were held for the purpose of discussing and clarifying the pro-
posals. The great majority of laymen and ministers in both
churches favored the constitution, while some of the Kumiai
delegates came instructed to the General Conference to vote
for a delay of six months. The two bodies met separately in
Ōsaka, November 23, 1888. The General Assembly of the
Itchi Kyōkai adopted the constitution by a unanimous vote.
The General Conference of the Kumiai group voted for a
postponement until May, 1889.[52] Subsequent postponements
finally terminated the negotiations.[53]

In spite of the failure of these efforts to unite the two
denominations the attempt was not without results. First,
the Christians were educated concerning the issues involved.
Second, the majority of the missionaries were shown to be
in sympathy with the movement.[54] Third, a general willingness to make concessions in the interests of an ideal was
demonstrated. Fourth, it was shown that something more
than logic and concessions was necessary to unite churches
with different polities.[55] Fifth, the Nippon Kirisuto Kyōkai
continued through a committee of the General Assembly a
study of creeds which had begun during the negotiations,
with the result that a simple, irenic confession of faith was
substituted in 1890 for the lengthy doctrinal statement then
in use.[56]

The failures of these three attempts to effect a united
Protestant church were due to a variety of factors. First,
the ideals exceeded the realities of the situation. The missionaries thought in catholic terms but acted according to
denominational patterns. They were able to agree in conference that the congregations they were to organize should
be of the same name, polity, and creed, yet when setting
them up, the Presbyterian-Reformed missionaries organized
according to the presbyterian form and the missionaries of
the American Board of Commissioners for Foreign Missions
according to congregationalism. Second, pressure from the

American churches was felt by all the missionaries concerned. Promotional agencies in America feared that support for projects abroad would be decreased unless definite results could be shown in return for money invested. Groups in the United States suggested that in event the union was consummated the Congregational Church might well withdraw its financial assistance.[57] Third, a majority of the missionaries favored the proposal, yet there was still much denominationalism within both missions.[58] Some missionaries were of the opinion that the merger would have split both churches.* Fourth, by the time the movement was under way denominational consciousness had become sufficiently strong among the Japanese to complicate the negotiations. By the middle '80's Japanese leadership, meanwhile having been permeated with the ideology of the missionaries, shared in the responsibilities for the decision.† Fifth, the proposed constitution sought to combine two types of polities which appeared mutually exclusive.‡ Sixth, many Kumiai congregations feared that liberty would be sacrificed as the price of unity.[59] Seventh, the General Assembly of the Nippon Kirisuto Itchi Kyōkai in taking action on the measure was representative of the churches affiliated with it, and was authorized to speak for them. The General Conference of the Kumiai Kyōkai was restricted by the autonomy of

---

* Mrs. T. True correspondence to the Board of Foreign Missions of the Presbyterian Church in the U. S. A., June 10, 1887. George Knox in correspondence to the Board of Foreign Missions of the Presbyterian Church in the U.S.A., July 27, 1887, denied that a split would eventuate. Niijima Jō in numerous letters to the American Board of Commissioners, about the same date, was certain that a few of the Kumiai congregations would refuse to enter the new church.

† This became even truer in later years as Japanese ministers studied in denominational seminaries in the west, and became recipients of certain privileges which accrued to them under the existing denominational framework.

‡ Imbrie, Wm., *Church Unity in Japan*, p. 28. When church union was effected in 1941 denominational blocks were retained, but the structure for the national church closely resembled that of the presbyterian system.

the local congregations, and thus could take no action bind-ing upon them. Eighth, the fact that the Plan of Union in the United States had finally been abandoned by the Presby-terian and Congregational churches, accounted for an inertia within both bodies which was not overcome within the churches in Japan for several decades.

The suggestion of Bishop Bickersteth has been omitted from this concluding analysis because it never reached the stage of negotiations. Had it done so it would doubtlessly have failed for all the reasons mentioned above save the last two. Matters did not extend beyond the exploratory stage in respect to the Seikōkai's suggestion because the other missions were of the opinion that union with the Episcopal bodies could be accomplished only on the terms of the latter.

EVANGELISM

As shown above, schools, Christian literature, medical and social welfare work and the organization of local and national churches contributed to the development of a popular opinion in favor of Protestantism, and introduced persons who were interested in the secondary benefits of Christianity in preference to its primary values. Evangelism in a general sense might be made to include all the above. Technically, however, the Japanese word for evangelism (*dendō*) refers more especially to certain direct means of propagating Christianity as distinguished from the educational, medical and social work approaches and it is to this activity that attention must now be directed.

Protestant missionaries to Japan were permitted by the terms of the treaties to conduct services in their own lan-guages for the foreign residents of the port cities. As the popular fears of Christianity were dispelled, inquisitive Japa-nese gathered about the chapels, to observe and to listen.

Missionaries requested the 1867 International Week of Prayer Committee to include petitions that open preaching might not be followed by ill consequences for the Japanese.[60] The 1872 prayer services held in Yokohama which culminated in the organization of the first Japanese church were conducted in the English language, save for the petitions of the students who participated.[61] Lectures in foreign languages there were at special meetings, and in school chapels, but most of the direct evangelism was carried on among the people by means of the national language. Sermons in Japanese became common after the removal of the anti-Christian edicts.* Chapels were specially constructed and houses were rented for the purpose, according to local convenience and needs.[62]

Beginning about 1881 missionaries and Japanese evangelists of several missions and churches began to conduct mass meetings at large public halls,[63] in order to disseminate information concerning Christianity and to stimulate public interest in the church. English and Japanese were both used depending upon the linguistic skill of the speaker. Some of the speeches were apologetic, while others attacked the local religions. As the relationship between religions and international morality gained prominence, this subject likewise was treated.[64] Each session was usually followed by an informal meeting for those whose interest had been aroused.[65] C. S. Eby, who promoted the Tōkyō series each year throughout the period of rapid growth, in 1890 erected a tabernacle in the heart of the city for purposes of continuing such public discussions.[66] Profiting by this experience a similar program was followed at Yokohama, then in many other cities and towns throughout the country.[67] Referring

---

* *Proceedings of the Osaka Conference*, pp. 67, 83. Missionaries stressed the importance of preaching, by word and example, to the strengthening of the Japanese ministry. Pastoral work, however, was left to the nationals, who with only a theoretical knowledge of the subject, did not adequately develop this type of evangelism.—*Tokyo Missionary Conference Report*, pp. 166–167.

no doubt to these popular meetings, Anesaki Masaharu said that the churches were crowded during the '80's with men and women who "listened to sermons delivered by missionaries—preferably in English.[68]

Among the most effective of the mass meetings was the series conducted at Kōchi, Shikoku, to which city missionaries were invited by the statesman Itagaki Taisuke, a political liberal and patriot who was ardent in his favors towards Christianity. Attracted by the famed patronage, hundreds of lawyers, doctors, teachers, politicians, and students, as well as common people, attended the meetings and post-lecture discussions. Within a short time, there were sufficient baptisms among the interested to form a church. As the incident was not duplicated elsewhere, this became the instance *par excellence* of the spread of Protestantism through its identification with western political idealism.[69]

Itineration was another technique employed by missionaries, Japanese evangelists, and theological students. There were several early instances of travel through the country on passports for the open purpose of preaching. In 1874 missionaries of the Methodist Episcopal Church probably preached when they paid visits to Hakodate and to the west coast of Japan,[70] (Dutch) Reformed Church missionaries visited a village 115 miles from Tōkyō in 1876 in answer to a request, preached and organized a church.[71] Dōshisha theological students followed a program of itineration near Kyōto in the same year.[72] During the period of rapid advance the Japanese and foreign preachers made extended trips outside the treaty ports, spending weeks and even months in completing a circuit.[73] Churches did not grow out of each of these meetings,[74] but the Christian message was broadcast among many people who would not have heard it otherwise. In addition to conducting services at established churches, lecturing at public halls and in homes where no church was available, and superintending the activities of the Christian followers,* the missionaries also by personal advice and sympathy strengthened the morale of the evangelists and Christians along the route.[75] The extent of itineration was enlarged by the development of highway, railway, and steamship lines, since the missionaries were able thereby to increase the number of outstations, and to visit isolated points regularly. While there were some instances of penetration outside the area of westernized travel, the expansion of the Christian movement generally followed the lines of communications. The reverent and impressionable attitude of the Japanese, the high respect they accorded to western scholars and civilization, made itineration outside the population centers feasible in spite of continuing anti-Christian prejudices.[76]

SUMMARY

An historical study such as this either should constitute an exhaustive account of the personnel and projects of the several Protestant missions engaged in Japan, provide a source book of letters, documents, and articles written by missionaries or Japanese Christians or both, narrate the evolution of the Christian life and institutions in Japan ; or it should display a cross section of the Christian movement and the factors which affected its development. The second alternative has provided the pattern for the material embraced in this chapter. Representative examples rather than

---

* J.B. Porter wrote in 1890 that the superintendence of Japanese workers was becoming less necessary or desirable; that the Japanese could in most cases supervise the churches and evangelists better than could the missionaries; that it was consequently becoming the policy of the foreigners to preach and visit churches only when invited or appointed to do so; that the Japanese were a high-spirited people, uneasy under foreign constraint and control, so that the time was not far distant when missionaries must cease holding the controlling power in the churches; and that the mission boards might soon find it advisable to make all monetary contributions directly to the Japanese mission boards.—*Church at Home and Abroad*, September 1890, p. 212.

exhaustive accounts have been employed to indicate the methods of Protestantism's spread in Japan. It has proved impossible to limit the historical account to the years between 1883 and 1889 inasmuch as the expansion of the church during these years was conditioned largely by the developments of the preceding quarter century. While 1883 marks the beginning of a new era both with reference to rate of growth and to privileges enjoyed by the Christians, it is not a chronological point of cleavage as to the characteristics of or the methods employed in the spread of Protestantism.

The processes characterizing the church's development in Japan proved to be strangely similar to those which marked the extension of the missionary movement elsewhere in Asia: personal rather than governmental resources marked the missionaries' *modus operandi*, women played an increasingly important role, the church admission standards were kept high, the influence of Protestantism was out of all proportion to its numerical strength, and there was decreasing missionary control due to the emergence of capable Japanese leadership and to the achievement of ecclesiastical self-support and independence.

Among the means employed to touch the life of the nation and to strengthen the Christian movement, the one engaging the largest number of workers was that which catered to the universal desire for knowledge. Schools for men and women, for adults and children, training them for professional Christian service, for church membership, for citizenship and for admission to higher government institutions were established to gain a foothold for missionary activities and then improved to provide a religious education calculated to offset the growing secular emphasis in education. In addition to their own schools, missionaries also taught at the Japanese founded and administered Dōshisha, in private and government colleges and universities, and in institutions of learning sustained cooperatively by missionaries and Japanese patrons.

The preparation and translation of Christian literature likewise loomed important in the total missionary program of expansion. The entire Bible was rendered into Japanese by a cooperative committee ; a hymnal was prepared jointly ; and tracts, books, and periodicals were published to convince the non-Christians and to instruct church members.

The efforts of the missionaries by 1883 had led to the establishment of numerous local congregations and a number of denominations which were multiplied and strengthened between 1883 and 1889. This period was characterized by a tendency on the one hand towards unity and on the other towards sectarianism. Two attempts prior to 1890 to consolidate the Christian forces proved abortive although families of missions with similar polities were drawn closer together. Cooperation with respect to specific projects proved easier to effect than organic union.

In addition to the educational and literary methods employed in the establishment and development of the church, preaching, public lectures, and extensive itineration were engaged in by both missionaries and Japanese. A rising interest in social and moral conditions culminated in the founding of temperance societies, orphanages and efforts to ameliorate the lot of prisoners. Applied medicine, which had been employed to advantage during the introductory period was abandoned by most of the mission agencies as Japanese physicians, surgeons and hospitals proved competent to care for the needs of the people. These were the principal methods by which Christianity spread in Japan prior to 1890.

Part III

RAPID GROWTH AND RETARDATION

Chapter VIII

REASONS FOR SPECTACULAR GROWTH

1883—1889

In 1883 a veteran foreign representative stated that the success experienced by the Protestant movement in Japan up to that time had probably never been surpassed in the history of Christian missions.[1] Nevertheless, the growth of the church during the years 1883–1889 far exceeded that of the preceding period.   The reasons underlying this expansion having been already pointed out, it is necessary to make a thorough analysis of the phenomena whereby the exotic faith partially surmounted the handicaps imposed by the past history of Kirishitan missions and for a short time quickened its rate of advance.

As a matter of fact the liabilities under which missionary operations were conducted were never completely overcome. Some of them were temporarily more or less quiescent, yet at no time was the Christian movement able to transcend entirely the difficulties which beset it.   Towards the close of the decade, Ebina Danjō, a Japanese pastor who subsequently became President of the Dōshisha, stated it would be difficult to exaggerate the ill will which the average Japanese had for Christianity.[2]

The anti-Christian sentiments did not disappear even during the time of its ascendency.   The edict boards having been removed Christianity was practically, if not officially, tolerated by the government, yet neither Christianity as a religion nor the Christian church as an organization enjoyed legal status. Following the proclamation of the Constitution with its guarantee of religious freedom, considerable discussion ensued as to whether or not the proviso concerning the right of conscience applied to Christians.[3]

Many of the inconveniences suffered by Christianity were not removed even during the era of greatest development. Takahashi Gorō, one of the Bible translators and editor of the *Rikugo Zasshi*, complained in 1888 that these amounted to virtual persecution. The specific charges were that Christians were excluded from certain privileges enjoyed by Shinto and Buddhist believers, that churches could not be built or possessed as the common property of Christians, and that pastors could not conduct funerals in their own capacity. It was alleged that these inconveniences hindered the propagation of Christianity and encouraged opponents to desecrate the churches and meeting places, to attack Christians, and to oppose Christian funerals.[4] This letter provoked considerable discussion in both the vernacular and English press, and it was claimed that since nothing had been said of these incidents in the local papers there was probably no basis for the protest.[5] There was agreement, however, that because the church lacked official recognition it did suffer certain disabilities. Churches paid taxes from which temples and shrines were exempt. In strong Buddhist centers Christian services often were obstructed, and difficulties were raised with reference to funerals.[6] Missionaries were aware of the existence of these handicaps, but refused to permit their activities to be determined by them. Critics of Takahashi argued that Christianity should concern itself with fitting the people for larger liberties rather than agitating for premature proclamations.[7]

The rapid spread of Protestantism during the years 1883–

1889 may or may not have been beneficial, taking the long view, for the growth of the church. As the connections between Christianity and western culture, especially in the capital and in large cities, accounted for much of the church's sudden growth, it was the discredit into which things occidental fell in the metropolitan areas which caused the retardation of Protestantism after 1889. What might have eventuated had the steady but slow progress which was the outcome of early caution and plodding continued, is not determinable. The expansion of the missionary forces in that event would not have been as great and there would have been no rapid increase in the size of the congregations, but neither would there have been the paralyzing shock of the reaction after 1889. Such historical conjectures lead to no dogmatic conclusions but do indicate tht the phenomena of rapid growth were not necessarily an asset to the Christian movement.

For seven or eight years following the Ōsaka Conference (1883) the Protestant movment in Japan enjoyed an era of prosperity. A popular interest in matters religious was manifested both in the cities and in the rural areas. Christianity was a common theme, proclaimed from platforms and discussed in public places. The home mission boards of the national churches and missionaries alike were overwhelmed with applications from towns and villages for preaching services.* Large numbers of Japanese professed a faith in terms satisfactory to the missionaries and Japanese who examined them, and were admitted into the churches. Numerous mission schools for boys and girls were crowded with patriotic, ambitious scholars.[8] A number of influences directed the attention of the people towards Christianity. Confucian morality

---

* *Church at Home and Abroad*, June 1887, pp. 566–567. The Baptist missionaries did not share this optimism. A characteristic opinion among them denied the claims made elsewhere that the Japanese people were willing to listen to preaching, and that the Bible was being read extensively by every class in the nation.—H. H. Rhees correspondence to the American Baptist Missionary Union, July 29, 1884.

had been temporarily invalidated by the rising vogue of things western. As the younger generation was accused of being deficient in ethical standards, a more adequate system of morality was demanded. The effort of the central government to reinstate the Confucian code in the educational system met with public dissatisfaction. Leading citizens urged that Christianity was the best existing system of morals, and that if everything else western was to be accepted Christianity likewise should be adopted. The vernacular press alleged that in appropriating the science but not the ethics of the occident Japan yoked herself to a carriage with one wheel. The contention was that in so-called Christian countries religion was the means whereby morality was promoted, while mental development was encouraged by teaching the arts and sciences; that the ancient religions of Japan were retarding influences which in recent times had not and could not promote the nation's welfare; that as the science and religion of a given civilization stood to each other as the wheels of a cart, Japan had erred in importing but a single wheel.[9] Brinkley claimed in 1884 that the time could not be far distant when the rulers of Japan would be compelled to grant complete freedom of conscience, that all impediments to the spread of Christianity had been removed but more than negative toleration was needed, and that as all peoples with superior physical and intellectual powers had chosen Christianity, it would be impossible for Japan to take the material and not adopt the moral civilization of the west.[10]

Much discussion thereby arose as to the relationship between Christianity and cultural development. Some claimed that Christianity lay at the root of progress, others that the latter (e.g., science) had developed despite rather than because of Christianity. The *Jiji Shimpō* was of the opinion that liberty of conscience, thought, speech and person was the sign and secret of western Christianity and the essence of the New Testament.[11] The *Mainichi Shimbun* in 1888 offered its congratulations that the popular reputation of Protestantism had been enhanced, but expressed dissatisfaction over its lack of official status. As the rapid and extensive diffusion of Christianity would be to the best interests of the nation, the newspaper recommended that the religion of the west be legally recognized. Such a step would necessitate, however, that Christian ministers abstain from all political activities. It was to be doubted, the *Mainichi* asserted, that the government withheld concessions to Christianity as bargaining points in its efforts to secure a favorable revision of the treaties.[12] While the Christians were gratified by the improved status they enjoyed, many of them deprecated the use of their religion as a political expedient,[13] and warned against the danger of wholesale conversions.[14]

Certain social trends also contributed to the spread of Protestantism. Students from abroad reported that Christianity was a civilizing factor which, contrary to rumor, did not destroy patriotism. They went further and urged that religion was basic in the development and superiority of western culture. Contacts of the people with foreigners strengthened this belief. It was only after 1880 that the Japanese were able to obtain a comprehensive view of western civilization. Popular attention previously had been focussed on the political, military and naval affairs of the nation almost exclusively.[15] Relatively speaking, much of the anti-Christian prejudice which persisted after the Restoration had decreased by the end of 1884. The Buddhist priests, who were in the forefront among the opposition, learned that to contest the advances of Christianity they also would have to combat the central government. Defending the missionaries against the charge that they were cloaks for imperialism, friends of the foreign representatives of the western churches urged on their behalf that Christian teachings exercised a wholesome restraint upon the dangerous elements in the local political situation. Considering the

165

liberal mood of the nation which the conservative government had to control, western morality appeared to many officials to be a valuable political instrument.[16] Two incidents illustrated the growing tolerance in the official attitude towards the foreign religion. An audience was granted by the emperor on September 12, 1885, to a papal delegate who was given assurances that the full measure of protection would be extended to Christian subjects. In December 1885, Japanese officials together with members and clergy of the Orthodox Church participated in the funeral services of the deceased Russian minister. Brinkley claimed that the latter event "amounted almost to an official recognition of the status of Christianity in Japan.[17]

Whether for good or ill, by the middle '80's many of the former enemies of Christianity conceded that the nation had benefited by its introduction. Whereas students, journalists, public speakers, lawyers, merchants, and officials had previously resisted its spread, their antagonism in many cases had turned to tolerance and even open acceptance. Even where there was no missionary or church, the people generally knew something concerning the western creed and acquiesced in its presence.[18] Churches were crowded with interested listeners. The appeals for missionaries to hold meetings and to teach English, with freedom to engage in religious propaganda, were greater than could be met. The rate of growth was such that many of the missionaries anticipated the day when they could permanently withdraw from Japan, confident that the national Christians would be competent to carry the responsibilities of the church. So certain were they of this development, mission boards were entreated to coordinate their forces and provide adequate workers and funds so as to make an experiment of the nation which would demonstrate that a non-Turanian land could be Christianized.* Missionaries contended that never had a people been more receptive or the opportunities more inviting than those of Japan; that it was criminal not to fully occupy Japan when the way had been so well prepared; that if the mission boards should act speedily and wisely, Japan might become a Christian nation in less than a quarter of a century; but that not to take advantage of the opportunities was to stand aside while error and false religions took the place that rightfully belonged to Protestant Christianity.[19]

The above outlined increase in the size of the church and the wave of popular enthusiasm enjoyed by the Christian movement throughout the period 1883 to 1889 are not to be explained by the processes of spread alone. Motivating the expansion of Protestantism in Japan were numerous personal, economic, political, cultural and religious factors, some of which were operative only during the particular years covered by this dissertation, while others dated from an earlier time and continued past 1889.

Among the general reasons which existed prior to and continued beyond this significant period, the first to be considered is the persistence and strategy of the missionaries in laying a foundation for the Christian movement in Japan. Foreign representatives of the church had been discreet and conciliatory during the years when their religion was under an official ban. The missionary pioneers necessarily had confined their efforts almost exclusively to the treaty ports for a decade. During this interval the pioneers had concentrated upon language study, translation and literary production. They thereby served to discredit popular suspicions that the Christian religion was a mask for western imperialism. The Japanese were anxious to learn; the mission-

---

* *Missionary Herald*, March 1884, p. 83; *Missionary Herald*, November 1888, p. 534; Arthur May Knapp, a Unitarian missionary to Japan was of the opinion that there was no historical justification for this expectation.—Knapp, *Feudal and Modern Japan*, (Yokohama, Kelly and Walsh, 1906) p. 187.

aries made use of this desire by establishing schools and by cooperating with government and private agencies in conducting educational institutions both in the treaty ports and in the interior. The passport regulations, which forbade extensive travel save for purposes of health and scientific investigation, remained a hindrance to missionary itineration both prior to and for several years after 1889. A considerable proportion of the missionary personnel accepted employment, nominal or actual, under individual Japanese or local governments, with the understanding that in addition to their teaching responsibilities they would be permitted to preach and teach Christianity. Companies of Japanese were organized to give positions to the missionaries, so that foreigners would be within the letter of the law. In the case of the Doshisha the company was far from being a fiction, although the salaries of the missionaries and a portion of the maintenance fund were supplied by the American Board of Commissioners for Foreign Missions. In certain other cases all the funds were furnished by the missionaries or the societies directly concerned, the nominal employer being actually in the hire of the missionaries. Though the latter differed among themselves as to the ethics of the methods, their social, medical and educational activities resulted in the establishment of numerous local congregations, the organization of nation-wide denominational groups, and the general enhancement of Protestantism's reputation.

The attitude assumed by the missionaries towards treaty revision likewise brought them into public favor. The resolutions forwarded to the western powers and the articles prepared for foreign language journals were evidence to the Japanese that the missionaries were on their side with reference to the restoration of Japan's tariff autonomy and to the removal of extra-territoriality. The conference of missionaries in 1884 voted unanimously to request the foreign diplomatic representatives in Tōkyō that greater liberality should be shown with regard to Japan's desires for judicial and tax autonomy.* This position, which was reaffirmed in 1890, helped to clear the reputation of the religion from those blemishes inherited from the days of Kirishitan missions. These actions were taken not only out of a sympathy which most of the missionaries felt for Japan's position, but also because of a fear that if the western nations refused to accede to Japan's requests, the effect upon the Christian movement would be disastrous.[20]

In this connection mention should be made of the fact that the missionary community included several outstanding scholars, linguists, organizers, musicians, teachers, and preachers. With few exceptions they were exemplary Christians and diligent workers. Among those who laid the foundations were several of advanced age and previous missionary experience. The opening of the nation had led several mission boards to appoint workers of demonstrated ability, particularly along lines of scholarship. The missionaries themselves stressed the need for talented recruits. Japan, they insisted, was no place for mediocre men.

Closely allied with the ability of the missionaries and the effectiveness of the strategy they employed was a second factor, namely, the quality and social status of the converts. Thirty percent of the Christians were from the *samurai* class, though they constituted five percent of the total population. Among the members and officials of the prefectural assemblies, and in the national Diet (which assembled first in 1890) the percentage of Christians was many times that in the nation at large.[21] The prestige which the new faith enjoyed in political and official circles attracted crowds of people throughout the nation to the public meetings.

---

* "We trust that the Christian nations will act in a Christian way in removing the obnoxious clause from their treaties with this empire . . . ."—*Japan Weekly Mail*, May 17, 1884, pp. 461–462, 465–466; *Missionary Herald*, August 1884, pp. 304–306.

The ability and zeal of the Japanese Christians was a third reason for the growth of Christianity in Japan. From the very beginning, the Japanese Christian churches were missionary minded, that is, the church members undertook the maintenance of branches in unchurched areas. Several home mission boards were established shortly after the national organizations were effected in order to intensify and supervise the efforts of the Japanese Christians. In one case the missionary was advised that the Christians were not ready for church organization inasmuch as all of them were not yet ready to preach.[22] Japanese ministers, teachers and editors relieved the missionaries of administrative responsibilities and the necessity for preaching, and supplemented their teaching and translation activities. The fact that the members of the Kumamoto Band chose to matriculate at the Doshisha helped to compensate for the tardiness in the decision of the American Board of Commissioners for Foreign Missions to establish a mission in Japan, and enabled the Kumiai Kyōkai, affiliated with this mission, shortly thereafter to become one of the strongest of the denominations. Niijima Jō and Sawayama Paul were among the national figures who bestowed status on the church. The Dōshisha, foremost among the Christian schools, would not have been attempted but for the foresight, patriotic zeal and demonstrated ability of Niijima. Uemura Masahisa was editor of the *Nippon Hyōron*, a theologian, preacher and educator. Uchimura Kanzō, a member of the Sapporo Band, became a nationally known writer, teacher, and preacher during the period under review. The fact that dozens of men and women of ability were attracted to the Christian faith gave it nationwide prestige, influence in official circles and validity among the student class.

Closely related to the two preceding items was a fourth factor which greatly accelerated the growth of the Christian movement, namely, the evolution of the ideal of self-support.* The policy adopted by the Kumiai Kyōkai and the Japan mission of the American Board of Commissioners for Foreign Missions was a stimulus to the development of independent congregations. The instructions given to D. C. Greene on October 8, 1869 charged him to hold as his one great object the promotion of independent and self-supporting churches.[23] Jerome D. Davis reported in 1875 that the Japanese Christians were desirous of freedom from foreign assistance. To this end they founded mission societies to carry the Christian message beyond the limits being reached by the missionaries. Local congregations and officers made unusual sacrifices to attain self-support, and pastors often engaged at other types of occupation in order to be independent of foreign funds. Money from abroad was accepted with a feeling of obligation to render an equivalent for it.[24]

A fifth general factor which helps to explain the rapid spread of Protestantism in Japan was the development of Christianity as an urban movement, urban because millions of people were uprooted and their associations broken as the basic economy of the nation was transformed from agriculture to one that was increasingly industrial, commercial, and city-dwelling. The main missionary efforts were confined to the open cities, that is, the areas in which the Japanese students, business and industrial groups were congregating.†

---

* Speaking at a conference in 1926 in China, R.Y. Lo used words which were applicable as early as the years 1883–1889: "Christianity in Japan has gone farther ahead than we have in becoming...indigenous because their church has attained self-support, self-government, and self-propagation much more than we have. The influence of the Christian Church in Japan has penetrated the social and intellectual life more than we have. Just why...I cannot say. Is it due to difference in government or racial fiber—I cannot say. But there must be some reasons . . . " *The Church in China Today* (Shanghai, 1926, pp. 166) p. 34.

† Compare the development in Japan with what Harnack says of religion in the Roman Empire: "All religions which made their way into the empire along channels of intercourse and trade were primarily religions of the city,

Schools both within and without the settlements attracted students from the rural districts, the children of national and prefectural officials and the sons and daughters of the wealthy merchant who resided in the cities. A large percentage of the early missionaries concentrated on students inasmuch as education was the sole avenue of approach open to the foreigner, and with the view that subsequently the church might be an educated one with a trained ministry. There is truth in the statement that Christianity has been from the first a student movement. Protestantism had its major success among the educated classes in urban districts, which fact placed a stamp upon the church that has altered but little during the intervening years.[25]

That Christianity was in a position to take advantage of the manifold revolution the nation was experiencing, was a sixth factor in the rapid development of the church. The decline of the shogunate and the restoration of the emperor to political power, the decadence of the ancient culture and the popularity enjoyed by western innovations, the rise of a new governing class from among the lower *samurai,* and the religious vacuum produced by the disestablishment of the old religions were among the developments which facilitated the propagation of Christian ideals and institutions. Religion entered into the revolution at a number of points. The internal changes which were attendant upon the transfer of authority and the preparation for a constitutional monarchy made for domestic disorganization. Younger and more liberal elements which were increasingly favorable to the ideas of the west came to the fore. People who had formerly been taught how and what to think now were permitted in numerous areas of life, including religion, to decide and choose

---

and remained such for a considerable period...In the main it (Judaism) continued to be a city religion, and we hear little about Jews who were settled on the land.''—Harnack, *The Mission and Expansion of Christianity,* Vol. I, p. 14.

for themselves. Christianity appealed to the Confucian-educated and now uprooted warriors who discovered in the exotic faith spiritual foundations for the civilization they wished to appropriate for their own country. It was not the Pauline doctrine of the forgiveness of sin but the magnitude of the Christian idea of God, the exalted notion of personality in the New Testament, and the Christian ethic, particularly in the province of social and sex morals, which the *samurai* comprehended and appreciated.[26] As these former warriors had taken the leadership in making the new Japan, these religious and ethical concepts were the means of extending the influence of Christianity far beyond the boundaries of the church. The adoption of Christianity, which appeared to be an integral part of western life and institutions, was urged on grounds of patriotism and expediency. Protestantism was also active in the areas where social change had created new human needs. The superiority of the Christian ethic was demonstrated in the schools, hospitals and orphanages which it founded. The fact of transition thus unabled Protestantism to gain a hold in what had been at other times a conservative, difficult field for new religions.

A seventh reason for the spread of Protestantism in Japan was that this, the dominant religion of America, felt in its expansion a particular obligation towards Japan. At the time the American Board of Commissioners for Foreign Missions was considering Japan as a possible area for operations, the needs and opportunities of the nation were urged particularly on the score that the European societies, in concentrating upon other fields, seemed to be leaving Japan as a special province of the United States.[27] Among the missionaries there were those who reasoned that whether Japan should be a Christian nation or a crude counterfeit, a people without creed, character, or permanence, was a question for the solution of which the American Christians were largely responsible.[28] It was from America that the largest part of the missionary funds and personnel came. England constituted the second largest source of support. Protestantism of both America and England stressed individual rather than group conversion,[29] and emphasized education, social service, the preparation of literature, and the translation of the Bible. The prominence of women's work, particularly characteristic of missions from America,[30] strengthened the Christian cause in Japan. While the government and other private institutions concentrated upon male education, the training of women was left almost exclusively to the mission schools.

The fact of American missionary dominance was fortunate for the spread of Protestantism in view of the relative favor which the culture, politics, and institutions of the United States enjoyed. The Japanese felt a debt of gratitude towards America because her friendly opening of the nations was regarded as having saved Japan from the partitioning or the compromise of national integrity, which had attended the activities of other western lands operating in the East.

American Christianity had much in common with the liberal currents of the day which were in vogue in Japan. Liberalism, political democracy, and western technological superiority were regarded as complementary to and in part the product of Christianity. A reciprocal relationship was engendered between liberal politics and Christianity. Among the leaders of Japan were those who sought to free their nation from the oppression of tradition and the drag of ancient customs by adopting liberalism and individualism. As Christianity preached the equality and inherent worth of all men irrespective of social position, status, or race it caught the imagination of many idealists, who either accepted the religion personally or sought to use it for political purposes.[31] The statesman and founder of the *Jiyūtō* (Liberal Party), Itagaki Taisuke, was one person, who though attracted by the religion, and sponsor of its debut into Kōchi, Shikoku,[32] resisted the arguments of Niijima Jō and other influential Christians that he should be baptized. To become Christian was to be a liberal, but in becoming a liberal one did not necessarily enter the church.[33] Nitobe Inazō and Ebina Danjō were attracted to Christianity in part through patriotic motives, and, having become apostles of liberal Christianity, influenced dozens of compatriots along similar lines.* It has even been alleged that the Christian movement became a tool in the hands of liberal party leaders. True or not, Christian growth during the period conduced toward the popularization of liberal political ideals.[34]

It is relevant to our present point that these influences were primarily American rather than continental or English. The American ideal of democracy, personal and religious in its foundations, impressed the Japanese more profoundly than abstract English thought concerning economic freedom, or the French theories of political liberation. After 1887 the greater part of the social idealists were either Christian or Christian educated, many of whom had been members of the Kumamoto and Sapporo Bands.[35] Even the growing emphasis upon the divinity of the emperor was interpreted in terms of democracy. The liberals claimed that by placing the ruler above the entire nation all the people thereby became his subjects and equality was established throughout the country.[36]

The expansion of Protestant Christianity in Japan during the latter half of the nineteenth century was thus modified by the position of western culture of which it was a constituent element as well as by the Japanese environment. Some of the conditioning details—the persistence and strategy of the missionaries, the educational qualifications and social status

---

* Ebina, for instance, while pastor of a Kumiai church in Tōkyō, won Yoshino Sakuzō, subsequently professor at Tokyo Imperial University and an advocate of democratic ideals during the World War, Bunji Suzuki, president of the Japan Federation of Labor, and Uchigasaki, a liberal member of the national Diet.—Oshimo, *op. cit.*, p. 195.

of the converts, the ability and zeal of the Japanese Christian and leaders, the achievement of self-support, the urban character of the growing movement and of the nation, the position which enabled Protestantism to exploit Japan's multiple revolution, the relation of Protestantism to American life and culture, and the favor the United States enjoyed in Japanese thought—and their contribution to the extension of the Christian movement have been indicated above. While most of these separate items were especially operative between the years 1883 and 1889, they were by no means limited to these dates. Hence they fail to account for the phenomena of rapid growth during that particular seven-year span. Consequently it is necessary to seek further in order to determine specifically why that period witnessed a rate of growth which has never been repeated.

One of the reasons why the church developed rapidly during these particular years was that throughout this relatively brief period Christianity was regarded as vehicle, creator and an essential element in western culture.* It is true that the mania for things from abroad was strong much earlier than 1883, yet there was a time-lag with reference to Christianity and its popularity. Whereas the westernization process was taking place under government supervision and by virtue of its subsidy even prior to the Restoration, religion was not allowed consideration as a matter of personal conviction until many years later. A choice, oftentimes costly, was required of those who dared accept a non-official creed. Missionaries and Japanese evangelists alike insisted upon the experience of Christian conversion as the condition for acceptance into the church, which requirement constituted a hurdle more formidable than the building of a telegraph by government fiat out of the public treasury. The Protes-

---

* "...Missions had been the chief agents in introducing modern ideas, up to the time of the national reaction towards the end of the eighties..."—Anesaki, *History of Japanese Religion*, p. 373.

tant church was an unique innovation, there being nothing resembling it among Japanese cultural institutions. The fact that thousands of persons attended Christian services and lectures was the religious counterpart of the process of westernization. There was, however, no precedent among the Japanese for uniting with a congregation. Missionaries complained that while large numbers would attend open meetings, few accepted baptism. The inertia against joining the church was never completely overcome. Another factor which created a time-lag in the acceptance of Christianity was that the government's anti-Christian policy had served during the Tokugawa period as the spear-head of national isolation. The thought habits and sentiments inculcated by more than two centuries of training were more basic than the mere absence of machines and schools. It it true that there was current some popular disfavor against westernization, but among the learned and commercial classes sufficient interest existed to insure its ultimate success. Christianity, on the other hand, enjoyed the favor of no official group. It gradually gained limited support among the *samurai* and educated classes, but this only after the mission schools had been established. While these considerations do not explain the exact date 1883, they in part account for the time-lag between the popularization of western culture and the wide acceptance of Protestantism.

A second reason operating between the years 1883 and 1889 was that Christianity during that period conflicted less with indigenous religious ideas than earlier or later. Down to the nineteenth century all religions in Japan ultimately had been forced to come to terms with Shinto. Prior to 1868, Protestantism struggled against official Buddhism, and thereafter until 1877 against Shinto as the recognized state cult. The termination of all official connections with Budhism and Shinto in 1882[37] reduced religion for the first time to a matter of personal choice.

A third factor augmenting specifically the rapid expasion of Protestantism between 1883 and 1889 was the freedom Japan enjoyed from fears of foreign invasion during that particular interval. Russia in 1875 had ceded the Kurile Islands to Japan for Saghalin (Karafuto), and was thereafter engaged in seeking a Mediterranean outlet. Germany was still in the process of securing her European position, and thus hardly looking overseas. France having been shattered by the War of 1870 was devoting her energies to preparing against another of Bismarck's attacks. The United States, following the Civil War, had dismantled its war machine; it had during the '80's an inadequate navy, and was absorbed primarily in the development of the continent rather than in rebuilding its merchant marine. England was following the leadership of Gladstone. The imperialistic ambitions of the western powers were largely absorbed in the partitioning of Africa. These facts contrived to make the years from 1883 to 1889 a period of relative freedom from fear of foreign invasion.[38]

More fundamental than any of the above mentioned causes to the spread of Protestant Christianity in Japan during the years 1883-1889 was the fact that after 1883 Japan made a special effort to free herself of the conditions imposed by the treaties with the nations of the west.[39] The practical denial of judicial and tariff autonomy imposed upon Tokugawa Japan by the occident was continued after the Restoration. The government of the Meiji period was quite different in personnel and attitudes from that of the Tokugawa era which had been required by threat and partial demonstration of force to accept the conditions proposed by the other nations. As the effects of these treaties dealing with tariff duties and lack of jurisdiction over foreign residents began to be felt, the nation made efforts to relieve the situation by agitating for treaty revision. The alterna-to open abrogation, which conceivably would have led to military retaliation, was to prove that Japan was as enlightened and as civilized as the occident. The strides along lines of westernization, education, and industrialization, were evidences that the nation was headed in the proper direction. The fact that the other powers refused to heed Japan's pleas despite her phenomenal cultural and technological progress, gave birth to the feeling that one thing yet was lacking, namely, the Christianizing of the nation. The advocacy by missionaries of revision in terms more favorable to Japan had a direct bearing upon the spread of Protestantism during these years. Patriotic Japanese, reasoning that the religion of the missionaries must be on a par with their political views, were kindly disposed towards them.[40]

Fukuzawa Yukichi was the first prominent personality in Japan to advocate the utilitarian values of Christianity as a basis for its official adoption. He concluded in 1884 from his observation of both Buddhism and Christianity that the latter was bound to triumph in Japan through its superiority in wealth, intelligence, virtue and ability to attract persons of rank. As Buddhism had the advantage only as to the habits of the people, Fukuzawa reasoned that Christianity would ultimately become the religion of Japan.[41] He, for a time, advocated its adoption as the national religion on the following grounds: America and Europe excel all other lands in religion as well as in political institutions; they despise any nations which lack the distinctive badge of Christianity; only by the adoption of their religion can Japan attain equality with them.[42] According to his plan, a sufficient number of Japanese people should accept baptism so as to make the nation nominally Christian. Having taken her place in Christendom, Japan would thereby present the same social appearance as the western powers and share equally with them the values of their civilization.[43] The suggestion received no official consideration, yet did provoke much discussion, coming as it did from a reputed editor and educator and one who had three years earlier opposed the expansion of Christianity.

While official recognition was not accorded Protestantism at that early date, much open favoritism was shown the missionaries and the Christian churches. The popular animus in favor of the western religion which followed from this situation accounted in large measure for the rapid growth. In an appeal against the local authorities for closing a Christian meeting, the Tokyo government advised the village prefect that foreigners might deliver religious discourses outside the treaty limits.[44] Buddhism discovered that only limited opposition could be offered to the spread of Christianity.

This then was the factor in the situation which more than any other explains the era of Protestant progress. To employ a chemical terminology, it was the catalyst which precipitated the other elements. The attempts to demonstrate that Japan was becoming similar to the Christian nations of the west, not only commercially, industrially and culturally, but also religiously, made for open receptivity of the Christian religion, While the missionaries, speaking generally, failed properly to comprehend the interplay between the religious and cultural forces bearing upon the situation, many of them expressed an awareness that the favorable conditions under which they labored were temporary, that the prosperity enjoyed by the Christian movement had grown out of efforts to please the west, and that unless the nations should abjure their extraterritorial privileges, and reinstate Japan in the power to revise her own tariffs, Christianity would suffer reverses.

Important as the factor of treaty revision was for the spread of Christianity in Japan during these years, it must be viewed against the background of the other reasons given: the persistence and strategy of the missionaries, the quality and social status of the Japanese Christians, the capabilities and energy which they brought into the church, the urban nature of the Christian movement, the ability of the missionaries to take advantage of Japan's multiple revolution, the dominance of American Christianity, and the fact that the numerical superiority of American missionaries coincided with official favoritism for America. As to particular causes for the spread during these years it is clear that certain phases of westernization and the extension of the church were parallel, but that there was a tardiness in the growing popularity of the religious faith, that prior to 1889 Christianity was less in conflict with indigenous ideas of loyalty, and that during the years 1883-1889 Japan was relatively free from fears of foreign invasion. Most important of all, the reason which explains the rapid program of Christianity in Japan from 1883 to 1889 was that these were years when efforts were being concentrated on securing a favorable revision of the treaties. As will be shown, it was the failure of the struggle in 1889 to secure this revision that precipitated the anti-foreign reaction and retardation in the growth of the church.

Chapter IX

GROWTH RETARDED BY RESURGENT NATIONALISM

From 1872 to 1889 the history of Protestantism in Japan was a record of fairly consistent success, although progress was made faster in some sections than in others. Anti-Christian books and pamphlets were distributed and antagonism was evidenced in areas where Buddhism held. Several scattered reactions of short duration occurred,* but in the wider perspective, until the autumn of 1889 the barriers to the spread of Christianity seemed crumbling to such a degree that the foreigners anticipated the day when they could transfer their obligations to the nationals. That the country

---

* *Missionary Herald*, September 1883, p. 353; *Missionary Herald*, January 1888, pp. 25–27; *Missionary Herald*, March 1886, p. 105; *Missionary Herald*, June 1889, pp. 250–251; *Missionary Herald*, April 1891, pp. 152–153. An image of Christ hanging on a cross was placed on a cart and drawn through the streets at a Japanese festival. Men carrying spears were scheduled to thrust the image, but when the time came no one dared to do so.—*Missionary Herald*. December 1883, p. 494. In 1884 the Japanese had become embittered by the withholding of their national rights by the treaty powers—*Japan Weekly Mail*, May 31, 1884, pp. 508–509, 515. Christians were the object of Buddhist demonstrations at Takasaki, Kyōto, and other interior cities in 1884. —*Japan Weekly Mail*, July 19, 1884, pp. 57, 58, 60, 81; *Missionary Herald*, October 1884, p. 404. The *Mainichi Shimbun* censured the demonstrators, pointing out that such affairs would affect Japan's foreign intercourse and

was to be made completely Christian or at least the scene of a firmly entrenched church was a certainty to many of the workers.*

Prior to 1889, there had been only vague hints as to the obstacles the growing church was to encounter. During the late autumn of that year, however, many of the mission schools suffered a great decrease in enrollment, in some instances as much as fifty percent of the total.† Attendance at lecture meetings in the rural districts did not manifest the reactionary effects so quickly, although in Tōkyō, the center of the political arena, this type of missionary activity registered an increasing ineffectiveness.[1] Statistics for 1889 revealed a gain of 5,677 new members throughout the nation in all the Protestant churches. For the year 1890 the number of additions dropped to 1,199[2] The period of increasing diffi-

---

reputation as a nation. The fact that Buddhist priests with official status participated laid a responsibility upon the Japanese government for the incidents.—*Japan Weekly Mail*, August 2, 1884, pp. 122-123.

* *Report of the Committee on the Japan Mission, American Board of Commissioners for Foreign Missions*, in *Missionary Herald*, November 1880, p. 457. E.g., George Knox, a missionary connected with the Nippon Kirisuto Kyokai anticipated that by 1900 there would be twenty presbyteries and 400 congregations in the Nippon Kirisuto Kyōkai in Japan, that the Japanese faculties would control the colleges and seminaries, and that thereafter the Christian task in Japan would be the responsibility of the national church.—*Church at Home and Abroad*, September 1887, pp. 280-284.

† *Annual Report of the Western Presbyterian Mission*, September 1890, p. 16; Knox in *Church at Home and Abroad*, September 1890, p. 218. Commenting on the decrease in mission school enrollments, the *Kirsutokyō Shimbun* indicated factors which contributed to the reaction: (1) The fact that foreigners either directly or indirectly administered the schools made them unpopular. (2) The instruction was more suited to western lands than to Japan. For instance, there was a major emphasis upon languages rather than upon practical knowledge. (3) The missionaries who made up the bulk of the faculty were not skilled as instructors, and were interested in religious propagation rather than in teaching. (4) The required attendance at chapel and Bible study deterred students who were not interested in Christianity. Brinkley added that the constant improvement in private institutions had enabled them to outstrip the mission schools.—*Japan Weekly Mail*, April 5, 1890, p. 345. Also see *Japan Weekly Mail*, April 12, 1890, p. 380 for a missionary's answer to these arguments.

culties and slow progress had begun. Thereafter, outstanding achievements were rare and discouragements numerous. The reaction was evinced both by a stifling apathy and an active opposition. Numbers of Christians returned to the native religions, left the church, grew rationalistic, and lost their earlier zeal.[3] Church services and public lecture meetings were no longer thronged with eager listeners. The sales of Bibles and Christian literature decreased. Political matters rather than religion came to the spotlight of attention. Several politicians were openly antagonistic to the new faith. A revived Buddhism countered the advances of its younger rival by instigating persecution.[4]

Christianity was regarded as being out of accord with the national system and its morality unsuited to the nation. Its belief in a single God was thought to abrogate the position of the imperial family and the various personal relationships taught by Confucianism.[5] Shintō, which inculcated loyalty to the emperor, became increasingly a center of opposition. The expectation for the Christianizing of the empire was moderated. Failure to unite the denominations brought the realization that a union national church was not to be easily created. The growth of anti-foreign feelings led to a dominance of Japanese in the mission schools and church councils for it was reasoned that the abolition of political extraterritoriality should be paralleled by the elimination of ecclesiastical extraterritoriality.* The missionary ceased counting the years before he would be able to leave, having learned that the main task, far from being finished, stretched into the indefinite future. The task of making the Christian message intelligible to individuals became more difficult and time-

---

* *Missionary Review of the World*, July, 1891, pp. 517–519. Of the twenty-six Christian schools only two were administered by missionaries.—*Japan Weekly Mail*, December 20, 1890, pp. 615–616; *Missionary Herald*, October 1890, pp. 401–405.

consuming. The only reason it could be urged that missionaries might ultimately be no longer necessary was that national self-assertion would not endure their presence.[6]

William Imbrie once remarked apropos the rate of the spread of Christianity in Japan that the explanations offered for the rapid growth and for the retardation were alike superficial since both phenomena were of God.[7] Such an explanation hardly satisfies the historian, however, whose duty is not only to record events but also to analyze what appear to be the causes of social phenomena. Accordingly it is appropriate at this point to determine what seem to be the reasons for the reaction of 1889. Some of them were latent within the environment, needing only the proper stimulus to bring them into the open. Others were created by the impact of western culture, institutions and ideas upon Japan. No one factor was responsible, nor is it possible to offer an absolute explanation as to why the reversal should have been precipitated in the autumn of 1889. As a matter of fact, some scholars place its beginning as early as 1883. The process was cumulative, a combination of causes, varying in import. The thought elements, for instance, were instrumental primarily in affecting general trends; whereas the failure of the treaty revision conferences, the political excitement accompanying the promulgation of the Constitution, and the opening of the Diet, had a more direct bearing upon the reaction against western culture in general and Christianity in particular.

The first of the causes for the transition from westernization to nationalization was that the Japanese fancy for customs and practises of the west gave way to an antipathetic mood.[8] The Japanese had taken to western culture and technocracy that they might overcome the handicaps which faced the nation after its reopening. At great cost and considerable loss of face they had borrowed almost every phase of western life. The process was accelerated after 1882 in seeking to induce the nations of the occident to revise the unequal treaties. The failure of the negotiations in 1889, and the discovery of the conditions which the government had contemplated as the price for revision, played into the hands of ultra-nationalists. Isolated incidents illustrated the popular animosity against foreigners.[9] In 1888 a boy opened the door of a carriage in which a foreign woman was riding and spat in her face.[10] William Imbrie, while walking across the campus of a government school in Tōkyō, was attacked by a group of students and received a cut across the face. The principal of the school and the four guilty persons subsequently made an apology.* A foreigner attending a procession in which the emperor was riding was struck on the head for failure to remove his hat.[11] Such incidents occurred only in the cities, that is, in places where the process of westernization had attained sufficient momentum to make possible a reaction.[12]

In this connection it should be mentioned that Christianity was made to play the role of a " scape-goat ". The failure of the *samurai* to better their conditions, and the economic distress which followed after they had dissipated the retirement funds granted to them by the government, caused them to look askance at everything which had helped produce the fact of westernization. Uchimura Kanzō declared later that Christianity failed because too little gospel and too much western civilization had been taught. Certainly the Christian movement suffered during the period of reaction as though the two things had been equated in the teachings of the missionaries and evangelists.[13]

---

* *Japan Weekly Mail*, May 24, 1890. A correspondent of the *Japan Weekly Mail*, called attention in 1888 to the *Yomiuri Shimbun* which was at that time anti-foreign in tendency, and even malicious in urging the cessation of intercourse with foreigners who were too clever for the Japanese.—*Japan Weekly Mail*, June 30, 1888, p. 609.

The second of the causes for the reaction was that the conservative element within the population was never completely won over to the national program which sought the renovation of Japanese life and cultural institutions. The process of westernization had proved too rapid for most of the people. The termination of the Satsuma Revolt (1877) had silenced these elements, but had not eliminated the causes for the disaffection which touched at least a third of the population.[14] While the course of westernization continued unabated, the forces of reaction smouldered, waiting for an incident to fan them into flames. The Buddhists alone among the organized enemies of Christianity continued to demonstrate against its progress during the years 1883–1889.

The third of the smouldering embers was nationalism, although the patriotism which cried *Sonnō Jōi* (Revere the Emperor; Expel the Barbarians) after the arrival of Commodore Perry, and *Kokusui Hozon* (Preserve the national characterics) in 1889 were quite different in comprehension. The former was born of a loyalty to a superior in a fragmentary society rife with suspicion and jealousy between clans. The latter was the reflection of a patriotism which, allied with chauvinism had become national in scope during the intervening years. Following the revolution of 1868 the imperial house had been promoted as the center of national loyalty. Patriotic emotion had been easy to stimulate because of the morbid self-consciousness of the people at the time;[15] nevertheless, only after the failure of the treaty revision efforts was the climax reached.* It was part of a world movement, however, rather than an isolated phenomenon, being in the words of

---

* The Kokusui Hozon-tō (Party for the preservation of national characteristics) organized in 1886, was scarcely known until the people became alarmed about the question of the nation's individuality. By 1889 it was one of the two largest political groups.—*Japan Weekly Mail*, October 12, 1889, pp. 329–330.

Nitobe, but "a wavelet in a universal wave."[16] Christian teachings which countered ancient notions of loyalty were regarded with suspicion and misgivings. The Biblical injunction to love one's enemies conflicted with the feudal principle that one should not live under the same sky with the murderer of his father or mother.[17] Anyone believing in Christianity was regarded as having lost his national spirit, for it was rumored that the growth of the foreign faith would endanger the future of the nation.[18]

The rise of patriotism, the *Yamato Damashii*, was attributed by a Japanese writer to the unfair treaties, and the refusal of the powers to revise them, to a reaction against the excessively high regard in which foreigners were held by many of the older generation, to the approaching international crisis in the Far East, and to the fact that Japanese civilization was then entering a creative mood. The impelling motive was not fundamentally a dislike for foreigners but a desire to be independent and original in national development.[19] Westerners had unwittingly helped to induce this state of affairs by manifesting their contempt for Japan's imitative tendencies. The *Mainichi Shimbun* asserted that Japan was visiting upon the west its own want of judgment.[20] The *Japan Weekly Mail* observed apropos of this mounting sentiment: "The international jealousies and diplomatic incapacity which have kept Japan in fetters for so many years are now bearing their inevitable fruit, and Japan is beginning to show unfamiliar and unpleasant aspects to foreign residents.[21]

A protest against denationalization, hardly audible save in the cautions of westerners prior to 1888, which became vocal after 1888, was a fourth factor which bears upon the reaction. For a decade the Japanese were obsessed with the idea that everything foreign was desirable, that change meant progress, and that progress was improvement.[22] By 1889, European culture had come to be regarded as frivolous. In

April 1889, the *Japan Mail* observed that the inclination of the Japanese was to develop their civilization along Japanese lines, to preserve and reassert the national individuality which appeared at one time in danger of being swept away by the tide of western innovations, and to resume the old landmarks after the iconoclasm of the previous two decades.[23] Western scholars and men of letters such as Ernest F. Fenellosa and Sir Edwin Arnold, by their fostering of an appreciation for the products of the nation's past, stimulated among the Japanese a pride in their own creations and institutions.[24] One of the more constructive expressions of the slogan *Kokusui Hozon* (Preserve the national excellencies) was a glorification of indigenous art, architecture, life, and customs.* American and European residents as well as the vernacular press had often cautioned against the implicit peril of accepting the bad with the good from abroad;† but after the cultural consciousness had become nation-centered, resentment was expressed against the west's superimposition of its modes upon the country.

The charge that Christianity aimed to denationalize Japan was a legacy from Kirishitan missions, revived first by the monarchists as an argument against the feudal government, the *bakufu*, and again after the failure of the treaty negotiations to discredit Protestantism. Mission schools were defended against the allegation by a commencement orator in 1887

---

* Ishihara, *loc. cit.* An official in the Department of Education called attention to the fact that with respect to morals, Japan was not inferior to any Christian nation, and therefore the country had no need of imported standards.—*Japan Weekly Mail*, April 17, 1886, p. 370. A Japanese editor set forth the claim that in the indigenous moral ideas could be found all that was necessary for the ethical nurture of the people.—*Japan Weekly Mail*, December 7, 1889, pp. 522–523.

† Berry, K. F., *A Pioneer Doctor in Old Japan* (New York, Fleming H. Revell Co., 1940, pp. 247), p. 196. The *Hochi Shimbun* admonished the nation in 1886 that Japan was still far behind the civilized states of the world, and that only by a careful discrimination in the adoption of foreign elements could national aspirations and ends be achieved.—*Japan Weekly Mail*, April 10, 1886, p. 360.

who contended that far from becoming disloyal subjects the students were being trained therein for a greater usefulness.[25] The reaction was directed not only towards Christianity, but also against all evidences of western culture except technology. For instance, Professor Kume of the Tōkyō Imperial University reached the conclusion by the application of scientific methods of historical research that Shinto was a monotheistic rather than a polytheistic faith. His finding being out of harmony with current trends, he was dismissed from the faculty of the university.[26]

A fifth factor which progressively hindered the activities of Christians after 1889 was the discredit into which the nations professing Christianity and the secular representatives of the creed fell in their intercourse with Japan.[27] The people discovered that western nations and people were Christian in name but not always in fact and that there was therefore no necessary correlation between Christianity and western technology.* France's seizure of Indo-China, and England's annexation of Fort Hamilton in Korea, during the years 1884–1885, impressed the Japanese with the contrast between the profession and the practise of the western religion. Students returning from study abroad brought reports which negated some of the missionaries' claims for their home lands.

The evidence is conflicting as to the way in which missionaries represented the countries of the west. In some instances the occident was described as a paragon of virtue, beside which Japan with her licensed prostitution and *sake* drinking represented a low level of culture. Christian civilization was often but not always identified with Christianity.[28]

---

* *The Hochi Shimbun* stated in 1884 that the Japanese were learning that whatever material advantages might accrue from accepting the civilization of the west, occidental moral civilization was incompetent to regulate the intercourse of nations, that westerners were selfish and arbitrary in their treatment of easterners, and that they set might and profit far above right and justice in their international dealings.—*Japan Weekly Mail*, March 1884, pp. 224–226, 230–231.

For example, when C. S. Eby was asked how the international policies of Christian nations could be reconciled with the moral principles of the religion, he answered that the nations of the west were not Christian.[29] Mark Hopkins, addressing the youth of Japan in 1884 pointed out that Christendom was not identical with Christianity, and that the corrupt forms of the religion, the ethical inconsistencies of nominal Christians, and the imperfections of church members were among the greatest obstacles to the spread of the faith. Despite these admissions, the treatment accorded to Japanese students abroad, and the general level of morality in the west they found to be little above that in their own country.[30] The general state of morals in Yokohama and other treaty ports* was disclaimed by the missionaries as a criterion of what Christianity could accomplish. Thus was discredited the demand that Japan needs must adopt the religion as well as the technology of the west. Just as Tokugawa Ieyasu had reached the conclusion that he might retain the trade of Portugal and Spain without the presence of Catholic priests, nineteenth century Japan began to realize that acceptance of Christianity was not the *sine qua non* for enjoying western technology and materialism.[31]

Anti-Christian thought which infiltrated from the occident combined with an indigenous agnosticism[32] to produce a sixth source of opposition. During the interval when the national religions were still moribund, missionaries felt that ration-

---

* J. J. Rein pointed out in 1874-5 that while the Japanese acknowledge the beauty of Christian morals they regard the superiority of the Christian peoples as a result of causes outside of religion; they compare the morality of the foreigners in the treaty ports with their own, contending with justice: "You foreigners cannot maintain that the Bible has much influence on you. You are there exhorted to be peaceable, sober, chaste, to render unto every one his own, to cherish no malice, not to bear false witness, not to slander anyone, to show yourselves humble, etc.; and you do the exact opposite of all this." —*Japan Weekly Mail,* July 26, 1884, p. 83.

alism and liberalism from the west constituted a more formidable opposition than Buddhism and Shinto.[33] The liberal ideas were attacked by the missionaries but to no avail, as they entered via the teachings of westerners in the Japanese educational institutions and in imported and translated books. While limited originally to the schools and intellectual classes, radical ideas penetrated even to the mountain villages.[34] First were such works as those of Spencer, Mill and Tyndall, which while not anti-Christian, actually set up a system contradictory to the supernaturalism preached by the missionaries of the day.[35] A second type of troublesome literature was that which took issue with some of the problems of Christianity. Translations of Paine and Ingersoll, and Japanese works such as *Yaso Bemmō* (Christian Superstitions), *Bemmō* (Superstitions), *Yasokyō Mudori* (Unreasonableness of Christianity), and *Yasokyō Benwaku* (Exposition of the Errors of Christianity), had a great influence among the intellectuals and the Christian ministers. [36] For instance, Sugiura Shigetake advocated that religion should be determined by the methods of science. He claimed this practise had been followed in the west to such an extent that religion exercised control only over rites and ceremonies. On the other hand, it was alleged that the high esteem in which science was held in Japan created *a priori* reasons for not accepting Christianity, and since the Japanese have no natural taste for religion, to urge upon the common people what the intelligentsia cannot accept would be to encourage them in folly.* More potent than these objections was the earlier hostility to Christianity on political grounds in the writings of Fukuzawa Yukichi. His books and editorials in the *Jiji*

* *Japan Weekly Mail*, March 3, 1888, pp. 199–200. Katō Hiroyuki, president of the Imperial University at Tōkyō, suggested that the various religions be introduced into the schools, taught by authorized teachers, the records be kept of the moral effects of the teachings and that religion be accepted which proved most productive of moral results.—*Japan Weekly Mail*, March 3, 1888, pp. 197–199.

Shimpō voiced a suspicion of Christianity as part and parcel of the culture of the countries which were refusing to amend the unsatisfactory state of relations with Japan. In 1881 Fukuzawa suggested that the government take steps to suppress the spread of the religion. In his *Jiji Shogen*, a work published during the same year, he revived the anti-Kirishitan argument that in the event of a struggle with the west, the Christian party in the nation would assist the invaders.[37] Missionaries had begun to realize by 1883 that much of the antagonism they encountered was at bottom political in character.[38] When finally the concert of opposition was organized against Christianity the attack was not so much a fear of it as a religion, as of its political and social connections.[39]

A seventh factor, more closely related chronologically to the reaction, was the introduction of liberal theology. The Unitarians and Universalists who arrived in 1887 challenged the teachings of the orthodox missionaries concerning miracles and immortality, and denied that the latter held a monopoly upon the person of Christ.[40] Their teachings, methods and claims were resented by many of the pastors and missionaries of the longer established churches and missions.* The Unitarians, patronized by Fukuzawa Yukichi, made a considerable impression upon the foreign community and the ultra-liberal intellectuals of Tokyo[41] As most of their work was conducted in the English language, their operations were probably not so detrimental to the work of the older established missions as might be inferred from the condemnation they provoked.

---

* *Japan Weekly Mail*, March 15, 1890, p. 269; *Japan Weekly Mail*, March 22, 1890, p. 305; *Japan Weekly Mail*, March 29, 1890, p. 331. *E. g.*, Yokoi Tokio in the *Kokumin no Tomo* criticized the newly arrived Unitarians for approving Japanese customs indiscriminately, and for seeking to destroy the results of the Protestant movement without offering any positive Christian substitute.—*Japan Weekly Mail*, May 10, 1890, p. 470. *Japan Weekly Mail*, April 19, 1890, p. 406.

A case in point was the effect of Unitarianism upon Nakamura Masano (Tsuchida), a scholarly member of the *Meirokusha* (the Meiji Six), a group of reformists which played an important role in the progress made during the final quarter of the nineteenth century. Nakamura was a champion of enlightenment to be attained by way of English thought. He insisted upon the adoption of the moral ideas of the west and reform through moral and cultural improvement. His religion was a combination of Confucianism and Christianity. Implementing his social and religious idealism he established the Nakamura Dōninsha, a school which at one time was larger than the Keiō Gijuku of Fukuzawa Yukichi or the Kōgyōkusha of Kondō Makoto, the three being the outstanding private educational institutions in Japan during the early Meiji Period. His translations of Martin's *Evidences of Christianity* inspired many Confucianists to accept Christianity, and of Smiles' *Self Help* impressed the young with the value of personal diligence, strength and initiative. After Nakamura came under the influence of Unitarianism about 1881, his early idealism and ardor for moral reform was lost and his school abandoned.[42] One Protestant minister became a convert to Unitarianism, but he carried no one in the church with him.[43] Radical German theology which entered after 1885 with the advent of W. Spinner, Muezinger and C. M. Schmiedel brought higher criticism and other aspects of liberal theology to the fore.[44] Liberalism chilled enthusiasm and caused many young leaders of the church to renounce their faith. All the denominations were adversely affected. Preaching became defensive and disproportionately apologetic and ethical.[45]

In fairness to the missionary innovators it should be admitted that the liberal tendencies which circulated in the Japanese church following their arrival should not be charged entirely to the Unitarian, Universalist, and German missionaries. It is true that they sought to establish a new phase in Christian theology, to promote the religious development of the Japanese race along somewhat different lines from those to which most of the other missionaries were accustomed, and to give more weight to good conduct than to theological dogmas.[46] While they provided some of the materials, Japanese Christians, notably Kanamori Tsūrin and Yokoi Tokio, supplied the animus which provoked the ensuing theological controversy.[47]

The critical attitudes expressed in respect to religion were not confined to Christianity. There were some who denied that Shinto ceremonies embodied the worship idea, claiming that they were mere forms by which reverence for ancestors was expressed. Buddhism came to lay more stress on the ethical element in religion. Tenrikyō and Remmon-kyō, indigenous religious sects based on rationalistic superstition, became popular.[48]

The emergence of types of indigenous Christian liberalism may be enumerated as an eighth cause for the retardation in the outreach of Protestantism. Nationalism was adopted into Christian thought, in part as a defense against the contention that Christianity engendered disloyalty.[49]

Japanese Christians became desirous of developing their new faith as an integral part of the nation's civilization.[50] Christians were pressed to take over elements from the indigenous older faiths.[51] Church members began to assert that just as their religion had developed characteristics in the other countries where it held sway, it should do likewise in Japan.[52] "Japanese Christianity" was interpreted to mean a Christianity without dogma or historical connections, which culminated in Asiatic syncretism.[53] Kanamori Tsūrin, one of the Kumamoto Band, and pastor in Okayama following his graduation from the Dōshisha, was one of the first to be deflected. In his *Nippon Genkon no Kirisutokyō Narabini Shōrai no Kirisutokyō* (Japanese Christianity : Its Present and

Future), published in 1891, he pointed out that the supernaturalism and miracles of the Bible, the austerities, the tendency towards denationalization, and the sectarianism of Christianity were stumbling blocks to the progress of the faith. Missionaries and orthodox evangelicals alike criticise the book for its radicalism, as, for instance, Kanamori's thought concerning Christ, "...It is not an historical personage whom we may accept as our Savior but the idealistic Christ embodying the perfection of the human species, and symbolizing the communion of God and man.[54] Yokoi Tokio, another of the Kumamoto Band, suggested in 1890 that Japanese Christians had gained sufficient knowledge of the faith to avoid copying after English and American Christianity; that Japanese Christianity should exhibit some qualities not discernible in the older stock, that it must stand on a pedestal of Buddhism and Confucianism, with theology, rites and ceremonies purely Japanese.[55] While these statements were not approved by the rank and file of the Japanese Christians,[56] they indicated the directions that the increasing national feeling within the church was to follow.

The divisions of Christendom constituted a ninth factor, which came into prominence during the period of reaction and helped to accentuate it. Generally speaking, relations between the various missions and churches in Japan had been friendly until the coming of the Unitarians, Universalists, German Evangelicals, and the various groups of Plymouth Brethren. Even so, non-Christians were puzzled by the differences in doctrine, polity, modes of baptism and the fact of division.[57] The Plymouth Brethren, representing various types of thought, denounced the corruption of the churches and the paid ministry fostered by the older missions, claiming that they alone, of all the Christian groups, were true to the historic faith. As they worked largely among the believers, seeking to win them to their convictions, the

Brethren aroused considerable antagonism among the established churches and missions.[58] As the teachings which had been set forth as immutable by one sect were shown to be contradictory to the tenets of opposing groups, the Japanese concluded that such an unsettled faith was hardly worth substituting for their traditional beliefs.

Buddhist opposition and competition was a tenth complicating influence. The teachings and methods of the Christians had been copied by the priests, whose sermons in many instances clearly echoed Christian discourses. The Sermon on the Mount was openly taught by priests as though it had been pronounced by Buddha. Organizations patterned on those of the churches and missions were introduced by the temples.[59] A conference of Buddhists determined to send missionaries to the lands of the west.[60] Col. Henry S. Olcott, the theosophist, conducted a series of eighty meetings in Japan at the invitation of the Buddhists in 1889, but with negative results. His system proved to be at variance with that of the Buddhists and he was disappointed with the priesthood.[61] Priests were warned that unless they stopped striving for profit and honors Buddhism would be dissolved.[62] Disturbances, apparently provoked by Buddhists,[63] became so numerous it was speculated that Japan might become a battlefield of Buddhism and Christianity.[64] Mob violence was demonstrated at Tōkyō when a group gathered around a worship place smashed the windows and injured some of the congregation.[65] In 1889 this agitation became united with the nationalistic fervor indicated above. " Revere the Emperor, worship Buddha, and unite on the main points of the Buddhist faith," was the rallying slogan. The objects of this nationalistic Buddhist movement was to decry Christianity, to secure the election of Buddhists to political offices, and to effect a reunion of the state with Buddhism. Members pledged themselves in the selection of representatives to the Diet, provincial assemblies, town councils and local offices, in the appointment of school teachers, officials of societies and business companies to exclude all who showed themselves disloyal to the emperor or adverse to Buddhism by embracing the foreign religion. Schools were established for the teaching of Buddhist theology and English. Priests were sent to Hawaii to minister to the Japanese immigrants.[66]

An extraordinary ascendancy of political discussion which diverted the nation's attention from social and religious topics constitutes another cause for the reaction.[67] Political events absorbed popular speculation. Preparations for the promulgation of the Constitution, political meetings, elections, the approaching opening of the Diet, and the excitement over the treaty revision and the question of mixed residence, attracted attention which had formerly been directed to the process of westernization and the growth of Christianity.* The diet was first convened November 28, 1890. During the first two years it was twice prorogued and four times dissolved. Conflict between the Cabinet and the Diet caused widespread popular discussion. To Christianity was ascribed some of the blame for the failure of efforts for treaty revision. Foreigners were accused of devising methods for evading customs duties to the detriment of the national income and it was alleged that such actions were the fruits of Christianity.[68]

Social conditions were aggravated by a financial crisis, which in turn reacted upon the Christian movement, to con-

---

* *Fourteenth Report of the Council of Missions Cooperating with the Church of Christ in Japan*, pp. 2-3; *Japan Weekly Mail*, May 9, 1891, pp. 552-554. The nation was in a state of agitation for months prior to the opening of the Diet; yet, because of the lack of tariff and judicial autonomy, the parliamentary institution was destined to be in many respects farcical. Duties it would not be able to set; legislation affecting foreign residents and ships was forbidden, and many of its normal functions were subject to veto by the foreign diplomatic corps. The editor of the *Japan Mail* pointed out that to inaugurate a national assembly under such humiliating conditions was a reproach to the nation.—*Japan Weekly Mail*, January 26, 1889, pp. 78-79.

stitute a twelfth retarding factor. The rice famine of 1890 caused suffering particularly among the lower and middle classes. The commercial failures of those former *samurai* who had entered the business world became so common that the term *bushi no shōbai* (literally : warrior's business) became a proverbial expression for mushroom commercial ventures. The number of poor and indigent increased as the processes of urbanization and industrialization continued apace. The family system, which throughout the feudal ages had functioned to prevent suffering, was itself undergoing disruptive changes, and there was no adequate public relief administration to care for the sick and the aged. According to the *Kokumin no Tomo*, there were in Tokyo in 1882, 6,047 persons known to the authorities as financially incapable of caring for themselves. By 1887 the number had increased to 15,-119.[69] In accounting for this trend, estimate must also be taken of the accumulation of wealth in the hands of the bankers of the nation. The decrease in the number of persons eligible for election to the local assemblies provides one index. Between the years 1880 and 1887 the number of persons owning sufficient quantities of land to qualify them to stand for election decreased by 320,000.[70] The financial crisis resulted in reduced school enrollments as families found it necessary to economize.[71] The numbers added to the church and the volunteers for church responsibilities, as well as the amount of contributions, were adversely affected. Newspapers which were critical of the government alleged that the financial crisis was attributable to over-expenditures on behalf of the program of westernization.

The growth of nationalism and the stabilizing of the central government by the proclamation of the Constitution resulted in policies which formed a thirteenth element of reaction upon the Christian movement. The enlargement and improvement of the system of government schools created academic competition which the Christian institutions were hard pressed to meet. The universal conscription law of 1883 placed an added handicap upon all private educational agencies since attendance at a government school postponed the period of military training for draftees, while other institutions were not so privileged.[72] In order that her own students might enjoy this immunity, the Dōshisha sought to raise an endowment of ¥50,000. Christians feared, and with reason, that unless their own schools maintained a standard equal to that of the government schools, the best students would avoid the mission institutions with the result that potential Christian leaders and ministers would be lost to the church.[73] The situation was further complicated by the increasing difficulties which graduates of Christian schools met in seeking admittance into the Imperial University.[74]

In 1886 *Yōgaku Kōyō* (Principles of Instruction for Youth), written thirteen years earlier by the Confucian moralist, Motoda, was made the commentary for a newly established program of education which emphasized national principles, a reverence for proper authority, and upheld the authority of the state as opposed to individual freedom.[75] On the grounds that the universalism of religion contradicted the ethical standards of the nation, an attempt was made to exclude all religious influences from the public schools, and attacks were made upon Buddhism and Christianity by public school instructors as outmoded superstitions.

The *Imperial Rescript on Education*, promulgated in October 1890, officially established the ancient Confucian virtues, filial piety and loyalty, as the ethical bases of Japan's national life. The document became authoritative for all schools which sought government recognition. Some Christians resented the reverence with which the Rescript was received as an infringement upon the authority of the Bible.[76]

The developments were paralleled by instances of religious persecution, both within and outside the educational system.

Uchimura Kanzō resigned from Tōkyō Dai Ichi Kōtō Chū Gakkō, the government college where he was a lecturer, due to the pressure of public opinion resulting from his refusal to pay homage to the Imperial signature affixed to then recently proclaimed Imperial Rescript on Education. When the subject was discussed in a Christian periodical, the paper was suspended on the grounds that religious journals were not licensed to treat political questions. Other teachers were removed for intimating that the emperor was only a mortal.[78] The governor of Kumamoto advised the primary school teachers against the acceptance of Christianity. When some among the student body were expelled for studying the Bible, a committee of Christians appealed on the grounds of unconstitutionality. In commenting upon the incident, secular periodicals protested against the arbitrary interference with liberty of conscience. The Department of Education informed a committee of inquiry that while moral training should accord with the terms of the Rescript, the teacher's religion outside the classroom was his own affair. The Minister of Home Affairs decreed that local governments should not interfere with the religious convictions of the people,[79] but the official pronouncement did not terminate the persecutions. The teacher of a prefectural normal school warned the students in 1893 that anyone found attending Christian preaching places or investigating the religion would be expelled.[80] Such an eventuality would have constituted a professional black-listing.

The discrimination growing out of reawakened nationalism was not confined to students and teachers. Viscount Mori Arinori, a Christian and Minister of Education, was assassinated on the day of the proclamation of the Constitution by a zealot, Nishiro Buntarō, who mistakenly believed the Viscount had desecrated the shrine at Ise. Upon the death of the perpetrator of the deed, the vernacular press lauded the romantic notions of patriotism which had led him to give his life in enforcing respect for emperor and country. Government officials contributed to the funeral funds for the assassin.[81] The incident attested the revived spirit of patriotism.

Important as are the thirteen factors outlined above, they do not fully explain why the retardation of the spread of Protestantism occurred in 1889. Each contributed to the regression, but some of them were effective in thwarting the progress of Christianity from the day of its reintroduction. To determine the event, or combination of influences which precipitated the reaction, is the task to which we will now turn. In attempting this analysis, it would be well to remind ourselves of several questions which bear upon the main problem. Were the anti-Christian and anti-foreign sentiments identical in cause? Was the general change in sentiment maneuvered by the Japanese government or was it a spontaneous popular expression of opinion? Would a more sympathetic attitude on the part of the treaty powers have forestalled the change in sentiment, or was this but a repetition of the traditional process by which Japan first adopted a foreign culture, then assimilated it during a period of seclusion? Partial answers to these and related questions will be given in the course of the analysis below.

The event which precipitated the reaction against western civilization and thereby the Protestant regression was the failure of the treaty negotiations.[82]

The treaties which the emperor had approved under duress on October 23, 1865, constituted the basis of Japan's relations with the west until 1894. Meiji diplomacy sought above all else to effect a revision of the instruments by which the inexperienced Tokugawa statesmen had signed away two of the nation's rights.[84] The Iwakura mission failed at this task, as did a Tōkyō conference in 1882. Foreign Minister Inouye Kaoru secured the consent of the government in 1886 to make another attempt. He proposed to convince the treaty powers that Japan's advances since 1853 had raised the nation to the cultural level of the occident.[85] The pace of westernization was accelerated. For several years Japan had been revising her legal codes, following the general pattern of the west. The system of jurisprudence was remodeled along Latin lines. Foreign language study was stressed in the schools. Intercourse between the western residents and the Japanese in Tōkyō was facilitated by the construction of a special club where they could meet. The inhabitants were advised to prepare for mixed residence which would follow the restoration of Japan's taxing and judicial powers.[86]

The representatives of the treaty nations were invited to confer at the Foreign Office on May 1, 1886, when the first of thirty-six conferences was held. The results of the negotiations remained a secret until the *London Times* printed an account of the terms under consideration. The condition which provoked the strongest reaction was that collegiate courts should be provided for the judging of cases involving foreign subjects, such courts to consist of both western and Japanese judges. General opposition against this concession was aroused among all classes of people. Young agitators (*sōshi*) from every prefecture assembled in Tōkyō. Outbursts of violence occurred. Popular pressure became so general that the conferences were abandoned and Inouye resigned in August 1887.[87]

Premier Itō Hirobumi filled the portfolio until February 1888, when Okuma Shigenobu, founder of the Progressive Party (*Kaishintō*), was invited to join the cabinet as Foreign Minister. Okuma reopened the conferences but dealt with the powers separately rather than as a unit. Meanwhile, pressure was brought to bear upon the western nations by enforcing the literal interpretation of existing treaties. Whereas Inouye had favored the west and had granted many concessions to foreign residents, the new government granted them only those considerations expressly provided by the agreements in force. Officials suddenly became exacting about passports.

Missionaries and teachers residing in the interior were required in many instances to withdraw to the treaty ports. The *Jiji Shimpo* observed editorially that since the foreign powers could not be induced by amicable persuasion and liberal concessions to alter their international agreements, westerners should be treated according to the strict letter of the covenants in order that they might thereby understand the odium with which the Japanese had long regarded them. Brinkley observed that this point of view was quite general in official circles and naturally so, in view of the past relations between Japan and the treaty powers.[88]

Okuma was successful in the negotiations, but his political adversaries made an issue of the conferences and remonstrated against the proposed revision terms, especially in respect to the revived plan for collegiate courts. These political criticisms among other things aroused public attention and resentment which served to sway government officials who had supported Okuma to the opposition. Okuma stood his ground until October 18, 1889, when a young agitator, Kurushima Tsuneki, made an attack upon his life. During the Foreign Minister's convalescence, the cabinet of which he was a member was forced to resign.[89]

Although implicit in the above statement of facts, it would be well to summarize the factors which made it impossible for Japan to alter her position *vis a vis* the west. First, no oriental state had ever been accorded sovereign rights over the lives and property of occidentals. Second, the efficacy of the nation's reorganized judicial machinery had yet to be demonstrated. The conferences were adjourned in 1887 in order that Japan might have time in which to translate the recently revised codes into English.[90] Third, the western business men in the port cities were opposed to any tariff alterations which would place them at a disadvantage, or deprive them of their immunity against Japanese jurisdiction.[91] Fourth, the Japanese agitators, emotional, patriotic young men, usually in the employ of political pressure groups, insisted that the foreigners relinquish their privileges and remain concentrated in the open ports. They resisted any compromise which would imply an inferior status on the Japanese side.[92] Fifth, an aroused public opinion made it impossible for the Japanese government to approve the only terms which were acceptable to the nations of the west. Jurists, politicians, journalists and officials denounced the conditions as unconstitutional, and the general public refused to sanction the administration of laws in their sovereign's name through the agency of foreigners. The Japan-for-the-Japanese reading of the Constitution was demanded.[93]

Viewed as a political issue, treaty revision had little reference to the spread of Protestantism in Japan;[94] but in view of the concessions which had been made to the west during the course of the negotiations, including special favors to the missionaries, the failure of the Japanese government to reach a satisfactory solution of the foremost political problem of the day reacted against western civilization in general and Christianity in particular. Ōkuma was injured in October. Within two months elements of opposition were manifested by the decreased enrollment in the mission schools. Tōkyō, the scene of the most extensive missionary operations, was the first city to register the reaction. By the winter of 1889–1890 the mass meetings which had in the previous year overflowed the largest auditoriums were drawing few people. The attendance at church services decreased. The missionaries were openly charged with responsibility for the failure of the treaty negotiations.

During the year 1892 Japanese periodicals and missionaries reported that the reaction was passing. To some, this signified a return to the earlier type of prosperity. Saner counsels diagnosed the task ahead as more difficult than that of the decade which had just passed. Anti-foreign sentiments gradually decreased and in the 1890's western technology regained its former prestige, trade increased and industry developed. The growth of the church, however, never again became spectacular. The spread of Christianity, while constant, depended to a considerable extent upon the foundations which had been laid during the less disturbed years preceding the period of rapid expansion.

In summary, retardation in the growth of the Christian movement after 1889 may be attributed to a series of elements precipitated by the failure of the treaty revision negotiations: an altered perspective with reference to the civilization of the west, the perpetuation of a conservative strain within the life of the nation, the maturation of national feeling with its protest against denationalization, the discovery of the difference between the theory professed and the practise exemplified by Christendom, anti-Christian thought, liberal theology, the emergence of indigenous elements of Christianity, the divisions which rose among the Christian workers and groups, Buddhist counteraction, the diversion of the peoples' minds from religious matters to heightened political interests, economic problems, and a more settled internal situation which afforded an exotic religion less opportunity to express itself. To these might be added the fact that the original enthusiasm of the Christian community had been lost, although this was more an outcome than a cause of the reaction.

Chapter   X

CONCLUSION

To interpret rather than catalogue the details relative to a segment of Protestant history in Japan has been the primary purpose of the preceding chapters. The significance rather than the occurrence of events in the evolution of the Christian movement between the years 1883 and 1889 has been the chief concern. In prodding below the surface of the historical phenomena, we have sought, but have not always been able to discover, complete explication. Varied forces have been and are shaping the Christian movement, and many of these, particularly the economic and political, have as yet to be interpreted adequately by secular historians. "The richness, the bewildering variety and sharp contrasts revealed in the history of Japan in recent times "[1] are no less true of Protestantism than of the whole of society.

The missionary expansion of the period under review must be viewed with respect to the entirety of the environment in which the process occurred. The older religions of the nation constituted only a fraction of the total medium which influenced the development of Protestantism. The fact of cultural evolution comprised the most important single force conditioning the religious evolution. For a quarter century prior to the beginning of the era of rapid growth, the nation had been undergoing a transformation in part out of a desire to share the material goods and technology of the west, but in larger part, in order to prove herself worthy of a place among the powers of the world and thereby recover her judicial sovereignty and customs autonomy. The concerted attempt made by Japan to demonstrate the parity of its renovated civilization with that of Christendom created a milieu that was especially well-disposed to the growth of the Christian church. The desire of the nation to achieve equality with the self-styled enlightened powers generated a spirit advantageous not only for the reproduction of the material aspects but for the propagation of the religion of western civilization as well. When the occidental powers showed a disinclination to recognize Japan's advances, the consequent frustration retarded even as the preceding receptivity had stimulated the spread of Christianity.

The year 1883 marked a quantitative rather than a qualitative point in the expansion of Protestantism in Japan. The missions which entered and the churches that were established prior to 1883 were the determinative institutions in the ensuing years. It was primarily American, and secondarily a British Protestantism which found its way to Japan, with few important differences between the two. Evidences of cooperation and the striving towards unity proved stronger than the tendency towards diversity, although the latter was able to obstruct organic union except in the case of denominations with similar polities, and cooperation in the conduct of joint meetings, Bible translations, and the preparation of a hymnal. The spread was almost exclusively in the urban areas. Except that medical missions decreased in importance and education demanded increasingly larger faculties and resources, the processes and methods differed little from those employed in other mission fields during the century.

This study having been brought to the end of the period of rapid growth, and the nature of the reaction which adversely affected the Christian movement having been indicated, the purpose as stated in our introduction has been achieved.

CONCLUSION

To conclude the narrative at this point, however, possibly creates the erroneous impression that the movements outlined in chapters three to seven were ended. Speaking generally, the activities of the missions and churches alike were influenced but not determined, retarded but not terminated, by the changing cultural forces. Despite the setback, the various Protestant activities continued with but little alteration. There were, as a matter of fact, some definite advances gained as by-products of the reaction. Although there was no effective compensation for the decrease in church membership, the loss of optimism and hope, the new obstacles which beset the progress of the weak young church, or the permanent slowing down of the rate of church increase, the situation was not completely lacking in elements of encouragement.

In the first place, the earlier gains were not entirely lost. Out of a rapid augmentation of a given hundred individuals, from a dozen to a score became devoted to the cause of the Christian movement, and most of the others remained friendly and contributed on special occasions for religious purposes. Likewise, of those who withdrew from church membership or never became identified with the church through their inability to harmonize its teachings with scientific knowledge and "higher criticism," many continued sympathetic and often contributed to its support.[2] Even during the period of extreme abatement a sympathetic though silent support was given the Christian movement by editors, educators, lawyers and others among the intellectuals.

A second advantage growing out of the reaction was the fact that the persecution purged the rolls of those who were half-hearted in their faith. Having passed the crisis, the church was stronger with a reduced membership than previously when it comprised a larger but partially Christianized community. In being forced to resort to and rely upon the spiritual supports of their religion, the leaders of the movement gained a power of endurance, courage and influence they might not otherwise have attained.[3] A higher conception of the Christian life evolved. More careful instruction was given to candidates for baptism. Greater caution was exercised in admitting applicants to membership. The cost of becoming Christian restrained many, giving assurance that those who did join possessed moral courage and stability of character.[4] The church acquired a consciousness of power and self-dependence.[5] Confidence replaced the doubts of those who remained in its communion.[6]

Third among the permanent contributions was the acquisition on the part of the church and the missionaries of a more realistic conception of the task they faced. They had learned that more hunger for culture had not the missionary significance many of them had thought to be the case, that the path of evangelism led from the small to the great, and from depth to height, rather than the contrary.[7] The decline of attendance at the public lecture meetings illustrated the difference between a civil hearing and a hearty acceptance of Christianity as a religion.

The Japanese people, in the fourth place, came to regard the church as a permanent establishment with its own sphere of influence. The truths it proclaimed were no longer popular, for they were not enhanced by a vogue for things western. Still, its peculiar claims and virtues were as widely recognized as ever. The church therefore depended primarily upon spiritual and personal rather than upon cultural and political resources. For all the opposition met by Christian candidates, their religious beliefs did not obstruct political advancement, as was proved in several instances. The gradual diffusion of Christian morals and the open profession of its sentiments tended to affect social conditions. Men entered the ministry although many were lost to law and other professions.[8] Church congregations, reduced in size though they were, persisted in assembling despite the lack of novelty. Support for local church expenses and home missions was maintained. Despite the loss of much of his status as leader, the missionary aided in keeping the church united and its agencies in operation. The romance, the enthusiasm, the peculiar difficulties and the triumphs of the first stage of the work had passed. Missionaries and Japanese Christians perceived that they had entered a more mature stage where there was less excitement, where renewed endeavors along the lines of education and evangelism, and constant watchfulness were the price to be paid for continued progress.[9]

Special attention is called to the fact that in the *Proceedings of the Osaka Conference* there are two sets of pages numbered 89–186, one set being identified with asterisks, hence the asterisks in the various *Osaka Conference* references cited below.

NOTES

Introduction

1. *Church at Home and Abroad*, September 1892, p. 223.
2. Latourette, K. S., *The First Five Centuries* (New York, Harper & Brothers, Publishers, 1937, pp. xxiv, 412) pp. x-xii.

Chapter I: The Religious Situation

1. *Japan Weekly Mail*, November 10, 1883, p. 669.
2. Speer, Robert E., *Missions and Modern History* (New York, Fleming H. Revell Co., 2 vols., 1904), Vol. II, p. 162.
3. *Tokyo Missionary Conference Report*, p. 236.
4. *Tokyo Missionary Conference Report*, pp. 236–237.
5. DeForest, John H., *Sunrise in the Sunrise Kingdom* (New York, The Young People's Missionary Movement, 1904, pp. 233), pp. 27–28.
6. *Tokyo Missionary Conference Report*, p. 237.
7. *Tokyo Missionary Conference Report*, p. 237.
8. *Japan Weekly Mail*, February 13, 1886, pp. 159–160; *Japan Weekly Mail*, March 3. 1888. pp. 197–201.
9. Sansom, G. B., *Japan* (London, The Cresset Press, 1932, pp. xvi, 537), pp. 77, 329.
10. *London Missionary Conference Report*, Vol. I, p. 246.
11. Sansom, *op. cit.*, p. 225.
12. Eliot, Charles, *Japanese Buddhism* (London, Edward Arnold & Co., 1935, pp. xxxv, 449), p. 236 note.
13. Reischauer, A. K., *Studies in Japanese Buddhism* (New York, The Macmillan Co., 1917, pp. xviii, 361), p. 295.
14. Aston, W. G., *Shinto* (London, Longmans, Green & Co., 1905, pp. 390), p. 362 note.
15. Sansom, *op. cit.*, p. 225.
16. Sansom, *op. cit.*, p. 118.
17. Tagawa, Daikichiro, *Kokka to Shūkyō* (English translation by Winburn

NOTES

7. Thomas in *Japan Christian Quarterly*, Vol. XIV, April, 1939), p. 5.
18. Sansom, *op. cit.*, p. 116.
19. See p. 33.
20. Sansom, *op. cit.*, p. 115.
21. Sansom, *op. cit.*, pp. 116, 120.
22. Sansom, *op. cit.*, pp. 411, 546.
23. Sansom, *op. cit.*, p. 227.
24. Aston, *op. cit.*, pp. 5, 210, 269, 285 ; Anesaki, Masaharu, *History of Japanese Religion* (London, Kegan Paul, Trench, Trubner & Co., Ltd., 1930, pp. xxii, 423), p. 4.
25. Anesaki, *op. cit.*, p. 8.
26. Anesaki, *op. cit.*, p. 109.
27. Eliot, *op. cit.*, p. 219.
28. Sansom, *op. cit.*, p. 18.
29. Brinkley, Capt. C. F.,*A History of the Japanese People* (New York, The Encyclopaedia Britannica Co., 1914, pp. xi, 784), p. 194.
30. Anesaki, *op. cit.*, pp. 109, 110, 112.
31. Eliot, *op. cit.*, p. 277.
32. Aston, W. G., *Japanese Literature* (London, William Heinemann, 1899, pp. xi, 408), p. 398.
33. *Nihongi*, English translation by Aston (*Transactions and Proceedings of the Japan Society of London*, 2 vols., Supplement I, 1896), Vol. II, p. 76.
34. *Kojiki*, English translation by Chamberlain (*Transactions of the Asiatic Society of Japan*, Vol. X, Supplement, 1882), pp. 15–25 describes the deification of the earth.
35. *Nihongi*, Vol. II, pp. 164, 351 ; *Kojiki*, pp. 99–110, 130–133.
36. *Kojiki*, Vol. II, pp. 135, 184 ff.
37. *Kojiki*, Vol. I, p. 132. This passage refers to the cross rafters which remain to this day a characteristic of the shrines.
38. *Kojiki*, pp. 39–43 ; *Nihongi*, pp. 333, 336, 338, 398. See the *Norito*, a collection of ancient rituals, translated by Satow, *Transactions of the Asiatic Society of Japan*, Vols. VIII and IX, 1880, 1881.
39. See Satow, E. M., *The Revival of Pure Shintau* (*Transactions of the Asiatic Society of Japan*, Vol. III, Part I, Appendix, 1875), *passim.*
40. Ozawa Saburō, *Shina Senkyōshi J. L. Nevius to Nippon to no Kankei* (*Kirisūtokyō Shi Kenkyū*, No. 6, November 8, 1939), pp. 34–35.
41. *Japan Weekly Mail*, May 12, 1883, p. 37.
42. *Japan Weekly Mail*, August 2, 1884, pp. 122–123 ; *Japan Weekly Mail*, August 16, 1884, pp. 159, 166 ; *Jiji Shimpo* in *Japan Weekly Mail*, August 23, 1884, p. 195 ; *Nichi Nichi Shimbun* in *Japan Weekly Mail*, August 30, 1884, pp. 217–218.
43. *Mainichi Shimbun* in *Japan Weekly Mail*, August 2, 1884, pp. 122–123; *Japan Weekly Mail*, August 16, 1884, p. 164 ; Hozumi Nobushige, *Ancestor Worship and Japanese Law* (Tōkyō, The Maruzen Kabushiki Kaisha, 1912, pp. xxx, 198), 91–92.
44. Holtom, *op. cit.*, p. 6.
45. Brinkley, *op. cit.*, p. 119.
46. *Nihongi*, Vol. I, pp. 262–263, 311 and note.
47. Murdoch, James, *A History of Japan* (London, Kegan Paul, Trench,

CHAPTER I : THE RELIGIOUS SITUATION

Trubner & Co., Ltd., 3 vols., 1925, 1926), Vol. III, pp. 91–124.

48. Murdoch, *op. cit.*, Vol. III, pp. 125–137.

49. Murdoch, *op. cit.*, Vol. III, pp. 467–497 ; Satow, *The Revival of Pure Shintau, passim.*

50. Aston, *Japanese Literature* (London, William Heinemann, 1899, pp. xi, 408), pp. 321, 326–330.

51. Murdoch, *op. cit.*, Vol. III, pp. 481, 487.

52. Sansom, *op. cit.*, pp. 487, 492.

53. Papinot, E., *Historical and Geographical Dictionary of Japan* (Tōkyō, Librairie Sansaisha, 1910, pp. xiv, 842), p. 52.

54. Sansom, *op. cit.*, p. 115; Anesaki, *History of Japanese Religion*, p. 206; Eliot, *Japanese Buddhism* (London, Edward Arnold & Co., 1935, pp. xxxv, 449), pp. 342, 385, 397.

55. *Nihongi*, Vol. II, pp. 59–60.

56. *Ibid.*, Vol. II, pp. 67.

57. *Ibid.*, Vol. II, pp. 60–61, 65.

58. *Ibid.*, Vol. II, pp. 66–67.

59. *Ibid.*, Vol. II, pp. 96, 101–102, 133 and note, and *passim.*

60. *Ibid.*, Vol. II, pp. 122, 149.

61. *Ibid.*, Vol. II, p. 123.

62. *Ibid.*

63. *Ibid.*, Vol. II, pp. 134–135, 421.

64. *Ibid.*, Vol. II, p. 203.

65. Eliot, *op. cit.*, pp. 218–232.

66. Eliot, *op. cit.*, pp. 233–253.

67. Eliot, *op. cit.*, pp. 254–274 ; *Shin Shiu Kio Shi*, English translation by James Troup, in *Transactions of the Asiatic Society of Japan*, Vol, XIV, 1886, pp. 1–17, pp. 3, 5, 11.

68. Eliot, *op. cit.*, pp. 275–282.

69. Eliot, *op. cit.*, pp. 282–288.

70. Summers, J., *Notes on Osaka* (*Transactions of the Asiatic Society of Japan*, Vol. VII, 1879), p. 377.

71. Eliot, *op. cit.*, pp. 289–304.

72. Eliot, *op. cit.*, pp. 305–317. Tokugawa Ieyasu had sought to terminate disputes by fiat. (See his Legacy, Article XXX I, cited in Murdoch, *op. cit.*, Vol. III, p. 801).

73. Tagawa Daikichirō, *Kokka to Shukyō*, English translation by Winburn T. Thomas in *Japan Christian Quarterly*, Vol. XIV, April 1939, p. 7.

74. *Proceedings of the Osaka Conference*, p. 55.

75. Reischauer, *Studies in Japanese Buddhism* (New York, The Macmillan Co., 1917, pp. xviii, 361), pp. 296–299, 303–306.

76. Lloyd, Arthur, *The Creed of Half Japan* (London, Smith, Elder and Co., 1911, pp. 393), pp. 160–167, 208–224; Anesaki, *History of Japanese Religion*, pp. 130 note, 148 note ; Eliot, *Japanese Buddhism*, 148, 338, 394.

77. Matsura, *Nagasaki Kokon Shūran* (English translation by Wooley, *Transactions of the Asiatic Society of Japan*, Vol. IX, 1881), p. 128 ; Satow, *The Church at Yamaguchi from 1550 to 1586* (*Transactions of the Asiatic Society of Japan*, Vol. VII, 1879), pp. 133 ff ; Gubbins, *Review of the Introduction of*

NOTES

Christianity into China and Japan (*Transactions of the Asiatic Society of Japan*, Vol. VI, Part I, 1878), p. 9.

78. Gubbins, *op. cit.*, p. 10.
79. *Saikoku Kirishitan Bateren Jitsu Roku*, quoted by Gubbins, *op. cit.*, pp. 11–12.
80. Annual Letter of 1882.
81. Gubbins, *op. cit.*, p. 13; Matsura, *op. cit.*, pp. 130–131.
82. *Ibuki Mogusa*, quoted by Gubbins, *op. cit.*, p. 13; Matsura, *op. cit.*, p. 131.
83. Satow, E. M., *The Church at Yamaguchi from 1550 to 1586* (*Transactions of the Asiatic Society of Japan*, Vol. VII, 1879), p. 153, quoting a letter from Froes.
84. One official document contained such a statement. Quoted in Satow, *The Church at Yamaguchi from 1550 to 1586*, p. 141.
85. Ebisawa, *Relation between the Ethics of Bushido and Christianity in Cultural Nippon*, Vol. VII, Nos. 3 and 4, Parts I and II, 1939, Part I, p. 22.
86. Ogawa Shumei, *Nihon 2600-Nenshi* (Tokyo, Ichi Shobo, 1939, pp. 342), pp. 255–268.
87. Gubbins, *op. cit.*, pp. 15–16. For an account of the confusion over the various papal pronouncements, see Satow, *The Origin of Spanish and Portuguese Rivalry in Japan* (*Transactions of the Asiatic Society of Japan*, Vol. XVIII, 1890), pp. 147 ff.
88. Sweet, Charles F., *The Arrest and Death of the Twenty-Six at Nagasaki*, February 1957 (*Transactions of the Asiatic Society of Japan*, Vol. XLIV, Part I, 1916), pp. 20 ff.
89. Gubbins, *op. cit.*, p. 17; a similar instance in the case of Hideyoshi is given in Satow, *The Church at Yamaguchi from 1550 to 1586*, p. 151
90. Gubbins, *op. cit.*, p. 19.
91. Gubbins, *op. cit.*, pp. 21, 30; Matsura, *op. cit.*, p. 134.
92. Satow gives a translation of the anti-Kirishitan edicts in *Transactions of the Asiatic Society of Japan*, Vol. VI, Part I, 1876, pp. 46–51.
93. Best known of these was Sidotti. See Dixon, J. M., *Christian Valley* (*Transactions of the Asiatic Society of Japan*, Vol. XVI, 1889), pp. 207–214.
94. Matsura, *op. cit.*, pp. 140–143; Geerts, *The Arima Rebellion and Koeckebacker* (Letters from Koeckebacker concerning the part he played in the affairs, translated in *Transactions of the Asiatic Society of Japan*, Vol. XI, 1883), pp. 61 ff.
95. Matsura, *op. cit.*, p. 136.
96. Satow in *Transactions of the Asiatic Society of Japan*, Vol. VI, Part I, 1878, p. 51.
97. Ogawa Shūmei, *op. cit.*, p. 284.
98. Ebisawa, *op. cit.*, Vol. II, p. 15.
99. Thomas, Winburn T., *Christian Relics* in *Japan Advertiser*, May 26, 1937.
100. Shimmura and Hamada, *Tombstone of the Christians in the Keichō Era found in Kyōto and its Neighborhood*, Chapter II, paragraph 3, in *Report Upon Archeological Research*, Department of Literature, Vol. VII, Kyōto Imperial University, 1923.
101. The Log of Captain Luke Bickel quoted in Harrington, C. K., *Captain*

Bickel of the Inland Sea (New York, Fleming H. Revell Co., 1919, pp. 301), pp. 70–71.

102. Marnas, F., *La Religion de Jésus Resuscitée au Japon* (Paris, Delhomme et Briguet, 2 vols., 1867), Tome Second, pp. 588.

103. *Japan Weekly Mail*, February 23, 1884, p. 169; *Japan Weekly Mail*, December 1, 1883, pp. 749–750.

104. Translations from the *Jiji Shimpō* in *Japan Weekly Mail*, May 12, 1883, p. 38; *Japan Weekly Mail*, May 26, 1883, p. 79; *Japan Weekly Mail*, June 9, 1883, p. 141; translation from the *Chōya Shimbun* in *Japan Weekly Mail*, June 2, 1883, pp. 102–103.

105. For reports of Buddhist sermons which show direct influence of Christianity see *Japan Weekly Mail*, March 8, 1884, pp. 218–219; for missionary activity of the bonzes see *Japan Weekly Mail*, April 5, 1884, p. 318; *Japan Weekly Mail*, May 3, 1884, p. 405.

106. *Missionary Herald*, November 1881, p. 444.

107. *Ibid.*, September 1882, p. 348.

108. *The Chrysanthemum*, October 1881, pp. 404–408.

109. *Hiogo News*, December 1, 1881, quoted by Cary, *op. cit.*, Vol. II, pp. 128–129.

110. *Missionary Herald*, 1882, p. 152.

111. *Ibid.*, 1878, p. 223; *Proceedings of the Osaka Conference*, p. 145*.

112. Cary, *op. cit.*, Vol. II, pp. 140–141.

113. *Missionary Herald*, 1880, p. 64.

114. *Japan Weekly Mail*, August 11, 1883, p. 354.

115. January 22, 1882.—*The Chrysanthemum*, April 1882, p. 179.

116. February 7, 1882.—*The Chrysanthemum*, April 1882, pp. 180–181.

117. *The Chrysanthemum*, July 1882, pp. 311–312.

118. *Missionary Herald*, April 1882, pp. 151–152.

119. Tagawa, *op. cit.*, p. 7.

120. Tagawa, *op. cit.*, pp. 2–3.

121. *Choya Shimbun* in *Japan Weekly Mail*, May 10, 1884, pp. 444–445; *Japan Weekly Mail*, May 8, 1886, pp. 448–452.

Chapter II: The Social Situation

1. Sakamaki Shunzō, *Japan and the United States, 1790–1853* (*Transactions of the Asiatic Society of Japan*, Second Series Vol. XVIII, December 1939, pp. xi, 204), *passim*.

2. Hawks, F. L., *Narrative of the Expedition of an American Squadron to the China Seas and Japan* (New York, D. Appleton & Co., 1856, pp. vii, 624), pp. 440–442.

3. *The Complete Journal of Townsend Harris* (New York, Japan Society, 1930, pp. xix, 616) pp. 571–573, 578–589.

4. The Treaty of Amity and Commerce between the United States and Japan, Article VIII, cited in *The Complete Journal of Townsend Harris*, pp. 582–583. See note on its acceptance, in *The Complete Journal of Townsend Harris*, p. 512.

5. Ii Kamon no Kami, *Memorial on Foreign Intercourse, 1853*.—Translat-

217

NOTES

ed in Gubbins, J. H., *The Progress of Japan* (Oxford, Clarendon Press, 1911, pp, 323), pp. 285–288 ; *Bakumatsu Gwaikodan.*—Translated in Gubbins, *The Progress of Japan*, pp. 289–291.

6. Oshimo, Raymond Kakuichi, *The Development of Social Idealism in Modern Japan* (Ph. D. Thesis, University of Chicago, 1931, pp. 221), p. 4.

7. *Shimonoseki Convention*, October 1864. Gubbins, *The Progress of Japan*, pp. 296–298.

8. *The Complete Journal of Townsend Harris*, pp. 209–210; *Japan Weekly Mail*, April 14, 1883, pp. 236–240 ; *Japan Weekly Mail*, January 5, 1884, pp. 9–11 ; the *Jiji Shimpō* in *Japan Weekly Mail*, May 23, 1885, p. 488 ; editorial in *Japan Weekly Mail*, June 6, 1885, pp. 524–525; speech by K. Sugi in Tōkyō, reported in *Japan Weekly Mail*, January 22, 1887, p. 77.

9. *Manifesto Announcing the Shogun's Resignation.*—Gubbins, *The Progress of Japan*, pp. 306–311.

10. *Memorial Surrendering Fiefs.*—Gubbins, *The Progress of Japan*, pp. 313–315.

11. *The Five Articles of the Imperial Oath*, translated in Hozumi, *Ancestor Worship and Japanese Law* (Tokyo, Maruzen Kabushiki Kaisha, 1912, pp. xxx, 198), pp. 92–93.

12. Oshimo, *op. cit.*, pp. 89–90.

13. *Imperial Notification No. 12*, April 16, 1883, translated in *Japan Weekly Mail*, April 21, 1883, pp. 255–256.

14. *Japan Weekly Mail*, March 31, 1883, p. 207 ; *Japan Weekly Mail*, May 12, 1883, pp. 38–39.

15. Koba Sadatake, *History of Japanese Penal Legislation* (English translation from *Oesterreichische Monatsschrift fur den Orient*) in *Japan Weekly Mail*, December 29, 1883, pp. 840–843. For a German view of the penal legislation see Mayor, Dr. S., in *Japan Weekly Mail*, November 3, 1883, pp. 648 ff.

16. *E. g.*, by the Iwakura Mission and treaty revision conferences in Tōkyō of 1882 and 1886–7. See Treat, Payson, J., *Diplomatic Relations between the United States and Japan*, 1853–1895 (California, Stanford University Press, 2 vols., 1932), Vol. I, pp. 399–449, Vol. II, pp. 221–265.

17. *Jiji Shimpō*, translated in *Japan Weekly Mail*, January 8, 1887, pp. 36–37.

18. Editorial in *Japan Weekly Mail*, May 30, 1885, pp. 504–506.

19. Nishi, *Japanese National Characteristics*, *Japan Weekly Mail*, September 29, 1883, p. 536 ; *Jiyu Shimbun*, *Japan Weekly Mail*, December 22, 1883, pp. 822–823.

20. Anesaki, *History of Japanese Religion*, pp. 329 ff.

21. *Home and Foreign Record*, October 1872, p. 305.

22. *Japan Weekly Mail*, February 20, 1886, pp. 174–175.

23. *Hōchi Shimbun* in *Japan Weekly Mail*, January 26, 1884, p. 86.

24. Most of the items were suggested by K. S. Latourette in his *The Great Century* (New York, Harper & Brothers, 1941, pp. viii, 516), pp. 9 ff.

25. Tsuchiya Takao, *An Economic History of Japan* (Tokyo, *Transactions of the Asiatic Society of Japan*, December 1937, pp. xviii, 269), *passim*.

26. Norman, E. Herbert, *Japan's Emergence as a Modern State* (New York, Institute of Pacific Relations, 1940, pp. xvi, 254), p. 4.

218

Chapter III: Christianity Re-enters Japan

1. Cary, *op. cit.*, Vol. I, p. 273.
2. Cary, *op. cit.*, Vol. I, p. 277.
3. Cary, *op. cit.*, Vol. I, pp. 376 ff.
4. *Japan Weekly Mail*, June 13, 1885, p. 541. For additional information on the Greek Orthodox Church consult Clement, *Christianity in Modern Japan* (Philadelphia, American Baptist Publication Society, 1905, pp. xv, 205), pp. 52–58; *Japan Christian Evangelist*, Vol. XVI, pp. 277 ff; *Japan Christian Evangelist*, Vol. XV, pp. 331 ff; *Japan Weekly Mail*, June 1, 1890, p. 521.
5. *Chrysanthemum*, October 1881, pp. 392–396.
6. *Tokyo Missionary Conference Report*, p. 912.
7. *Home and Foreign Record*, November 1881, pp. 378–380.
8. *Proceedings of the Osaka Conference*, p. 65.
9. *Missionary Review of the World*, September 1892, pp. 655–656.
10. See clause XXXIII in the *Additional Articles to the Treaty of Commerce...1856...Between the Netherlands and Japan.*—Gubbins, *op. cit.*, p. 262; and clause VIII in the *Treaty...between the United States and Japan of 1858*—Gubbins, *op. cit.*, p. 275.
11. Williams, Frederick Wells, *The Life and Letters of Samuel Wells Williams* (New York, G.P. Putnam's Sons, 1888, pp. vi, 490), p. 284; *Missionary Herald*, March 1864, p. 66; *Proceedings of the Osaka Conference*, p. 89.
12. Griffis, W.E., *Verbeck of Japan* (New York, Fleming H. Revell Co., 1900, pp. 376), p. 62.
13. *Proceedings of the Osaka Conference*, pp. 25–26.
14. *Ibid.*, pp. 26–27.
15. *Ibid.*, p. 27.
16. *Ibid.*, p. 28.
17. *Ibid.*, p. 29.
18. *Ibid.*, p. 29.
19. *Ibid.*, p. 62.
20. *Ibid.*, pp. 64–66.
21. *Ibid.*, p. 66.
22. *Ibid.*, p. 71.
23. *Ibid.*, p. 83.
24. *Ibid.*, statistical table.
25. *Ibid.*, p. 94*.
26. *Ibid.*, p. 112.
27. *Ibid.*, pp. 112–113.
28. *Ibid.*, p. 125.
29. *Ibid.*, statistical table.
30. *World Atlas of Christian Missions* (New York, Student Volunteer Movement for Foreign Missions, 1910, pp. 172), p. 86; Cary, *op. cit.*, Vol. II, p. 220.
31. *Tokyo Missionary Conference Report*, pp. 922–923; G.F. Albrecht correspondence to the American Board of Commissioners for Foreign Missions, April 9, 1891.
32. *Ibid.*, p. 883.
33. *Ibid.*, p. 919.

34. *Ibid.*, p. 932.
35. *Ibid.*, p. 917.
36. *Ibid.*, p. 919.
37. Cary, *op. cit.*, Vol. II, p. 179.
38. *Tokyo Missionary Conference Report*, p. 911.
39. *Proceedings of the Osaka Conference*, pp. 112*–113*, 125.*
40. Japan Christian Yearbook, 1904, p. 184.
41. Latourette, K. S., *The Great Century*, pp. 34 ff.
42. *Missionary Herald*, December 1883, p. 494.
43. *Proceedings of the Osaka Conference*, pp. 52–53.
44. *Missionary Herald*, May 1883, p. 192; *Ibid*, August 1883, pp. 299, 299–300, 300–301; *Ibid.*, September 1883, pp. 352–353; *Ibid.*, August 1884, pp. 310–311.
45. *Ibid.*, July 1883, p. 271.
46. *Church at Home and Abroad*, August 1883, pp. 271–272.
47. Cary, *op. cit.*, Vol. II, p. 171.
48. *Tokyo Missionary Conference Report*, p. 924; *Japan Weekly Mail*, December 10, 1884, p. 598.
49. *Ibid.*, pp. 926–927.
50. *Ibid.*, pp. 931–932.
51. *Proceedings of the Osaka Conference*, pp. 143–152.
52. Greene, D.C., *The Missionaries in Japan* (reprint from the Japan *Weekly Mail*, March 26, 1892); *Annual Report of the American Board's Mission Cooperating with the Kumiai Churches of Japan*, June 1900, p. 43; *Japan Weekly Mail*, May 17, 1884, p. 466.
53. The outline of this section was suggested by Latourette, K. S., *The Great Century*, Chapter IV.
54. *Home and Foreign Record*, August 1863, p. 177.
55. *Missionary Herald*, November 1872, p. 337.
56. *Ibid.*, February 1872, pp. 61–62.
57. *Japan Weekly Mail*, May 17, 1884, pp. 453, 461–462, 465–466; *Japan Weekly Mail*, May 31, 1884, pp. 508–509, 515; *Japan Weekly Mail*, June 21, 1884, pp. 582–583.
58. *Tokyo Missionary Conference Report*, p. 137.
59. *Ibid.*, p. 138.
60. Hepburn correspondence to Board of Foreign Missions of the Presbyterian Church in the U. S. A., March 1884.
61. *Tokyo Missionary Conference Report*, p. 131.
62. *Ibid.*, p. 132.
63. *Ibid.*, p. 132.
64. *Ibid.*, pp. 133–134.
65. *Proceedings of the Osaka Conference*, statistical tables.
66. *Missionary Herald*, April 1888, p. 169.
67. J. C. Hepburn correspondence to Board of Foreign Missions for the Presbyterian Church in the U. S. A., April 2, 1888.
68. *Tokyo Missionary Conference Report*, p. 135.
69. *Ibid.*, pp. 134–135.
70. More commonly known by his western name, Joseph Hardy Neesima.

CHAPTER IV: EDUCATION

See Nakamura, C., *op. cit.*, *Japan Evangelist*, Vol. V, p. 57.
71. *Proceedings of the Osaka Conference*, p. 149*; Cary, *op. cit.*, Vol. II. p. 112.
72. *Proceedings of the Osaka Conference*, p. 149*.
73. *Missionary Herald*, October 1884, pp. 384–385.
74. *Proceedings of the Osaka Conference*, pp. 100*, 126*.
75. Uchimura, Kanzō, *Diary of a Japanese Convert* (New York, Fleming H. Revell Co., no date, pp. 6, 212), p. 60; *Proceedings of the Osaka Conference*, pp. 306–309; Naruse Jinzō, *A Modern Paul in Japan* (Tōkyō, The Keiseisha, 1893, pp. 117), p. 37.
76. *Proceedings of the Osaka Conference*, p. 144*.
77. *Ibid.*, p. 147*.
78. Uchimura, *op. cit.*, p. 83; *Proceedings of the Osaka Conference*, p. 148*.

Chapter IV: Education

1. Latourette, K. S., *A History of Christian Missions in China* (New York, The Macmillan Company, 1929, pp. xii, 930), p. 416.
2. *Proceedings of the Osaka Conference*, p. 89*.
3. Keenlyside and Thomas, *History of Education in Japan* (Tōkyō, Hokuseidō, 1937, pp. xiv, 385), p. 257.
4. *Tokyo Missionary Conference Report*, pp. 240–241.
5. *Ibid.*, pp. 242–243.
6. *Proceedings of the Osaka Conference*, statistical table.
7. Latourette, K. S., *A History of Christian Missions in China*, pp. 214, 441 ff.
8. *Tokyo Missionary Conference Report*, p. 245.
9. Keenlyside and Thomas, *op. cit.*, p. 257.
10. *Japan Weekly Mail*, January 11, 1890, p. 30.
11. *Tokyo Missionary Conference Report*, pp. 248–249.
12. *Church at Home and Abroad*, May 1887, pp. 473–474; *Tokyo Missionary Conference Report*, pp. 892, 919.
13. *Proceedings of the Osaka Conference*, 164*, *Tokyo Missionary Conference Report*, p. 919.
14. *Proceedings of the Osaka Conference*, p. 45.
15. *Church at Home and Abroad*, September 1890, p. 213; *Proceedings of the Osaka Conference*, p. 135*; *Sixth Annual Report of the Missions Cooperating with the Church of Christ in Japan*, p. 17.
16. *Proceedings of the Osaka Conference*, p. 138*.
17. *Ibid.*, p. 59.
18. *Ibid.*, p. 66.
19. *Ibid.*, p. 163*.
20. Tucker, *op. cit.*, p. 146.
21. *Proceedings of the Osaka Conference*, p. 74; *Japan Weekly Mail, January* 11, 1890, p. 30.
22. *World Atlas of Christian Missions*, p. 70.
23. *Proceedings of the Osaka Conference*, pp. 143*–144*.
24. *Ibid.*, pp. 110*, 157*; *Japan Weekly Mail*, January 1, 1887, pp. 11–12.

25. *Proceedings of the Osaka Conference*, pp. 45, 72–73, 137*–138*.
26. *Japan Christian Yearbook*, 1908, pp. 153 ff ; *Proceedings of the Osaka Conference*, p. 70.
27. *Proceedings of the Osaka Conference*, pp. 45, 79.
28. *Ibid.*, pp. 59, 84, 135*.
29. *Ibid.*, p. 100*.
30. *Ibid.*, p. 126*.
31. *Ibid.*, p. 69.
32. *Ibid.*, p. 71. By the end of 1882 there were "homes" at Tōkyō, Yokohama, Nagasaki, and Hakodate, with day and boarding students.—*Ibid.*, pp. 160*–161*.
33. Tucker, Henry St. George, *The History of the Episcopal Church in Japan* (New York, Charles Scribner's Sons, 1938, pp, 228), pp. 96, 155.
34. *Proceedings of the Osaka Conference*, pp. 74, 92*, 128*, 101*, 142*–143*.
35. *Tokyo Missionary Conference Report*, p. 892. A learned clergy is needed to command the respect and confidence of a rapidly growing learned laity, due to a growing dissatisfaction with old institutions and craving for new ideas.—*Proceedings of the Osaka Conference*, p. 172.
36. *Proceedings of the Osaka Conference*, p. 99*.
37. *Ibid.*, pp. 45–46, 67, 101*.
38. C. W. Fisher correspondence to the Board of Foreign Missions of the Presbyterian Church in the U. S. A., February 2, 1885.
39. *Ibid.*, pp. 74, 108*.
40. *Ibid.*, pp. 88–90*, 106*, 131*, 166*.
41. *Ibid.*, p. 68.
42. *Ibid.*, p. 91*.
43. *Ibid.*, pp. 98*–99*, 104*–105*, 163*.
44. *Ibid.*, pp. 125*, 168*.
45. *Ibid.*, p. 141*.
46. *Ibid.*, p. 157*.
47. *Ibid.*, pp. 171*–172*.
48. *Ibid.*, statistical tables.
49. *Tokyo Missionary Conference Report*, p. 893.
50. *Ibid.*, pp. 899–900.
51. *Ibid.*, pp. 915, 916.
52. *Ibid.*, p. 922.
53. E. g., *Proceedings of the Osaka Conference*, pp. 109*, 151*, 168*; *Tokyo Missionary Conference Report*, 899–911 ; *Missionary Herald*, June 1881, p. 222.
54. Latourette, K. S., *A History of Missions in China*, p. 426 and note.
55. *Proceedings of the Osaka Conference*, pp. 76, 99*–100*.
56. *Ibid.*, p. 99*.
57. *Ibid.*, statistical tables.
58. *Ibid.*, p. 141*.
59. *Ibid.*, p. 149*.
60. *Ibid.*, p. 155*.
61. *Ibid.*, p. 168*.
62. *Ibid.*, p. 171*.
63. *Tokyo Missionary Conference Report*, pp. 138–139.

CHAPTER V: LITERATURE

64. *Japan Christian Yearbook* 1910, p. 201; *Tokyo Missionary Conference Report*, p. 738.

65. *Tokyo Missionary Conference Report*, pp. 290–291, 900.

66. *Ibid.*, p. 294.

67. *Proceedings of the Osaka Conference*, pp. 125*, 168*.

68. Mizuno Tsunekichi, *The Kindergarten in Japan* (Boston, The Stratford Co., 1917, pp. ix, 62), p. 31.

69. *Proceedings of the Osaka Conference*, pp. 68–69.

70. Cary, *op. cit.*, Vol. I, p. 98.

71. *Proceedings of the Osaka Conference*, pp. 80, 112*, 125*, 135*, 138*, 142*, 154*, 157*, 162*, 167*, 168*, 461–464.

72. *Ibid.*, pp. 457–458.

73. *Ibid.*, pp. 459–460.

74. *Church at Home and Abroad*, June 1889, pp. 557–559.

75. *Proceedings of the Osaka Conference*, pp. 59, 142*, 151*, 163*, 62, 63, 67.

76. *Ibid.*, p. 28.

77. *Ibid.*, p. 83.

78. *Ibid.*, p. 71; see Chapter IV, pp. 182–183.

79. *Japan Weekly Mail*, May 3, 1890, pp. 452–453.

80. *Proceedings of the Osaka Conference*, p. 79.

81. Correspondence from the field, Board of Foreign Missions for the Presbyterian Church in the U. S. A., July 12, 1886.

82. *Home and Foreign Record*, March 1880, pp. 78-80.

83. *Ibid.*, November 1883, pp. 379–380; *Ibid.*, February 1884, pp. 58–59; *Ibid.*, October 1884, pp. 379–380.

84. *Proceedings of the Osaka Conference*, p. 93*.

85. Carrothers, Julia D., *The Sunrise Kingdom* (Philadelphia, Presbyterian Board of Publication, 1879, pp. 408), pp. 400-401.

86. Uchimura Kanzō, *The Diary of a Japanese Convert* (New York, Fleming H. Revell Co., no date, pp. 212), pp. 12 ff; *Proceedings of the Osaka Conference*, pp. 159*–160*.

87. Cary, *op. cit.*, Vol. II, p. 123; *Proceedings of the Osaka Conference*, pp. 81, 108*.

88. *London Missionary Conference Reports*, Vol. II, p. 205.

89. *Japan Weekly Mail*, October 24, 1891, p. 497.

90. *Missionary Herald*, October 1887, pp. 393–396.

91. DeForest, Charlotte B., *The Evolution of a Missionary* (New York, Fleming H. Revell Co., 1914, pp. 299) pp. 181–182.

92. *Japan Weekly Mail*, October 24, 1891, p. 497; *Japan Weekly Mail*, October 31, 1891, pp. 531–532; *Japan Weekly Mail*, November 14, 1891, p. 590.

Chapter V: Literature

1. *Tokyo Missionary Conference Report*. pp. 436–437.

2. *Home and Foreign Record*, August 1867, p. 178.

3. *Ibid.*, May 1867, p. 107.

4. Nakamura, *op. cit.*, *Japan Evangelist*, Vol. V, pp. 54–55; *Proceedings of the Osaka Conference*, pp. 113*–117*; *Tokyo Missionary Conference Report*

pp. 800–804 ; *Japan Weekly Mail*, February 11, 1888, pp. 123–124, 130–132.

5. The account of the translation of the Bible into Japanese has been given often by the mission press.—See *Church at Home and Abroad*, June 1888, pp. 612–615; *Missionary Herald*, March 1883, p. 113; *Home and Foreign Record*, April 1883, pp. 120–121 ; *Japan Christian Yearbook*, 1909, pp. 152 ff.

6. *Tokyo Missionary Conference Report*, pp. 504, 505.

7. *Ibid.*, p. 522.

8. *Ibid.*, p. 528.

9. *Ibid.*, pp. 522–524.

10. Cary, *op. cit.*, Vol. II, pp. 85–86. The first published copy of this is on display in the museum of the Kyō Bun Kwan (Christian Literature Society) in Tōkō.—*Kirisutokyō Bunken Karimokuroku*, an unpublished bibliography of Japanese books prepared by Winburn T. Thomas, item 33.

11. *Tokyo Missionary Conference Report*, p. 439 ; *Kirisutokyō Bunken Karimokuroku*, item 83.

12. *Ibid.*, pp. 440–441.

13. *Ibid.*, pp. 438–439.

14. *Ibid.*, pp. 442–443.

15. Otis, Cary, in *Japan Evangelist*, Vol. V, p. 76.

16. *Tokyo Missionary Conference Report*, p. 444.

17. *Kirisutokyō Bunken Karimokuroku*, *passim*.

18. Uchimura Kanzō, *Diary of a Japanese Convert*, pp. 66–68.

19. *Tokyo Missionary Conference Report*, pp. 447–448 ; *Proceedings of the Osaka Conference*, p. 147*; *Kirisutokyō Bunken Karimokuroku*, items 168, 460, 865.

20. *Tokyo Missionary Conference Report*, pp. 448–449 ; *Proceedings of the Osaka Conference*, pp. 102*, 178*.

21. Verbeck in *The Chrysanthemum*, April 1881, pp. 150–152.

22. *Proceedings of the Osaka Conference*, p. 178*.

23. *Kirisutokyō Bunken Karimokuroku*, item 148.

24. *Proceedings of the Osaka Conference*, p. 126*; Tucker *The History of the Episcopal Church in Japan*, p. 116.

25. *Tokyo Missionary Conference Report*, p. 447.

26. *Ibid.*, pp. 449–451 ; *Japan Weekly Mail*, March 22, 1890, pp. 295–300.

27. *Tokyo Missionary Conference Report*, p. 452.

28. *Japan Weekly Mail*, November 8, 1884, p. 447.

29. *Tokyo Missionary Conference Report*, p. 467.

30. *Ibid.*, p. 477.

31, The history of this subject had been compiled by Allchin in *Ibid.*, pp. 461–502 ; for a list of Protestant hymn books published in Japan, see *Ibid.*, pp. 970–973. The most complete account of the development of hymnology in the church in Japan is by Matsumoto Tsuyoshi, *Hymnology in Japan:* An Historical Study...(M.S.M. Thesis, Union Theological Seminary, 1935, pp. 47 and plates).

Chapter VI : Social Welfare Activities

1. *Home and Foreign Record*, January 1862, p. 18, says 1878; J.C. Hepburn correspondence to the Board of Foreign Missions of the Presbyterian Church

CHAPTER VI : SOCIAL WELFARE ACTIVITIES

in the U. S. A., January 6, 1888, gives the date when the dispensary was abandoned as 1877.

2. *Proceedings of the Osaka Conference*, p. 44 ; *Home and Foreign Record*, January 1862, p. 18.

3. *Proceedings of the Osaka Conference*, p. 48.

4. *Ibid.*, p. 58.

5. *Ibid.*, p. 63.

6. *Ibid.*, p. 75.

7. *Ibid.*, pp. 107*-108*.

8. Cary, *op.*, *cit.*, Vol. II, p. 108.

9. *Proceedings of the Osaka Conference*, pp. 108*, 145*.

10. *Ibid.*, pp. 67, 99*; Tucker, *op. cit.*, pp. 117, 157.

11. *Ibid.*, pp. 71, 110*, 322.

12. *Ibid.*, p. 165*.

13. *Ibid.*, pp. 71, 124*.

14. *Ibid.*, p. 164*.

15. *World Atlas of Christian Missions*, p. 70.

16. *Home and Foreign Record*, April 1882, pp. 126–127.

17. Tucker, *op. cit.*, pp. 116–117 ; *Proceedings of the Osaka Conference*, pp. 165, 320–324.

18. *Missionary Herald*, February 1888, p. 64 ; *Japan Weekly Mail*, July 14, 1888, pp. 27–28.

19. J. C. Hepburn correspondence to the Board of Foreign Missions of the Presbyterian Church in the U. S. A., April 26, 1884.

20. J. C. Berry correspondence to the Board of Foreign Missions of the Presbyterian Church in the U. S. A., December 16, 1884.

21. *Proceedings of the Osaka Conference*, pp. 145*-146*.

22. Cary, *op. cit.*, Vol. II, pp. 133–135; *Missionary Herald*, July 1877, p. 216.

23. Cary, *op. cit.*, Vol. II, pp. 206–207.

24. Cary, *op. cit.*, Vol. II, p. 208 ; *Church at Home and Abroad*, April 1889, pp. 379–380.

25. *Missionary Herald*, January 1881, p. 25.

26. *Japan Weekly Mail*, June 15, 1889, p. 566 ; *Ibid.*, July 13, 1889, p. 27; *Ibid.*, July 27, 1889, pp. 79-80 ; *Missionary Herald*, February 1882, p. 70 ; *Ibid.*, July 1883 ; pp. 269–270. Members of the First Kumiai Church in Kobe, sold their smoking apparatus and donated the proceeds to the Christian movement.—*Ibid.*, May 1884, p. 194 ; Nakamura Keiu sought to promote a temperance society as early as 1884.—*Japan Weekly Mail*, December 20, 1884, p. 585.

27. *Japan Weekly Mail*, December 14, 1889, pp. 547, 551; *Ibid.*, December 21, 1889, p. 567.

28. *Tokyo Missionary Conference Report*, p. 935.

29. *Ibid.*, p. 934; *Japan Christian Yearbook*, 1907, p. 166; *Ibid.*, 1908, p. 306.

30. *Missionary Herald*, September 1889, pp. 358–359 ; *Japan Weekly Mail*, June 15, 1889, p. 566 ; *Ibid.*, July 13, 1889, p. 27 ; *Ibid.*, July 27, 1889, pp. 79–80.

31. *Tokyo Missionary Conference Report*, p. 937.

32. *Ibid.*, p. 928 ; *Japan Christian Intelligencer*, *Vol. I*, p. 62.

Chapter VII: The Churches and Evangelism

1. *Proceedings of the Osaka Conference*, p. 52.
2. *Ibid.*, p. 53.
3. This term refers to the part of the Yokohama Foreign Concession along the water front, popularly known as The *Bund*.
4. *Proceedings of the Osaka Conference*, p. 53; Cary, *op. cit.*, Vol. II, p. 77
5. *Ibid.*, p. 59.
6. Imbrie, Wm., *Church Unity in Japan*, p. 3.
7. *Ibid.*, p. 4; *Proceedings of the Osaka Conference*, p. 85; *Japan Weekly Mail*, July 16, 1887, pp. 58–59.
8. Nakamura, C., *op. cit.*, *Japan Evangelist*, Vol. V. p. 77; *Proceedings of the Osaka Conference*, pp. 79–81.
9. Nakamura, C., *op.*, *cit.*, *Japan Evangelist*, Vol. V, pp. 78, 79; Imbrie, *Church Unity in Japan*, p. 5; *Proceedings of the Osaka Conference*, pp. 60, 67, 72, 79, 99*, *et. seq.*
10. *Proceedings of the Osaka Conference*, pp. 85, 86.
11. *Ibid.*, p. 70.
12. Cary, *op. cit.*, p. 109 has a note correcting the implication given by the *Missionary Herald*, 1874, p. 273 that the creed had been prepared by members of the Kōbe church.
13. Nakamura, *op. cit.*, *Japan Evangelist*, Vol. V, p. 58; *Proceedings of the Osaka Conference*, p. 86.
14. *Proceedings of the Osaka Conference*, p. 86.
15. *Proceedings of the Osaka Conference*, p. 86.
16. Imbrie, *Church Unity in Japan*, p. 7; *Proceedings of the Osaka Conference*, p. 87.
17. *Tokyo Missionary Conference Report*, p. 106.
18. Imbrie, *Church Unity in Japan*, pp. 8 12.
19. Imbrie, *Church Unity in Japan*, p. 10.
20. Imbrie, *Church Unity in Japan*, pp. 9, 12.
21. *Tokyo Missionary Conference Report*, p. 106.
22. *Proceedings of the Osaka Conference*, p. 89*; *Japan Christian Yearbook*, 1903, p. 79. For minutes of the organization of the *chūkai* see *Home and Foreign Record*, January 1878, pp. 21–22.
23. *London Missionary Conference*, Vol. I, pp. 246–247.
24. Nakamura, C., *op. cit.*, *Japan Evangelist*, Vol. V, p. 79.
25. *Proceedings of the Osaka Conference*, pp. 166*–167*.
26. *Tokyo Missionary Conference Report*, pp. 106–107, 888–889.
27. *Proceedings of the Osaka Conference*, pp. 98*–99*.
28. *Proceedings of the Osaka Conference*, pp. 232–278; *Tokyo Missionary Conference Report*, pp. 601, 603–610.
29. Tucker, *op.*, *cit.*, p. 123.
30. *Proceedings of the Osaka Conference*, pp. 306–309.
31. *Proceedings of the Osaka Conference*, p. 101*; Speer, *Studies in Missionary Leadership* (Philadelphia, Westminster Press, 1914), pp. 114, 126; De-Forest, J. H., *Sunrise in the Sunrise Kingdom*, p. 117.
32. *Japan Weekly Mail*, February 21, 1885, pp. 174–175.

CHAPTER VII: THE CHURCHES AND EVANGELISM

33. *Tokyo Missionary Conference Report*, p. 895.
34. *Tokyo Missionary Conference Report*, p. 881.
35. *Missionary Herald*, March 1883, p. 86.
36. *Tokyo Missionary Conference Report*, pp. 103–105, 879–884; Tucker, *op. cit.*, pp. 136–139; Cary, *op. cit.*, Vol. II, p. 191.
37. Tucker, *op. cit.*, p. 138.
38. *Tokyo Missionary Conference Report*, p. 106; Imbrie, Wm., *Church Unity in Japan*, p. 6; *Sixth Annual Report of the Council of Missions Cooperating with the Church of Christ in Japan*, p. 2.
39. *Tokyo Missionary Conference Report*, pp. 888–889; *Ninth Annual Report of the Council of the Three Missions* (1885). [MSS.]
40. *Tokyo Missionary Conference Report*, p. 913.
41. *Tokyo Missionary Conference Report*, pp. 912–913.
42. *Tokyo Missionary Conference Report*, pp. 898–900.
43. *Tokyo Missionary Conference Report*, pp. 898, 919–920.
44. *Tokyo Missionary Conference Report*, p. 912.
45. *Tokyo Missionary Conference Report*, pp. 915–917.
46. *Japan Weekly Mail*, October 15, 1887, pp. 378–379.
47. *Japan Weekly Mail*, May 7, 1887, p. 439.
48. Tucker, *op. cit.*, pp. 138–139. Much of the correspondence in connection with this incident was reproduced in the *Japan Weekly Mail* of the following dates in 1887; May 7, pp. 447–448; May 14, pp. 466–467, 474–475, 475; May 21, pp. 486, 493; May 28, pp. 516, 517; June 18, p. 593; July 9, p. 30; July 16, pp. 59–60. See also Imbrie, Wm., *Church Unity in Japan*, pp. 14–17.
49. London Missionary Conference, Vol. I, p. 257.
50. Imbrie, Wm. *Church Unity in Japan*, pp. 18–20; *Japan Weekly Mail*, June 4, 1877, pp. 546–547.
51. Imbrie, Wm. *Church Unity in Japan*, p. 21.
52. *Ibid.*, pp. 22–23.
53. *Ibid.*, p. 27.
54. *Tokyo Missionary Conference Report*, p. 885; *London Missionary Conference Report*, Vol. II, p. 364.
55. Imbrie, Wm., *Church Unity in Japan*, pp. 30–31.
56. *Tokyo Missionary Conference Report*, p. 106, 886.
57. Cary, *op. cit.*, p. 194; Imbrie, Wm., *Church Unity in Japan*, p. 28.
58. William Imbrie correspondence to the Board of Foreign Missions of the Presbyterian Church in the U. S. A., June 21, 1886.
59. Imbrie, Wm., *Church Unity in Japan*, p. 28.
60. *Proceedings of the Osaka Conference*, pp. 49–50.
61. *Ibid.*, p. 52.
62. *Ibid.*, pp. 72, 76, 80, 103*, 104*, 110*, 124*.
63. *Missionary Herald*, February 1881, p. 57; *Ibid.*, August 1881, pp. 297–300; *Ibid.*, September 1884, p. 349; *Church at Home and Abroad*, May 1887, pp. 478–479.
64. *Japan Weekly Mail*, May 31, 1884, p. 503.
65. *Home and Foreign Record*, August 1883, pp. 271–272.
66. *Proceedings of the Osaka Conference*, p. 162*; *Japan Weekly Mail*, July 5, 1890, p. 12.

67. For the account of a similar gathering at Matsue, one of Japan's most conservative cities, see *London Missionary Conference Report*, Vol. I, p. 241; *Missionary Herald*, March 1853, p. 109.

68. Anesaki, *History of Japanese Religion*, p. 356.

69. Imbrie, *The Church of Christ in Japan*, p. 91; *Home and Foreign Record*, March 1885, pp. 105-107.

70. *Proceedings of the Osaka Conference*, p. 70.

71. *Ibid.*, pp. 79-80.

72. *Ibid.*, p. 82.

73. *Missionary Herald*, May, 1881, pp. 180-184.

74. *Tokyo Missionary Conference Report*, p. 137.

75. *Ibid.*, p. 166.

76. *Proceedings of the Osaka Conference*, pp. 141-142.

Chapter VIII: Reasons for the Spectacular Growth 1883-89

1. *Proceedings of the Osaka Conference*, p. 138.

2. *Missionary Herald*, May 1889, p. 177; *Church at Home and Abroad*, June 1889, p. 591.

3. *Seventeenth Report of the Council of Missions Cooperating with the Church of Christ in Japan*, pp. 5-6.

4. *Japan Weekly Mail*, September 29, 1888, p. 300.

5. *Ibid.*, October 6, 1888, pp. 323-324.

6. *Ibid.*, October 13, 1888, pp. 348-349.

7. *Ibid.*, October 20, 1888, p. 372.

8. *Tokyo Missionary Conference Report*, p. 109.

9. *Nichi Nichi Shimbun* and *Jiji Shimbun* in *Japan Weekly Mail*, May 12, 1883, p. 38.

10. *Japan Weekly Mail*, February 16, 1884, p. 115; *Ibid.*, August 16, 1884, p. 159.

11. *Ibid.*, May 21, 1887, pp. 490-492.

12. *Ibid.*, March 10, 1888, p. 217.

13. *London Missionary Conference Report*, Vol. I, p. 239.

14. *Japan Weekly Mail*, September 15, 1888, p. 258; *Missionary Herald*, June 1885, pp. 222-223.

15. *Japan Weekly Mail*, May 8, 1886, pp. 448-452.

16. *Ibid.*, May 12, 1883, p. 38.

17. *Ibid.*, December, 12, 1885, pp. 571-572, January 9, 1886, p. 33.

18. *Ibid.*, May 8, 1886, pp. 448-452.

19. *The Church at Home and Abroad.*, September 1887, pp. 284-285; *Missionary Herald*, November 1888, p. 534.

20. *The Church at Home and Abroad*, December 1889, pp. 482-483; *Missionary Herald*, May 1886, pp. 174-176.

21. *Japan Weekly Mail*, March 26, 1892, reprinted as *The Missionaries in Japan*, by D. C, Greene; *Annual Report of the American Board's Mission Cooperating with the Kumiai Churches in Japan*, June 1900, p. 43.

22. *Missionary Herald*, May 1875, p. 132.

23. Correspondence, Secretary American Board of Commissioners for Foreign Missions, October, 8, 1869.

24. *Missionary Herald*, May 1875, p. 132.

25. Iglehart, C. W., *Points of Contact with Shinto in the Approach of Christianity to Rural Japan* (S. T. M. Thesis, Union Theological Seminary, New York, 1933) p. 23.

26. Gundert, Wilhelm, *Japanische Religionsgeschichte* (Tokyo, Japanisch-Deutsches, Kulturinstitut, 1935, pp. xviii, 267) pp. 166–167.

27. *Missionary Herald*, November 1869, pp. 380–384.

28. *The Church at Home and Abroad*, June 1887, p. 548.

29. Gulick in *Missionary Herald*, April 1872, pp. 123–125.

30. Latourette, K. S., *The Great Century* (1941, Harper & Brothers, New York, pp. viii, 516), p. 98.

31. *Japan Weekly Mail*, May 8, 1886, pp. 448–452.

32. Imbrie, Wm., *The Church of Christ in Japan* (Philadelphia, Westminster Press, 1906, pp. 122) p. 91.

33. Oshimo, *op. cit.*, pp. 94–95, 193–195; Fisher, Galen, *Creative Forces* in Japan, p. 152.

34. Speer, *op. cit.*, Vol. II, pp. 403–404; *Chōya Shimbun in Missionary Herald*, April 1882, pp. 151–152.

35. Oshimo, *op. cit.*, pp. 77–79.

36. Takahashi Kamekichi, *Nihon Shihon Shugi Hattatsushi*, p. 24, quoted in Oshimo, *op. cit.*, pp. 61–62.

37. See Chapter I, p. 14, note 2.

38. Noss, George S., *The Rise of Nationalism in Japan and the Christian Movement* (M. S. T. thesis, Union Theological Seminary, 1937, pp. 140), pp. 31–32.

39. Brinkley, *A History of the Japanese People*, p. 709.

40. *Missionary Herald*, March 1886, p. 105.

41. *The Future of Religion in Japan*, which sets forth Fukuzawa's reasons for this view, appeared first in the *Jiji Shimpō*, June 18, 19, and 20, 1884. It was published in translation in the *Japan Gazette*, July 26, 1884.

42. *Japan Weekly Mail*, July 12, 1884, pp. 24–26, 35; *Ibid.*, July 26, 1884, pp. 92–93; *Ibid.*, January 24, 1886, pp. 84–85, 90–91.

43. *Ibid.*, March 3, 1887, pp. 197–201.

44. *Ibid.*, April 27, 1889, p. 396.

Chapter IX: Growth Retarded by Resurgent Nationalism

1. *Missionary Herald*, September 1890, p. 370; *Ibid.*, February 1891, p. 48.

2. DeForest, John H., *Sunrise in the Sunrise Kingdom* (New York, The Young People's Missionary Movement, 1904, pp. 233), p. 190.

3. *Seventeenth Annual Report of the Council of Missions Cooperating with the Churches of Christ in Japan, passim.* Churches of a hundred members dropped to thirty or forty.—*Tokyo Missionary Conference Report*, p. 607.

4. *Church at Home and Abroad*, September 1890, p. 221.

NOTES

5. Katakozawa Chiyomatsu, *Meiji Gannen no Kirisutokyō ni Okeru Shisō no Ichikōan* in *Kirisutokyō Shi Kenkyū*, No. 6, November 8, 1939, p. 19.

6. Knox, George W., in *Church at Home and Abroad*, September 1892, pp. 224-225.

7. *Tokyo Missionary Conference Report*, p. 896.

8. Uemura Masahisa in *Nippon Hyōron* in *Japan Weekly Mail*, November 7, 1891, p. 546 ; *Missionary Herald*, October 1887, pp. 308-309 ; *Missionary Review of the World*, September 1891, p. 719.

9. *Japan Weekly Mail*, December 6, 1890, p. 551.

10. *Ibid.*, June 2, 1888, p. 505.

11. *Japan Weekly Mail*, May 24, 1890, pp. 528-529, 532-533.

12. *Church at Home and Abroad*, September 1891, pp. 219-220.

13. *Japan Christian Intelligencer*, Vol. I, No. 2, p. 52.

14. *Missionary Herald*, December 1880, p. 509; Norman, E.H., *op. cit.*, p. 96.

15. Warneck, Gustav, *Outline of a History of Protestant Missions* (New York, Fleming H. Revell Co., 1901, pp. 13, 364), p. 313.

16. *Tokyo Missionary Conference Report*, pp. 96-97.

17. DeForest, *Sunrise in the Sunrise Kingdom*, pp. 185 ff.

18. *Church at Home and Abroad*, November 1892, p. 386.

19. *Japan Weekly Mail*, June 22, 1889, pp. 599-601.

20. *Ibid.*, April 27, 1889, pp. 404-405.

21. *Ibid.*, January 26, 1889, p. 78.

22. *Ibid.*, July 1887, p. 18.

23. *Ibid.*, April 20, 1889, pp. 371-372.

24. Anesaki, *History of Japanese Religion*, pp. 360 ff.

25. *Church at Home and Abroad*, July 9, 1887, pp. 37-38.

26. *Thirteenth Annual Report of the Missions Cooperating with the Church of Christ in Japan*, p. 14 ; Church at Home and Abroad, September 1894, pp. 219-221.

27. *Japan Weekly Mail*, April 4, 1891, p. 397.

28. *Home and Foreign Record*, February 1872, pp. 49-51.

29. *Japan Weekly Mail*, May 31, 1884, p. 503.

30. Berry, K. F., *A Pioneer Doctor in Old Japan* (New York, Fleming H. Revell Co., 1940, pp. 247), pp. 196-197.

31. Anesaki, *Religious and Social Problems of the Orient* (New York, Macmillan, 1923, pp. xi, 77), p. 27.

32. *Japan Weekly Mail*, March 16, 1890, pp. 260-261.

33. *Missionary Herald*, November 1880, p. 471.

34. *Proceedings of the Osaka Conference*, p. 122.

35. *Ibid.*, pp. 118-119 ; *Japan Weekly Mail*, April 4, 1881, p. 397.

36. *Proceedings of the Osaka Conference*, p. 120 ; *Chrysanthemum*, May 1882, pp. 227-228.

37. *Japan Weekly Mail*, January 21, 1882 ; *Ibid.*, July 12, 1884, p. 35.

38. *Proceedings of the Osaka Conference*, p. 121.

39. Anesaki, *History of Japanese Religion*, p. 361.

40. *Japan Weekly Mail*, March 15, 1890, pp. 266-267, 272-274; *Ibid.*, March 29, 1890, pp. 330-331; *Ibid.*, April 5, 1890, pp. 355; *Ibid.*, May 3, 1890, p. 458.

41. *Ibid.*, December 27, 1890, pp. 650-653.

CHAPTER IX: GROWTH RETARDED

42. Oshimo, Raymond Kakuichi, *The Development of Social Idealism in Modern Japan* (Ph. D. Dissertation, University of Chicago, 1931, pp. 221), pp. 68–69; Anesaki, *History of Japanese Religion*, pp. 350–353.

43. *Missionary Review of the World*, September 1891, p. 648.

44. J. D. Davis correspondence to the American Board of Commissioners for Foreign Missions, November 15, 1890.

45. *Tokyo Missionary Conference Report*, pp. 92–93; Anesaki, *History of Japanese Religion*, p. 358; *Japan Weekly Mail*, April 4, 1891, p. 397.

46. *Japan Weekly Mail*, December 20, 1890, pp. 611–612.

47. *Missionary Review of the World*, September 1891, p. 645; *Missionary Review of the World*, November 1891, p. 850. G. E. Albrecht correspondence to the American Board of Commissioners for Foreign Missions, April 9, 1891. It was also noted in the same communication that Spinner, a German missionary, was a warmhearted, wholesouled Christian and a scholar of high rank.

48. *Tokyo Missionary Conference Report*, p. 93 and note.

49. *Seventeenth Annual Report of the Missions Cooperating with the Church of Christ in Japan*, pp. 17–18.

50. *Japan Weekly Mail*, December 20, 1890, pp. 615–616.

51. Kozaki Nariaki, *Christian Thought in Japan*, in *Japan Weekly Mail*, August 8, 1891, p. 619.

52. Uchimura Kanzō's confession, *Japan Weekly Mail*, December 5, 1891, p. 676; *Japan Weekly Mail*, May 9, 1891, p. 555.

53. Warneck, *op. cit.*, p. 314.

54. Reviewed and summarized in the *Rikugō Zasshi*. Translation in Japan *Weekly Mail*, October 3, 1891, pp. 400, 411–413; *Ibid.*, November 7, 1891, pp. 561–562; *Missionary Review of the World*, August 1892, pp. 604–606.

55. Epitomized and translated from the *Rikugō Zasshi* in *Japan Weekly Mail*, July 19, 1890, pp. 59–60.

56. Uemura Masahisa, in the *Nippon Hyōron*, states that Yokoi himself was dissatisfied with his theological position.—*Japan Weekly Mail*, November 7, 1891, p. 546.

57. F. G. Harrington correspondence to the American Baptist Missionary Union, April 14, 1890.

58. *Church at Home and Abroad*, September 1890, p. 219; *Missionary Review of the World*, September 1891, p. 643.

59. *Seventeenth Report of the Missions Cooperating with the Church of Christ in Japan*, pp. 12–13.

60. *Missionary Herald*, June 1886, p. 208.

61. *Missionary Review of the World*, May 1890, p. 329; *Missionary Herald*, May 1889, p. 204; *Missionary Herald*, August 1889, pp. 315–317.

62. Shinagawa, Yajirō, Minister of Home Affairs, in *Japan Weekly Mail*, September 12, 1891, p. 304.

63. As at Nagoya in January 1891. See *Japan Weekly Mail*, January 24, 1891, p. 92, and January 31, 1891, p. 118.

64. Itō Sōsui, in *Yomiuri Shimbun*, *Japan Weekly Mail*, July 25, 1891, p. 93.

65. *Seventeenth Report of the Council of Missions Cooperating with the Church of Christ in Japan*, pp. 3–4.

66. *Missionary Herald*, May 1889, p. 178.

231

NOTES

67. Uemura Masahisa, in *Nippon Hyōron, Japan Weekly Mail,* November 7, 1891, p. 546.

68. *Seventeenth Report of the Council of Missions Cooperating with the Church of Christ in Japan,* pp. 8–9.

69. *Japan Weekly Mail,* May 17, 1890, p. 495.

70. *Ibid.,* May 17, 1890, p. 501.

71. *Fourteenth Report of the Council of Missions Cooperating with the Church of Christ in Japan,* pp. 8–9 ; *Missionary Herald,* September 1890, p. 370.

72. *Japan Weekly Mail,* February 20, 1886, p. 172.

73. *Home and Foreign Record,* July 1885, pp. 268–269; *Missionary Herald,* January 1888, p. 4 ; *Missionary Herald,* February 1888, p. 67; correspondence of D. W. Stevens, counsellor of the Japanese Legation, Washington, to the American Board of Commissioners for Foreign Missions, April 14, 1888.

74. Cary, *op. cit.,* Vol. II, p. 221.

75. *Japan Weekly Mail,* July 4, 1891, pp. 15–16.

76. Holtom, *The Political Philosophy of Modern Shinto,* in *Transactions of the Asiatic Society of Japan,* 1922, Vol. XLIX, part II, pp. 73–75 ; Anesaki, *History of Japanese Religion,* pp. 362–365.

77. *Missionary Herald,* May 1891, p. 182.

78. *Church at Home and Abroad,* September 1892, pp. 219–221 ; George Allchin correspondence to the American Board of Commissioners for Foreign Missions, June 2, 1885.

79. *Sixteenth Report of the Missions Cooperating with the Church of Christ in Japan,* pp. 11–13.

80. *Seventeenth Report of the Council of Missions Cooperating with the Church of Christ in Japan,* p. 23.

81. *Japan Weekly Mail,* March 2, 1889, pp. 201–202; *Ibid.,* March 16, 1889, pp. 254, 255–256 ; *Ibid.,* July 6, 1889, p. 8.

82. See pp. 35–36.

83. *Japan Weekly Mail,* November 9, 1889, pp. 421–422.

84. Norman, Herbert, *Japan's Emergence as a Modern State,* p. 198 note ; *Japan Weekly Mail,* October 22, 1887, p. 399.

85. McLaren, W. W., *A Political History of Japan During the Meiji Era* (London, George Allen & Unwin, Ltd., 1916, pp. 380), p. 165.

86. Okuma Shigenobu, compiler, *Fifty Years of New Japan* (New York, E.P. Dutton & Co., 2 vols., 1909), Vol. II, p. 89.

87. Gubbins, J. H. *The Making of Modern Japan* (London, Seely, Service & Co., 1922, pp. 316), p. 179.

88. *Japan Weekly Mail,* September 22, 1888, pp. 272–273.

89. Okuma, *op. cit.,* Vol. I, pp. 162–163 ; McLaren, *op. cit.,* pp. 165–168.

90. Brinkley, *op. cit.,* 708–709 ; *Japan Weekly Mail,* August 6, 1887, p. 124.

91. Greene, E. B., *A New Englander in Japan* (Boston, Houghton Mifflin Co., 1927, pp. x, 374), pp. 213–214 ; *Japan Weekly Mail,* September 27, 1890, pp. 294, 298, 300 ff.

92. Greene, *op. cit.,* p. 243.

93. *London Times,* May 30, 1890, reprinted in *Japan Weekly Mail,* July 12, 1890, pp. 43–45.

94. Okuma, *op., cit.,* Vol. II, p. 89.

Chapter X: Conclusion

1. Norman, E. H., *op. cit.*, p. 209.
2. DeForest, *op. cit.*, pp. 191–192.
3. DeForest, *op. cit.*, p. 193.
4. *Seventeenth Report of the Council of Missions Cooperating with the Church of Christ in Japan*, p. 4.
5. Reischauer, A. K., *The Task in Japan* (New York, Fleming H. Revell Co., 1926), pp. 51–52, 181.
6. Uemura Masahisa in *Nippon Hyōron*, *Japan Weekly Mail*, November 7, 1891, p. 546.
7. Warneck, *op. cit.*, p. 316.
8. *Japan Weekly Mail*, April 4, 1891, p. 397.
9. *Church at Home and Abroad*, September 1892, pp. 224–225.

GLOSSARY

Amida (*Amirita, Amidabaya, Mida*) The supreme Buddha of the Paradise of the Pure Land of the West, the deity specially honored by the Jōdo and Shin sects.

Ashikaga A branch of the Minamoto family, fifteen of whom as *shōgun* ruled Japan between the years 1338 and 1573, designated as the Ashikaga period.

Bakufu Literally, government of the tent. In this paper the term refers to the Tokugawa government at Yedo, between the years 1603 and 1868.

Bemmō "Superstitions," by Yasui Sokken (1873).

Bukai Local association of pastors and delegates functioning as subsidiary bodies to the Sōkai of the Kumiai Kyōkai.

Bummei Kaika "Enlightenment and Civilization," the motto of the decade of westernization.

Bushi no shobai Literally, warrior's business.

Chōrō Elder or Presbyter.

Chōrō Kōkai or *Kyōkai* Presbyterian Church.

Chūkai Presbytery, the regional organization of the Nippon Kirisuto Kyōkai.

Daikai General Assembly, the national organization of the Nippon Kirisuto Kyōkai. There is nothing equivalent to the Synod in Japan. See also *Chūkai*.

Daimyo Literally, great name. A noble, a lord in feudal times, the possessor of great domains, whose revenue exceeded 10,000 *koku* of rice. Ieyasu divided them into *fudai* (hereditary), the 176 who had sided with him before the campaign of Sekigahara, and *tozama* (non-hereditary), the 86 who had submitted to his authority only after being defeated.

Dendō Zasshi "The Evangelist," a Christian magazine.

Dendōkyoku Board of Home Missions.

Fujin Kyōfukai The Women's Christian Temperance Union.

Fukuin Dōmeikai The Japan Evangelical Alliance.

Fukuin Shimpō "Gospel News," a Christian periodical.

Gagen Classical language.

Gaimushō Foreign Office.

Hokekyō The Lotus sutra.

Honkyō Gaigen "Compendium of Fundamental Foreign Teachings," by Hirata Atsutane.

Itchi Kyōkai Union Church.

Iesu Kyōkai Jesus Church.

Iesukyō A colloquial term meaning Christianity.

Jiji Shimpo A daily newspaper published in Tokyo, edited by Fukuzawa Yukichi.

Jiji Shogen "A Word for the Times," By Fukuzawa Yukichi, published in 1881.

235

GLOSSARY

Jinja A Shintō shrine; Shrine (ethnic) Shintō as distinguished from sect (religious) Shintō.

Jisha Bugyō Official of Shōgunate in charge of ecclesiastical affairs.

Jiyū Freedom.

Jōdo A Buddhist sect founded in 1174 by the priest Genkū (Enkō Daishi), or Hōnen Shōnin.

Jogakkō Girls' School.

Kaidō Shimbun A Buddhist newspaper published during the Meiji period.

Kamakura A small town near Tōkyō, for several centuries the military capital of Japan.

Kami God. The polytheistic concept of the Japanese is described in the dissertation, pp. 33-34.

Kana Japanese syllabary.

Kirishitan The romanized form of the Japanese term by which Roman Catholicism was known in Japan prior to 1859.

Kojiki "Chronicle of Ancient Events." The first Japanese history, compiled in 711-712 from the recollections of an aged woman. The account traces the development of Japan from the time of creation through 628 A.D.

Kokka A state, a country, a nation.

Koku 4.9629 bushels.

Kokumin no Tomo "Friend of the People," a periodical.

Kokumin Shimbun A daily newspaper.

Kokusui Hozon "Preserve the national characteristics," the motto of the period of reaction.

Kūkai Known better by his posthumous title, Kōbō Daishi. Kūkai founded the Shingon sect of Buddhism on Mt. Kōya in 816.

Kumiai Association.

Kumiai Kyōkai Congregational Church (in Japan).

Kyōbushō Ecclesiastical Department.

Kyōdōshoku Literally, teaching leaders. Official priests of the state cult.

Kyōha Literally, a teaching group. Referring to Shintō, indicates sect (religious), as distinguished from shrine (ethnic) Shintō.

Kyōkai Shimbun "Church Newspaper," a Christian periodical.

Mainichi Shimbun A daily newspaper.

Maishū Shimpo "Weekly News," a periodical.

Makoto no Michi wo Shiru no Chikamichi "A Short Cut to an Understanding of the True Way," by J.D. Davis; the first original tract in Japanese.

Meikio Shinshi A Buddhist periodical published during the Meij period.

Meirokusha "The Meiji Six," a group of reformers during the Meiji period. (See Anesaki, *History of Japanese Religion*, pp. 350-351 note.)

Minamoto Family name given to numerous sons and grandsons of emperors. The four most important branches were descended from the emperors Saga, Seiwa, Uda, and Murakami. For details see Papinot, *op. cit.*, pp. 373 ff.

GLOSSARY

Naimushō Home Office.

Namu Amida Butsu Literally, "Adoration to the Buddha Amida," the invocation (*nembutsu*) of the Jōdo and Shin sects.

Namu Myōhō Rengekyo Literally, "Adoration to the Lotus of Perfect Truth."

Nembutsu Literally, "Thinking of Buddha" See Anesaki, *History of Japanese Religion*, p. 178).

Nichiren Literally, lotus of the sun. A celebrated Buddhist priest, founder of the Nichiren Sect, (1222–1282).

Nihon or *Nippon*, Japan.

Nihon Kumiai Kyōkai, Japan Congregational Church.

Nihongi (or *Nihon Shoki*) "The Chronicles of Japan." A collection of the ancient chronicles of Japan written with Chinese ideographs in 720. The records purport to trace the history of the nation from the time of its origin to 697 A.D.

Nippon Hyōron A monthly review.

Nippon Kirisuto Ichi Kōkai (*Nippon Kirisuto Ichi Kyokai*) The Union Church of Christ in Japan

Nippon Kirisuto Kyōkai The Church of Christ in Japan.

Nippon Rengō Kirisuto Kyōkai The Federated Church of Christ in Japan, the proposed title for the union church which was to be formed by the merger of the Kumiai Kyōkai and the Nippon Kirisuto Kyōkai.

Nippon Seikōkai Holy Catholic Church of Japan (Episcopal).

Nippon Seisho no Tomo Scripture Union of Japan.

Norito Shinto prayers.

O-Yōmei Japanese transliteration of the Chinese name Wang Yang Ming; a philosopher who was born in 1472; he interpreted the classics idealistically, insisted upon the intuitive nature of knowledge, the omnipresence of the mind, and the correlation of knowledge to action.

Rebaiburu Revival.

Rikkyō Daigaku St. Paul's University.

Rikugō Zasshi "The Cosmos," a Christian magazine.

Rinki-kō Circle talks.

Ryōbu Literally, double aspect or dual. Applied to Shintō or Buddhism, *Ryōbu* refers to the synthetic religion: a blend of the two, which emerged after the ninth century.

Ryōchi The prime or universal conscience, according to the philosophical system of Ō-yōmei.

Saichō Better known by his posthumous title, Dengyō Daishi. Saichō founded the Tendai sect of Buddhism on Mt. Hiei after his return from China in 805.

Sake Rice wine.

Samurai Warrior, man of arms.

Sonnō-Jōi "Revere the Emperor, expel the barbarians," the slogan of the

GLOSSARY

monarchists prior to the Restoration.

San yōbun "Three Essential Documents," an early tract for the instruction of young Christians.

Sat-chō Shortened form of the names of the Satsuma and Chōshū clans.

Seiyō-Kibun "Strange Stories of the Occident," by Arai Hakuseki.

Shajikyoku Bureau of Shrines and Temples.

Shichi Ichi Zappō "Weekly Miscellany," a religious paper.

Shindō-sōron "Introduction to the Divine Way," by J.L. Nevius.

Shingon A sect of Buddhism founded by Kūkai about 816.

Shinri Ekichi "The True Doctrine Made Plain," a pamphlet.

Shinshū Shin, Ikkōshū, or Montoshū A Sect of Buddhism founded by Shinran Shōnin in 1224.

Shōgun A general. The Minamoto, Ashikaga, and Tokugawa, holders of this title and rank, each in turn exercised unlimited power to which the emperors themselves were obliged to yield. This fact caused foreigners in the nineteenth century to regard Japan as being ruled by two persons, one in seclusion in Kyōto and the other as acting sovereign in Yedo. The investiture of the *shōgun* was always at the hand of the emperor, and reserved to the descendants of Minamoto Yoritomo (1147–1199).

Shūkyō Religion.

Sōkai General Conference of the Kumiai Kyōkai.

Sōshi A bravo, a political bully, a hooligan.

Teishu Japanese transliteration of Chu Hsi, a system of Confucianism as taught by the Hayashi school. In 1608 *Teishu* became the official code of the *samurai* class.

Tendai A sect of Buddhism introduced in 806 by Saichō (Dengyō Daishi), and established in a monastery on Mt. Hiei near Kyōto.

Tendo Sakugen "Evidences of Christianity," by J.L. Nevius.

Tokugawa A family which descended from Nitta Yoshishige and was thus in the Minamoto line. Tokugawa Ieyasu was appointed *shōgun* in 1603, which title was retained in the family until 1868, the time of the Restoration. The years between these dates are known as the Tokugawa period.

Umayado Shōtoku Taishi, the prince- regent under whose patronage Buddhism was integrated into the national life of Japan.

Yamato Damashii The spirit or heart of Japan.

Yasokyō Bemmō "Christian Superstitions," an anti-Christian book by Tajima Shōji published in 1874.

Yasokyō (*Iesukyō* or *Yesukyō*) The romanization of the Japanese term for Jesus' teaching or religion.

Yasokyō Benwaku "Exposé of the Errors of Christianity," an anti-Christian book published by a professor at the Tokyo Imperial University about 1880.

Yasokyō Mudori "Unseasonableness of Christianity," by Fujishima Ryōon, an anti-Christian pamphlet published in 1881 to counteract the success of Christianity in Kyōto and Ōsaka.

GLOSSARY

Yasokyō Seidō Nyūmon "Introduction to the Righteous Way of Christianity."

Yedo The capital of the Tokugawa rulers, which name was altered to Tōkyō at the time of the Restoration.

Yen Unit of Japanese currency ; in 1887 equal to approximately $ .80.

Yōgaku Kōyō " Principles of Instruction for Youth," a text in education by Motoda.

Yorokobi no otozure, " Good Tidings." a Christian periodical.

Zokugo Colloquial language.

A BIBLIOGRAPHY CONCERNING
THE POST-RESTORATION DEVELOPMENT
OF CHRISTIANITY IN JAPAN

American Baptist Missionary Union, Correspondence from Japan. (MSS).

American Board of Commissioners for Foreign Missions, Correspondence to Japan. (MSS.)

American Board of Commissioners for Foreign Missions, Correspondence from Japan. (MSS.)

Anesaki Masaharu, *A Concordance to the History of Kirishitan Missions*, Catholic Missions in Japan in the Sixteenth and Seventeenth Centuries (Tokyo Office of the Academy, 1930, pp. 225).

Anesaki Masaharu, *History of Japanese Religion* (London, Kegan Paul, Trench, Trubner & Co., Ltd., 1930, pp. xxii, 423).

Anesaki Masaharu, *Religious and Social Problems of the Orient* (New York, The Macmillan Co., 1923, pp. xi, 77).

Aston, W. G., *Japanese Literature* (London, William Heinemann, 1899, pp. xi, 408).

Aston, W. G., *Shinto: The Way of the Gods* (London, Longmans, Green & Co., 1905, pp. 390).

Axling, William, *Kagawa* (London, Student Christian Movement, 1932, pp. 237).

Beach, Harlan P., and Fahs, Charles H., editors, *World Atlas of Christian Missions* (New York, Student Volunteer Movement for Foreign Missions, 1910, pp. 172); includes a directory of missionary societies, statistics and maps.

Berry, K. F., *A Pioneer Doctor in Old Japan* (New York, Fleming H. Revell Co., 1940, pp. 247).

Boxer, C. R., *Jan Compagnie in Japan, 1600–1817* (The Hague, Martinus Nijhoff, 1936, pp. xvi, 190).

Brinkley, Capt. C. F., *A History of the Japanese People* (New York, The Encyclopaedia Britannica Co., 1914, pp. xi, 784).

Brown, A. J., *The Mastery of the Far East* (New York, Charles Scribner's Sons, 1919, pp. x, 671).

Brown, A. J., *One Hundred Years* (New York, Fleming H. Revell Co., 1936, pp. 1140).

Carrothers, Mrs. J. D., *The Sunrise Kingdom* (Philadelphia, Presbyterian Board of Publication, 1879, pp. 408).

Cary, Otis, *A History of Christianity in Japan* (New York, Fleming H. Revell Co., 2 vols., 1909).

Chamberlain, Basil Hall, *Things Japanese* (London, Kegan Paul, Trench, Trubner & Co., Ltd., 6th ed., 1939, pp. xvi, 584).

Chrysanthemum, The, 1881–1882.

Church in China Today (Shanghai, 1926, pp. 166).

BIBLIOGRAPHY

Church at Home and Abroad, 1887–1893.

Clement, Ernest W., *Christianity in Modern Japan* (Philadelphia, American Baptist Publication Society, 1905, pp. xv, 205).

Davis, J. D., *A Sketch of the Life of Rev. J. H. Neesima* (New York, Fleming H. Revell Co., 1895, pp. 156).

DeForest, Charlotte B., *The Evolution of a Missionary* (New York, Fleming H. Revell Co., 1914, pp. 299).

DeForest, John H., *Sunrise in the Sunrise Kingdom* (New York, The Young People's Missionary Movement, 1904, pp. 233).

Dewey, John, *Characters and Events* (New York, Henry Holt, 2 vols., 1929)

Dixon, J. M., *Christian Valley* (*Transactions of the Asiatic Society of Japan*, Vol. XVI, 1889).

Ebisawa Arimichi, *Relation between the Ethics of Bushido and Christianity* in *Cultural Nippon*, Vol. VII, Nos. 3 and 4, parts I and II, 1939.

Eby, Rev. C. S., *Christianity and Humanity* (Yokohama, 1883).

Eby, Rev. C. S., *The Immediate Christianization of Japan* (Yokohama, 1884).

Eliot, Charles, *Japanese Buddhism* (London, Edward Arnold & Co., 1935, pp. xxxv, 449).

Finck, Henry T., *Lotos-Time in Japan* (New York, Charles Scribner's Sons, 1895, pp. xvii, 337).

Fisher, Galen, *Creative Forces in Japan* (New York, Missionary Education Movement, 1923, pp. viii, 248).

Geerts, A. J. C., *The Arima Rebellion and Koeckebacker* (Letters from Koeckebacker concerning the part he played in the affair, translated in *Transactions of the Asiatic Society of Japan*, Vol. XI, 1883).

General Conference of Protestant Missionaries in Japan, held in Tokyo in October, 1900 (Tokyo, 1901, pp. 1048); contains on pp. 740–959 a history of Protestant missions in Japan since 1854 by G. F. Verbeck.

Gordon, M. L., *Thirty Eventful Years* (Boston, American Board of Commissioners for Foreign Missions, 1901, pp. iv, 119); story of the American Board's Mission in Japan 1869–99.

Greene, Evarts Boutell, *A New-Englander in Japan* (Boston, Houghton Mifflin Co., 1927, pp. x, 374).

Griffis, William Elliot, *Verbeck of Japan* (New York, Fleming H. Revell Co., 1900, pp. 376).

Gubbins, J. H., *The Progress of Japan 1853–1871* (Oxford, Clarendon Press, 1911, pp. 323).

Gulick, Sidney L., *Evolution of the Japanese* (New York, Fleming H. Revell, Co., no date, pp. 457).

Gundert, Wilhelm, *Japanische Religionsgeschichte* (Tokyo, Japanisch-Deutsches Kulturinstitut, 1935, pp. xviii, 267).

Harada Tasuku, *The Faith of Japan* (London, New York, The Macmillan Co., 1914, pp. xiv, 190).

Hardy, A. S., *Life and Letters of Joseph Hardy Neesima* (Boston, Houghton, Mifflin Co., 1891, pp. 350).

BIBLIOGRAPHY

Harnack, Adolph, *The Mission and Expansion of Christianity in the First Three Centuries* translated and edited by James Moffatt (New York, G. P. Putnam's Sons, 2d ed., 2 vols., 1908).

Harrington, C. K., *Captain Bickel of the Inland Sea* (New York, Fleming H. Revell Co., 1919, pp. 301).

Harris, Townsend, *The Complete Journal of Townsend Harris* (New York, Japan Society, 1930, pp. xix, 616).

Hastings, James, *Encyclopedia of Religion and Ethics* (New York, Chas. Scribner's Sons, 1921, VI 428b).

Hawks, F. L., *Narrative of the Expedition of an American Squadron to the China Seas and Japan* (New York, D. Appleton & Co., 1856, pp. vii, 624).

Hildreth, Richard, *Japan as It was and Is*, edited with supplementary notes by Ernest W. Clement (London, Kegan Paul, Trench, Trubner & Co., Ltd., 2 vols., 1907).

Hiyane Antei, *Nippon Kinsei Kirisutokyō Jimbutsushi* (Biographies of Modern Japanese Christians Tōkyō, Kirisutokyō Shisō Sōsho Kankōkai, Holtom, 1935, pp. 558).

Holtom, D. C., *The National Faith of Japan* (New York, E. P. Dutton & Co., 1938, pp. xiii, 329).

Home and Foreign Record, 1867–1886.

Hozumi Nobushige, *Ancestor Worship and Japanese Law* (Tōkyō, The Maruzen Kabushiki Kaisha, 1912, pp. xxx, 198).

Iglehart, C. W., *Points of Contacts with Shinto in the Approach of Christianity to Rural Japan* (S. T. M. Thesis, Union Theological Seminary, New York, 1933).

Imbrie, *The Church of Christ in Japan* (Philadelphia, Westminster Press, 1906, pp. 122).

Imbrie, *Church Unity in Japan* (Tōkyō, Kyo Bun Kwan, 1914, pp. 42, 11).

Japan Christian Yearbook, 1902–1941 (Tōkyō, Kyo Bun Kwan).

Japan Evangelist, The (Tōkyō, 1893–1925); continued as *The Japan Christian Quarterly:* an independent monthly magazine in the interest of Christian work in Japan.

Japan Weekly Mail, 1883–1891.

Katakozawa Chiyomatsu, *Meiji Gannen no Kirisutokyō ni Okeru Shisō no Ichikōan* (A study of Anti-Christian Thought in Early Meiji, in *Kirisutokyōshi Kenkyū*, No. 6, November 8, 1939); the latter being an occasional publication issued by Christian historians.

Kawai, Michi, *Japanese Women Speak* (Boston, The Central Committee on the United Study of Foreign Missions, 1934, pp. 20, 204).

Keenlyside and Thomas, *A History of Education in Japan* (Tōkyō, Hokuseidō, 1937, pp. xiv, 385).

Kirisutokyō Bunken Karimokuroku, an unpublished bibliography of books on Christian subjects in Japanese, compiled by Winburn T. Thomas.

Knapp, Arthur May, *Feudal and Modern Japan* (Yokohama, Kelly and Walsh, 1906).

IBBLIOGRAPHY

Knox, G. W., *The Development of Religion in Japan* (New York, G. P. Putnam & Sons, 1907, pp. 21, 204).

Kojiki, English translation by Basil Hall Chamberlain (*Transactions of the Asiatic Society of Japan*, Vol. X, Supplement, 1882).

Latourette, Kenneth Scott, *A History of Christian Missions in China* (New York, The Macmillan Co., 1929, pp. xii, 930).

Latourette, Kenneth Scott, *The Development of Japan* (New York, The Macmillan Co., 1918, pp. xi, 237).

Latourette, Kenneth Scott, *The Great Century* (New York, Harper and Brothers, 1941, pp. viii, 516).

Lloyd, Arthur, *The Creed of Half Japan* (London, Smith Elder and Company, 1911, pp. 393).

London Missionary Conference Report. *Report of the Centenary Conference on the Protestant Missions of the World, 1888* (New York, Fleming H. Revell, 2 vols., no date).

Mabie, Henry C., *In Brightest Asia* (Boston, W. G. Corthell, 1891, pp. 175).

Marnas, Francisque, *La Religion De Jésus Ressuscitée au Japon* (Paris, Delhomme et Briguet, 2 vols., 1867).

Matsumoto Tsuyoshi, *Hymnology in Japan;* An Historical Study of the Hymnals Used in the Protestant Churches in Japan Excluding the Protestant Episcopal Church in Japan (M. S. M. Thesis, Union Theological Seminary, 1935, pp. 47 and plates).

Matsura To, *Nagasaki Kokon Shūran* (Notes on Nagasaki, English abstract by W. A. Wooley, *Transactions of the Asiatic Society of Japan*, Vol. IX, 1881).

Missionary Herald, 1869–1894.

Missionary Review of the World, 1881–1890.

Mizuno Tsunekichi, *The Kindergarten in Japan* (Boston, The Stratford Co., 1917, pp. ix, 62).

Moule, G. H., *The Spirit of Japan* (London, Student Volunteer Missionary Union, 1913, pp. 300).

Murdoch, James, *A History of Japan* (London, Kegan Paul, Trench, Trubner & Co., Ltd., 3 vols., 1925, 1926).

Nakamura, C., translator, *A History of the Church of Christ in Japan (The Japan Evangelist*, Vol. 5, 1898).

Naruse Jinzō, *A Modern Paul in Japan* (Tōkyō, The Keiseisha, 1893, pp. 117).

Nihongi, English translation by W. G. Aston (*Transactions and Proceedings of the Japan Society of London*, 2 vols., Supplement I, 1896).

Norito, translated by Ernest M. Satow (*Transactions of the Asiatic Society of Japan*, Vols. VIII and IX, 1880, 1881).

Norman, E. Herbert, *Japan's Emergence as a Modern State* (New York, Institute of Pacific Relations, 1940, pp. xvi, 254).

Noss, George S., *The Rise of Nationalism in Japan and the Christian Movement* (M. S. T. Thesis, Union Theological Seminary, 1937, pp. 140 and appendices).

BIBLIOGRAPHY

Ogawa Shūmei, *Nihon 2600-Nenshi* (Two Thousand Six Hundred Years of Japanese History, Tōkyō, Ichi Shobō, 1939, pp. 342).

Osaka Conference, Proceedings of the, General Conference of the Protestant Missions of Japan, Osaka, April 1883 (Yokohama, R. Meiklejohn & Co., 1883, pp. xviii, 468).

Oshimo, Raymond Kakuichi, *The Development of Social Idealism in Modern Japan* (Ph. D. Thesis University of Chicago, 1931, pp. 221).

Ozawa Saburō, *Shina Senkyōshi J. L. Nevius to Nippon to no Kankei* (The Relation of J. L. Nevius, Missionary to China, with Japan, in *Kirisutokyōshi Kenkyū*, Studies in the History of Christianity, No. 6, November 8, 1939).

Papinot, E., *Historical and Geographical Dictionary of Japan* (Tōkyō, Librairie Sanseisha, 1910, pp. xiv, 842).

Pascoe, C. F., *Two Hundred Years of the Society for the Propagation of the Gospel in Foreign Parts* (London, 1901); an historical account of the society from 1701 to 1900, based on a digest of the society's records. Chapter 91, pp. 717-727b, contains the history of the Church of England Mission in Japan.

Presbyterian Church in the U. S. A., Board of Foreign Missions, Correspondence from Japan. (MSS.)

Presbyterian Church in the U. S. A., Board of Foreign Missions, Correspondence to Japan. (MSS.)

Proceedings of the Osaka Conference. See *Osaka Conference.*

Reischauer, A. K., *Studies in Japanese Buddhism* (New York, The Macmillan Co., 1917, pp. xviii, 361).

Reischauer, A. K., *The Task in Japan* (New York, Fleming H. Revell Co., 1926).

Reischauer, Robert Karl, *Japan: Government and Politics* (New York, Thomas Nelson, 1939, pp. xiv, 221).

Report of the United Missions in Japan, 1886-1887.

Report of the Missions Cooperating with the United Church of Christ in Japan, 1888-1889.

Report of the Council of Missions Cooperating with the Church of Christ in Japan, 1890-1892.

Ritter, H., *History of Protestant Missions in Japan,* English translation by G. E. Albrecht, revised and brought up to date by D. C. Greene and M. Christlieb (Tokyo, Methodist Publishing House, 1898, pp. xv, 446).

Saitō Sōichi, *A Study of the Influence of Christianity upon Japanese Culture* (Tōkyō, Japan Council, Institute of Pacific Relations, 1931).

Sansom, G. B., *Japan* (London, The Cresset Press, 1932, pp. xvi, 537).

Sakamaki Shunzō, *Japan and the United States, 1790-1853 (Transactions of the Asiatic Society of Japan,* Second Series, Vol. XVIII, December 1939, pp. xi, 204).

Sakurai Tadasu, *Nippon Kirisutokyōshi* (History of Christianity in Japan, Tō-kyō, Ryūshōkaku, 1933, pp. 3, 467).

Satow, Ernest M., *The Church at Yamaguchi from 1550 to 1586 (Transactions of the Asiatic Society of Japan,* Vol. VII, 1879).

BIBLIOGRAPHY

Satow, Ernest M., *The Origin of Spanish and Portuguese Rivalry in Japan* (*Transactions of the Asiatic Society of Japan*, Vol. XVIII, 1890).

Satow, Ernest M., *The Revival of Pure Shintau* (*Transactions of the Asiatic Society of Japan*, Vol. III, Part I, Appendix, 1875).

Satow, Ernest M., translation of anti-Kirishitan edicts (*Transactions of the Asiatic Society of Japan*, Vol. VI, Part I, 1878).

Scott, Robertson, *The Foundation of Japan* (London, John Murray, 1933).

Shimmura and Hamada, *Tombstones of the Christians in the Keicho Era found in Kyoto and its Neighborhood*, in *Report upon Archeological Research* (Department of Literature, Volume VII, Kyoto Imperial University, 1923).

Shin Shiu Kio Shi (A Synopsis of the Doctrines of the Shin sect, English summary by James Troup in *Transactions of the Asiatic Society of Japan*, Vol. XIV, 1886, pp. 1–17).

Shūkyōron (Treatise on Religion, in *Meiji Bunka Zenshū*, Collection of Works on Meiji Culture, Vol. XI, Tokyo, Nippon Hyoronsha, 1928, pp. 4, 568).

Society for the Propagation of the Gospel in Foreign Parts, Classified Digest of the Records of the, 1701–1892 (London, 1893).

Speer, R. E., *Missions and Modern History* (New York, Fleming H. Revell Co., 2 vols., 1904).

Speer, R. E., *Studies in Missionary Leadership* (Philadelphia, Westminster Press, 1914, pp. 283).

Summers, J., *Notes on Osaka* (*Transactions of the Asiatic Society of Japan*, Vol. VII, 1879).

Sweet, Charles F., *The Arrest and Death of the Twenty-Six at Nagasaki, February 1597* (*Transactions of the Asiatic Society of Japan*, Vol. XLIV, Part I, 1916).

Tagawa Daikichirō, *Kokka to Shūkyō* (State and Religion, English translation by Winburn T. Thomas in *Japan Christian Quarterly*, Vol. XIV, April 1939).

Takeuchi Tatsuji, *War and Diplomacy in the Japanese Empire* (New York, Doubleday, Doran & Co., Inc., 1935, pp. xix, 505).

Thomas, Winburn T., *Christian Relics* (*Japan Advertiser*, May 26, 1937).

Tokyo Conference Report. See *General Conference of Protestant Missionaries.*

Treat, Payson J., *Diplomatic Relations between the United States and Japan,* 1853–1895 (California, Stanford University Press, 2 vols., 1932).

Tsuchiya Takao, *An Economic History of Japan* (Tōkyō, *Transactions of the Asiatic Society of Japan*, December 1937, pp. xviii, 269).

Tsurumi Yūsuke, *Present Day Japan* (New York, Columbia University Press, 1926, pp. 114).

Tucker, Henry St. George, *The History of the Episcopal Church in Japan* (New York, Charles Scribner's Sons, 1938, pp. 228).

Uchimura Kanzō, *The Diary of a Japanese Convert* (New York, Fleming H. Revell Co., no date, pp. 6, 212).

Warneck, Gustav, *Outline of a History of Protestant Missions from the Reformation to the Present Time*, authorized translation from the seventh German edition, edited by George Robson (New York, Fleming H. Revell

BIBLIOGRAPHY

Co., 1901, pp. 13, 364).

Williams, Frederick Wells, *The Life and Letters of Samuel Wells Williams* (New York, G. P. Putnam's Sons, 1888, pp. vi, 490).

Wright, W. B., *The Capture and Captivity of Père Sidotti in Japan*, (*Transactions of the Asiatic Society of Japan*, Vol. IX, 1881).

INDEX

A

Ackerman, Jessie 134
Adams, Dr. Arthur H. 130
Akasaka Hospital 131
Akita 80
Allchin, George 126
Allegemeine Evangeliche-protestantischer Missionsverein 80, 81, 106, 196
American Baptist Convention 106, 147
American Baptist Free Missionary Society 77, 78
American Baptist Missionary Union 75, 78, 106, 107, 120, 147
American Bible Society 119–20
American Board of Commissioners for Foreign Missions 16, 71–78, 92, 94, 110, 123–24, 130–32, 137n, 142–43 147, 150–51
   see also Doshisha University
           Kumiai Kyōkai
           Nihon Kirisuto Kōkai
           Niijima, Jō
American Christian Convention Mission 80
American Episcopal Missions 72, 76, 77, 100, 103, 125, 130
American Methodist Theological and Training School 106
American Mission Home 78
American Tract Society 122
American Unitarian Association 80
Anglo-Japanese University—see Aoyama Gakuin
Amherst College 73n, 113
Andover Theological Seminary 73n
Anesaki, Masaharu 152
Anglican Missionaries 89
Aoyama Gakuin 102, 106
Arai, Hakuseki 123
Arima, Shinousuke 133n
Arnold, Sir Edwin 189
Aston, W. G. 31n, 123n

B

Ballagh, J. H. 78, 138
Baptists 72, 74, 75, 120, 163
   see also American Baptist Convention
           American Baptist Free Missionary Society
           American Baptist Missionary Union
           English Baptists 147
           Southern Baptist Convention 81, 147
Bennett, A. A. 106
Berry, Dr. J. C. 78, 110, 130–32
Bettelheim, B. J. 117
Bible, Translation of 118–21
Bible Women 104ff
Bickersteth, Bishop Edward 144, 148–49, 152

INDEX

INDEX

Edinburgh Medical Mission 79, 80, 131
Education 96–116
Emperor 166, 175, 186, 187, 200–201
English Baptist Mission 79, 147
English Episcopal Missions 101
Ensor, George 78
Episcopal Missions 72, 77, 104, 106, 149–50
    see also Book of Common Prayer
          Church Mission Society
          Nippon Seikokai
          Protestant Episcopal Church, U. S. A.
          Society for the Propagation of the Gospel
Episcopal Church of Canada Mission 80
Evangelical Association of North America 79, 106, 108, 110, 148
Evangelism 152–157

F

Faulds, Henry 130
Fenellosa, Ernest P. 112, 189
Ferris Seminary 91, 103
French 48, 89
Friends, Society of 80, 129
Fujin Kyōfukai, 133
Fukuin Shimpō (Gospel News) 124
Fukuin Dōmei Kai (Japanese Evangelical Alliance) 124
Fukuzawa, Yukichi 112, 179, 192–93
Fyson, E. K. 118
Gardiner, Mrs. J. McD. 103
General Convention of Protestant Missionaries (1872) 118, 138
German Evangelical Protestant Missionary Society of Switzerland and Germany
    80 81, 82n, 196
German Reformed Church Missions—see Reformed Church in the U. S.
Ginza School—see Hara Jogakkō
Goble, Jonathan 77, 118
Gordon, M. L. 78, 101
Graham Seminary 103
Greek Orthodox Church 70, 89, 93, 166
Greene, D. C. 78, 101, 118
Greene, Mrs. D. C. 110
Gulick, L. H. 118
Gulick, O. H. 78, 111, 123
Guthrie, Mrs. L. M. 78
Gutzlaff, K. F. A. 117

H

Hakodate, 70, 78, 85, 154
Hara, Taneaki 103, 133
Hara Jogakkō 103
Harrington, F.G. 121n
Harris, Townsend 50, 76
Hattori Chiyo 134
Heidelberg Catechism 140
Hennig, Liemar 82n

251

INDEX

Hepburn, Dr. J.C. 77, 92, 103, 111, 117-19, 121, 126, 129
Hepburn, Mrs. J.C. 103
Hikari Kindergarten 110
Himeji 130,
Hiroshima 80, 86
Hokkaidō 133
Hokkaidō Temperance Society 134
Hopkins, Mark 190
Hymns 126
Hyogo 85
Hyogo Prefectural Hospital 130

I

Ibuka, Kajinosuke 123, 125
Ichikawa, Enosuke 111
Imamura, Kenkichi 123
Imbrie, William 185, 186
Imperial Rescript on Education 200-1
Inouye, Kaoru 202
Ise Shrine 201
Ishii, Jūji 132
Ishinomaki 80
Itagaki, Taisuke 154, 174
Itō, Hirobumi 52
Itō, Kazutaka 134
Iwai, Shinroku 134
Iwakura Mission 202
Iwamoto, Zenji 125

J

Janes, L. L. 113-14
Japan Weekly Mail 16
Jesuits 89, 93
Jiyūtō 174
Jones, D. F. 80

K

Kaidō Shimbun 48
Kaigai Iesu Kōkai 133, 138, 153
Kaishintō 203
Kami No Ōinaru Ai 121
Kanagawa 77, 78, 85, 129
Kanazawa 86, 110, 112
Kanamori, Tsūrin 83, 94, 105, 110, 123, 142, 194, 195
Karafuto—see Saghalin
Katei Gakkō 133n
Katō, Hiroyuki 192n
Keiō, Gijuku 112
Keiseisha 124
Kidder, Mary E. 78, 91, 103
Kindergarten 109-110
Kirishitan Missions-see Catholicism

252

INDEX

253

INDEX

INDEX

INDEX

Tomita, Tetsunosuke 114, 115
Tracts 121–22
Treaties 50–3, 89, 168, 175, 181, 202, 205
Tsukiji (Tokyo) 102, 103, 131
Triennial Conference (1883) 94

U

Uchimura, Kanzō 73, 74, 83, 113, 115, 123, 125. 170, 186, 200
Uchigasaki, Sakusaburō 175n
Ueda 139
Uemura, Masahisa 73, 119, 123–25, 170
Ukita, Kazutami 124
Union College 100
Union Theological School 100, 105–6
Unitarians 80, 81, 105, 148, 193–94, 196
Union Church of Christ in Japan 140
United Presbyterian Church of Scotland 79, 80, 130
United States 89, 90
Universalists 196, 197

V

Verbeck, G. F. 49n, 77, 111, 118

W

Wakamatsu 133
Waller, J. G. 80
Westminster Confession 117
White, W. G. 120
Williams, Bishop C. M. 76, 77, 104, 144
Williams, S. Wells 117
Wolfe, W. J. 112
Woman's Christian Temperance Union 133–34
Woman's Union Missionary Society for Heathen Lands 78, 91, 103, 108, 124, 140
Wycoff, Mr. 100
Women Missionaries, 92
Women Workers (Japanese) 90, 107

X

Xavier, St. Francis 89

Y

Yasokyō, Seido Nyūmon 121
Yajima, Kajirō 134
Yamamoto, Kakuma 84n
Yano, Riu 111n
Y. M. C. A. 83, 124
Yōgaku Kōyō (Principles of Instruction for Youth) 200
Yokohama General Convention 117, 138
Yokohama Temperance Magazine 133
Yokoi, Tokio 193n, 194, 196

INDEX

Date Due

APR 26 '61			